D1780536

Micronesia Under American Rule

MICRONESIA UNDER AMERICAN RULE

An Evaluation of the Strategic Trusteeship (1947-77)

HAROLD F. NUFER
Foreword by Maynard Neas

An *Exposition-University Book*

Exposition Press   Hicksville, New York

First Edition

© 1978 by Harold F. Nufer

All rights reserved, including the right of reproduction in whole or in part, in any form or by any means, electronic or mechanical, including photocopying, recording, or by any information storage and retrieval system. No part of this book may be reproduced without permission in writing from the publisher. Inquiries should be addressed to Exposition Press, Inc., 900 South Oyster Bay Road, Hicksville, N.Y. 11801

Library of Congress Catalog Card Number 77-90658

ISBN 0-682-49021-0

Printed in the United States of America

*To Robert R. Robbins: A skillful professor,
compassionate legislative counsel,
and abiding friend*

Contents

FOREWORD by Maynard Neas	ix
PREFACE	xi
INTRODUCTION	3
1. "To Foster the Development of Political Institutions . . ."	36
2. "To Promote Economic Advancement and Self-Sufficiency . . ."	114
3. "To Promote the Social Advancement of the Inhabitants . . ."	164
4. "To Promote the Educational Advancement . . ."	203
5. Japanese Interests in Micronesia at Present and in the Future?	218
CONCLUSIONS	229
INDEX	235

Foreword

It has been my good fortune to live and work in the United States Trust Territory of the Pacific Islands for the past twenty-six years. For four years prior to 1951, I was a member of the Philippines War Damage Commission, in Manila. The reader of this book will become well acquainted with many of the best Americans and islanders who have lived and worked in the only strategic trusteeship formed by the United Nations in that international organization's history, which dates back to its founding in 1945.

Professor Nufer has evaluated the efforts of all of us who have taken part in this unique experience and found us wanting in many respects and outstanding in a few instances. This is the way those of us who have spent a substantial part of our lives here have found it.

His work is unique in many ways. One of those that stands out is that he inspected the whole of Micronesia and wrote his book after seeing and hearing the people of Micronesia. Based on my experience over the past thirty years in the western Pacific, I recommend this book as truly accurate and an honest account of the activities of those of us who have spent a major part of our working lives in the Trust Territory of the Pacific Islands.

The reader may reach the conclusion that the United States could and should have done better in its efforts to carry out its commitments in these islands. However, I feel as *New York Times* correspondent Robert Trumbull did in 1959, when he concluded his book on the Territory, *Paradise in Trust:* "No country, I thought many times while I was in the islands, could govern the Trust Territory better than it was being done, except possibly the United States."

MAYNARD NEAS,
*Saipan,
Mariana Islands*

Preface

As recently as the late 1960s, an American congressman, in greeting at his Capitol Hill office a group of Micronesian students attending college on the mainland, had to turn to his staff—and an atlas—to find the location of Guam and the Trust Territory of the Pacific Islands (or, collectively, "Micronesia"). Surprisingly, this occurred *after* that elected legislator had served for a year on the Interior and Insular Affairs Committee—a congressional group responsible for overseeing, from the Legislative Branch's standpoint, the conduct of the Department of the Interior in administering that Trust Territory of some 2,200 islands spread over a three-million-square-mile area of the central and western Pacific. (Guam is a U.S. territory and has been since 1898.)

I will not belabor other—possibly excusable—misunderstandings about the physical location of Micronesia by Americans less informed than their elected representatives in Washington, D.C. Still, it is remarkable that such confusion exists when one considers that the U.S. Government has been involved in Micronesia *continuously* since the invasion of the Marshall Islands by American armed forces in early 1944. Even before that fighting, the sneak attack on Pearl Harbor had been launched by vessels of the Imperial Japanese Navy stationed in the Truk Lagoon of the eastern Caroline Islands.

The temptation in this book is to attempt a *detailed* retelling of events which have transpired in the Trust Territory of the Pacific Islands during the past three decades; however, the reader, instead, will be directed to such comprehensive sources as Commander Dorothy E. Richard's three volumes on the U.S. Naval Administration in Micronesia from World War II to 1951 (totaling some 2,700 pages),[1] and to Professor Norman Meller's in-depth analysis of legislative bodies in the Trust Territory, appropriately entitled *The Congress of Micronesia*.[2]

Thus, the focus here will be to *evaluate* how well the U.S. Governmen has *fulfilled* the four major goals of trusteeship established in Chapter XII of the United Nations Charter and reiterated in Article 6 of the Trusteeship Agreement of 1947, under which the far-flung islands of Micronesia are administered by the United States under the overall supervision of the U.N. Security Council.

The *uniqueness* in my evaluation of Micronesia under American rule since 1947 is that I have relied heavily on the *candid* reflections of a multitude of American, Micronesian, and Japanese officials, advisers, businessmen, scholars, and others who have had varying periods of living in the Trust Territory and other parts of the Pacific Basin over the past three decades (or longer, in the case of some Japanese businessmen). Their opinions—sometimes expressed in this book by name, other times, indirectly, and occasionally (on request), anonymously—are highly valued by me. I gleaned these views mostly during my year's sabbatical leave from Michigan Technological University, 1976-77, which found me spending a month in the Tokyo area and six weeks in Micronesia (including Guam).

Previously, I had made a tour of familiarization to the Trust Territory during the summer of 1970, accompanied on that occasion by my wife, Marian, whose own explorations, interviews, and commentaries provided added insights and broader bases for recall. I also engaged in correspondence with a number of Americans and Micronesians over the years as I prepared my doctoral dissertation, submitted to Tufts University in 1974.[3]

Where Micronesians, Japanese, or Filipinos are quoted in this book either directly from informal interviews which I tape-recorded during the fall of 1976, or from earlier or later correspondence, the *syntax* is maintained as expressed by those individuals. I feel strongly that the reader may appreciate the unpretentious speech patterns of those from the Pacific Basin areas. For example, many islanders speak in the *present* tense when referring to *past* happenings. For purposes of this book, all such quotations will occur in the *present* tense, with no footnoting involved for these interviews of 1976.

I am especially indebted to those who so warmly assisted me during my year's leave. First, to Professor Lawrence Rakestraw, at Michigan Tech, whose scholarly pursuits inspired me to apply for the sabbatical; to Professor A. Spencer Hill, my departmental head, who also encouraged and supported my application; to the Hans J. Heim family in Tokyo, who opened their home and extended their friendship to me during my stay in that country; to Izumi Kobayashi, Secretary General of the Japan Micronesia Association, who was instrumental in my contacting valuable sources in the Tokyo area; to Suekazu Hamanaka, Consul General of Japan on Guam; to Michael F. and Sue Caldwell, also on Guam, who made me their house guest in early October and again in November, 1976, and introduced me to their fellow University of Guam faculty members and Micronesia Area Research Center (MARC) officials; and to Strik Yoma, Director of Public Affairs in the Trust Territory Government Headquarters, on Capitol Hill, Saipan, who initially introduced me to his counterparts and generously provided me with office space for my month's stay on that island.

It is impracticable, unfortunately, to list here all those who so graciously permitted me to tape-record their views on subjects relating to the strengths and weaknesses of the American rule in the Trust Territory. They are mentioned at points throughout the following chapters and in the Index. I am indebted to Maynard Neas, not only for his Foreword to this book, but for his clear recall of events dating back to 1951, when he first came to Micronesia as an American official; and to Samuel McPhetres, Researcher for the Education for Self-Government Program in the Political Affairs Division of the Department of Public Affairs, for his guidance in sources I should consult.

Jackson Professor of Political Science Emeritus Robert R. Robbins, to whom this book is dedicated, was the first Legislative Counsel to the Congress of Micronesia in 1965. He successfully kindled in me—through a graduate seminar at Tufts University in the fall of 1966—a deep and doubtless abiding interest in Pacific Island peoples. Professor Robbins' respect for the islanders and concern for their welfare and advancement have continued since World War II, a period during much of which it has been in keeping with liberal thought to worry about their well-being and advancement toward self-government.

To Edward Uhlan, Publisher of Exposition Press, Inc., I owe a particular debt of gratitude. He perceived the possible value of such a book as this even before the manuscript was written. I appreciated his personal involvement in all the stages leading to the final product.

Finally, to my family and mother-in-law, Ardith G. May, I am grateful for their patience and love. Ardith opened her home to my family and me so that this manuscript could be prepared in the warm clime that is Ojai, California.

For whatever factual errors occur in the book, as well as the overall conclusions reached, I take full responsibility.

NOTES FOR PREFACE

1. Dorothy E. Richard, Cdr., USNR, *United States Naval Administration of the Trust Territory of the Pacific Islands* (3 vols.; Washington, D.C.: Government Printing Office, 1957.)
2. Norman Meller, *The Congress of Micronesia* (Honolulu: University of Hawaii Press, 1969).
3. Harold F. Nufer, "Unifying Factors in the Trust Territory of the Pacific Islands: An Analysis for the Period of 1963-72" (unpublished Ph.D. dissertation, Tufts University, 1974).

Micronesia Under American Rule

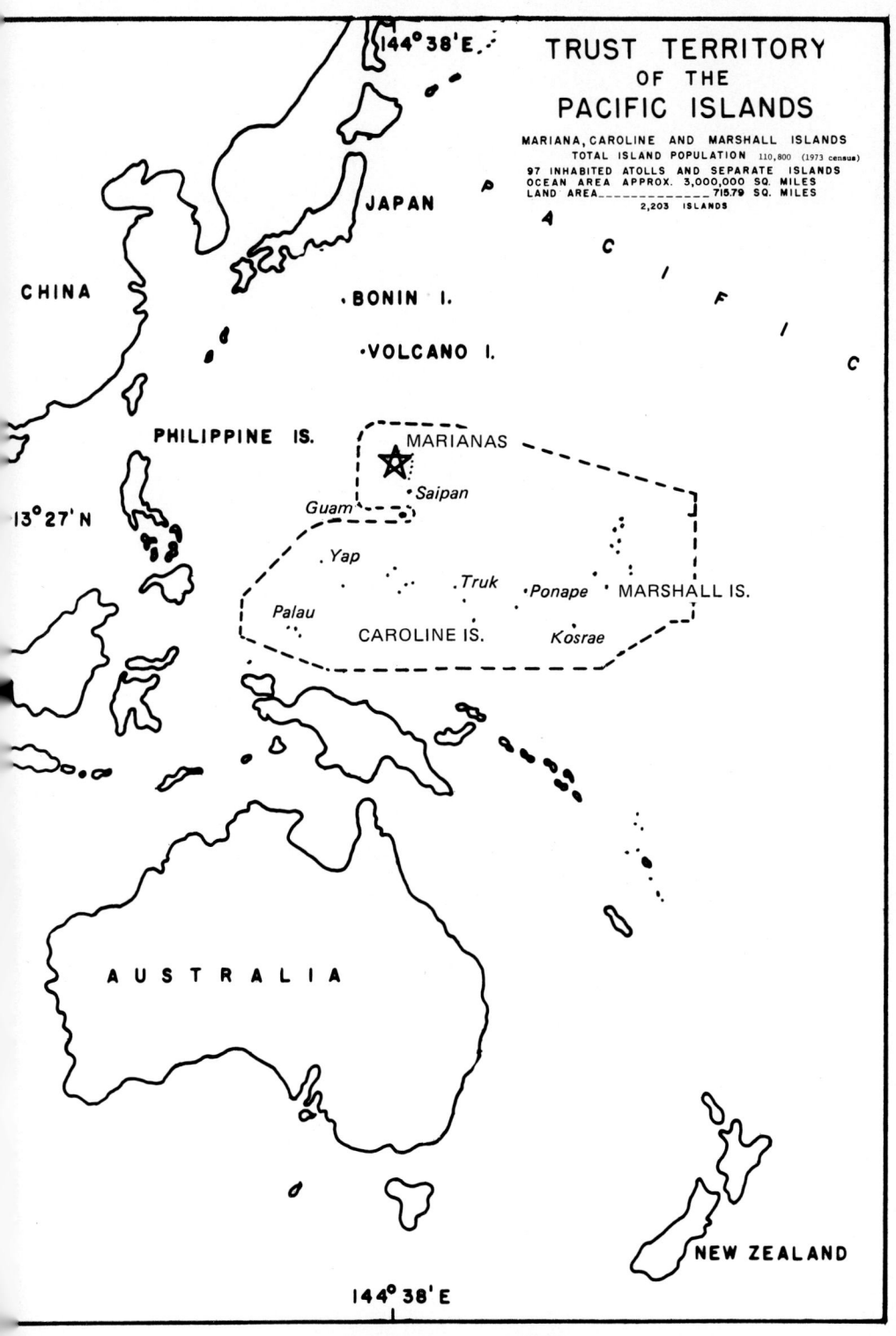

VICINITY MAP

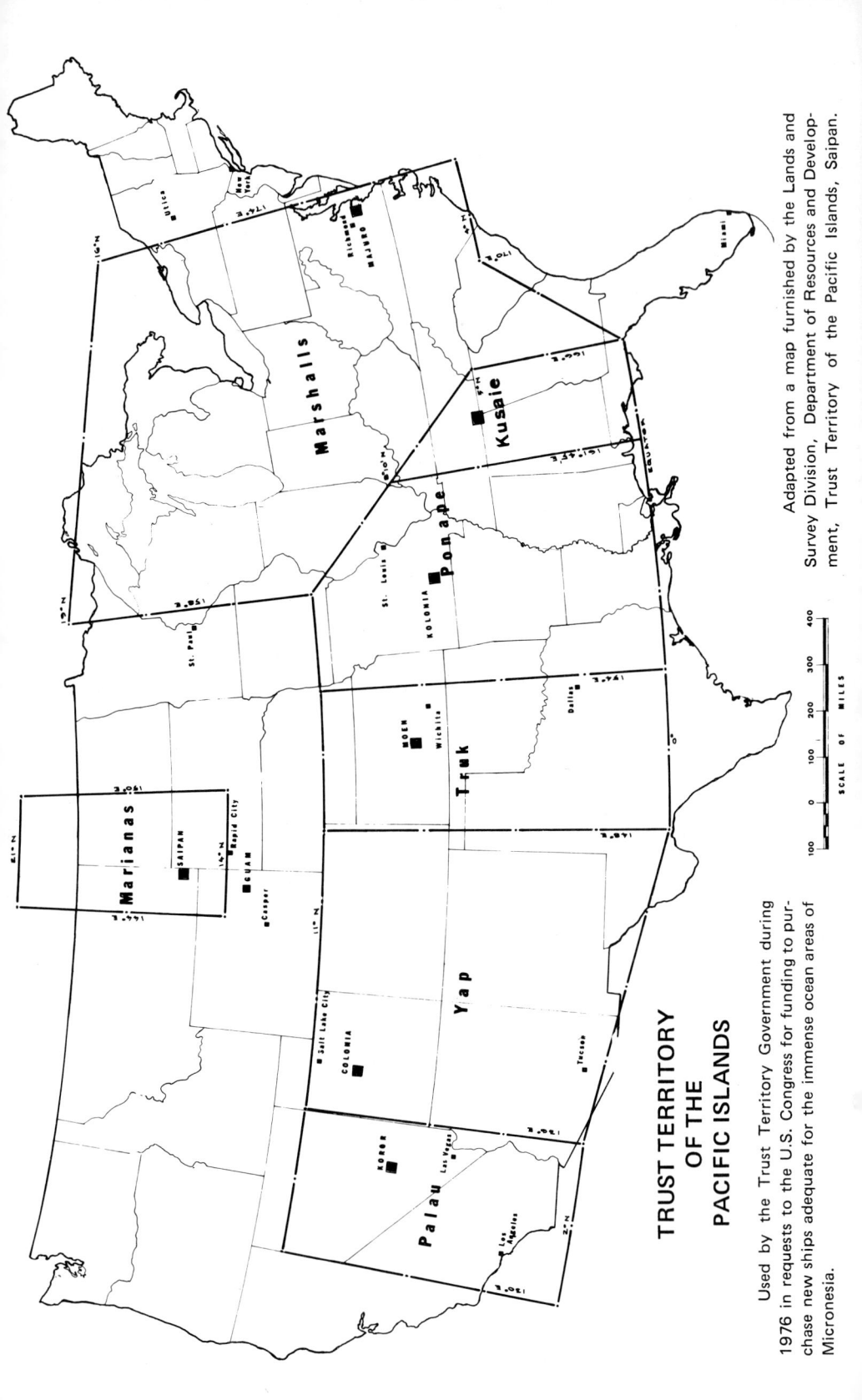

Introduction

A "SPAN-GER-JAP-AMER" ISLAND LINGUIST?

This is rather difficult to do in the late 1970s, but at least the thought is entertaining. Should you find a Micronesian who is a nonagenarian, or possibly an octogenarian, that person may be able to converse with you in *four* foreign languages, in addition to a dialect of one of the nine indigenous languages found in the Trust Territory of the Pacific Islands today. Such might not seem a great feat for a Scandinavian or a European, having been schooled for several years in two or three foreign languages and possibly traveled widely to other nations, not to mention being exposed to the saturation that is television programming these past three decades. However, the elderly Micronesian in the above situation may not have traveled beyond the confines of his own island grouping and possibly only seen a TV show once or twice in his lifetime, if at all.

The approximately 120,000 Micronesians in mid-1977,[1] living on but 97 of some 2,200 islands and islets over an expanse of the central and western Pacific (some 1,500 miles southwest of Hawaii for the Marshall Islands, and the northern Marianas being within 1,200 miles southeast of Japan, with the whole of Micronesia being north of the equator) comparable in size to the contiguous 48 United States—but with a total land area of only about 700 square miles—have been ruled successively since the sixteenth century by the Spanish (some 300 years), Germans (for 15 years), Japanese (almost 31 years), and finally, in the post-World War II era, under a strategic trusteeship administered on behalf of the U.N. Security Council by the Americans.

This introductory chapter will briefly review those prior administrations dating back to the Spanish and set the stage for the unfolding of the Trusteeship Agreement of 1947, which has resulted, to date, in a 31-year rule in Micronesia by the American Government.

MICRONESIA UNDER SPANISH RULE

While the Treaty of Tordesillas, in 1494, indicated that Spain was "responsible for all the islands of the Pacific,"[2] the dating for the advent of the Spanish in the central and western Pacific areas generally begins in the mid-sixteenth century, a few decades after the Portuguese navigator, Ferdinand Magellan, made his historic voyage across the vast Pacific Ocean and reached Guam in 1521. Later Spanish explorers visited the Pacific islands, usually bringing missionaries with them. An American anthropologist, Lessa, recounts an event in 1543 which occurred in the outer island area of the present Yap District, in the western Carolines, involving the Spanish explorer Ruy Lopez de Villalobos: "He [Villalobos] came across a small island that appears to have been Fais, a short distance east of Ulithi. He did not anchor there, but the natives came out in boats, making the sign of the cross and saying, in Castilian, *'Buenos días, matalotes!'* or 'Good day, sailors!' "[3]

The Spanish Government claimed Guam as a colony in 1565, using this largest of the islands in the Marianas as a "watering place" for the annual voyages of Spain's galleons en route from Florida to the Philippines via South and Central America. (Maynard Neas indicates that, on the return voyages, the galleons would sail "north from Manila and used the west winds direct to the California coast and then to Acapulco."[4]) The Spanish, unlike the Germans who were to follow them in the late nineteenth century, were not traders. Spain was interested in searching for gold, but found little in Micronesia. Purcell, in an excellent article on pre-American involvement in the islands other than Guam, said that, from the 1660s to 1898, Spain's emphasis in Micronesia was "on saving souls, and any effort at exploiting the area's resources was at best half-hearted. The Spanish were more interested in the economic potential of the Philippines and focused their attention there."[5]

Spain laid claim to the whole of the northern Mariana Islands after the arrival of the Jesuit missionaries in 1668 and the establishing of missions on Rota, Tinian, and Saipan. The Chamorros, who were the indigenes in the Marianas when the Spanish arrived, were to see their own culture submerged as the Spanish used soldiers and force, when necessary, to ensure that the Chamorros were Christianized. The Jesuit Order introduced, in 1669, the first form of formal education to be experienced by Micronesians.[6] A relocation program was instituted whereby the Chamorros were removed from their island homes in the northern Marianas and placed on Guam. Surprisingly, the Rotanese were able to escape this Spanish "sweep" at the time the rest of the Chamorros were taken to Guam. From 1700 to 1816, nobody was living on Saipan (some 75 miles northeast of Guam). The present Director of the Office of Territorial Affairs (DOTA), Van Cleve, wrote that, "by the middle of the nineteenth century, no pure Chamorros remained, their ancestry by then being heavily mixed with Filipino and Spanish contributions."[7] Father Arnold Bendowske, Associate Pastor of the Mt. Carmel Church on Saipan, and a Capuchin Franciscan, indicates that when the mission was reopened on Saipan in 1856, nine Chamorro families returned from Guam. Father Arnold further says that the population of Saipan in 1900 was only between 500 and 600 at the most, of whom only about 100 were Chamorros; the majority of the northern Mariana Islanders were Carolinians.

How extensive were the Spanish efforts in other parts of Micronesia? Educationally speaking, the Spanish, "for whom religion and culture were inseparable (but not identical), left such formal education as was to be provided for the natives in the hands of their missionaries. Religious instruction was the heart of the curriculum, but it was almost always supplemented with training in the trades."[8] Father Hezel identified the "trades" as being in "agriculture and carpentry, in particular;" and he wrote that "the rudiments of the Spanish language" would be added if the Micronesian students showed a capacity to learn such. He concluded: "Formal education during the Spanish regime, although conducted under the auspices of religious priests and brothers, and centered on the catechism, was concerned with those practical skills that the padres felt would help natives advance materially;" hence, the emphasis on the above vocational education approach.

While the Spanish concentrated their colonizing and Christianizing efforts in the western Carolines and the Marianas, American Protestant missionaries first arrived on the island of Kusaie (since January 1, 1977, the Kosrae District) in the eastern Carolines during the early 1850s. Boyer noted that "New England whalers also used to come here [to Kusaie] for food and water."[9] Starting in 1856, a series of "Morning Star" sailing ships brought those early Protestant missionaries from Boston Harbor to Micronesia. Price records that the first "Morning Star" sailing initiated a "romantic and pioneering venture. American Sunday-School children contributed their dimes to make possible the great square-rigged ship *Morning Star*, which should carry their missionaries to the South Seas to convert the heathen."[10]

Development of a copra trade in the latter part of the nineteenth century acted as a catalyst for a political struggle between Germany and Spain, with the Germans, in 1885, declaring a "protectorate" over the Marshall Islands. Germany also took control of Yap and claimed Truk, Ponape, and Kusaie within its sphere.[11] Pope Leo XIII was called upon that year (1885) to "adjudicate" a "political settlement" of the above squabble between the Spanish and the Germans. The Pope's decision "confirmed Spain's sovereignty over the Carolines while the Germans were "awarded" the "right to trade, fish, and establish settlements and coaling stations" in those islands. Germany also kept the Marshalls. Within a year of that adjudication, the spread of Catholicism to the eastern Carolines occurred, which, by 1887, lead to a "cold war" between Protestant and Catholic missionaries on Ponape. Father Hezel candidly wrote that the Protestant ministers in the eastern Carolines did not share in the "universal joy" which seemed to greet the arrival of the Spanish in 1886, the Congregationalists anxious to know what the "policy" of the new civil government of Catholic Spain would be toward the Protestant mission which had been cultivated carefully since its establishment in the early 1850s. Unfortunately for the Protestant clergy, their fears were justified: "They could expect little sympathy from a colonial government that regarded itself as responsible for the Hispanicization and Catholicization of those under its jurisdiction;" thus, with the judgment of the Spanish Capuchins on the American Protestants never very kindly, relations between the two factions worsened with time and mutual distrust led to a religious "cold war" which would head into "open hostilities between the two Christian groups."[12]

To summarize the Spanish experiences in the islands of Micronesia over a 300-year period, one may point to the absence of islander participation in the running of the government; the institution of a limited form of education, mostly in the trades; and economic development which was almost nil. The Spanish, in the opinion of Neas, "were not traders. They were missionaries more than anything else, and the pride of Spain and the glory of the Catholic Church." Parenthetically, in mid-1977, approximately half of the population of the Trust Territory of the Pacific Islands (and about 98 percent of the inhabitants in the northern Marianas, alone) were Roman Catholic and displaying a Hispanic influence in their family names and customs.

AN INTERMEDIATE PHASE: THE GERMANS

As mentioned previously, the Germans already occupied the Marshall Islands from 1885. Following the Treaty of Paris in 1898, when Guam was ceded to the United States as a result of the Spanish-American War settlement, Germany (in 1899) paid the sum of $4.5 million to Spain for acquisition of the Carolines and the Marianas (sans Guam, which was already a U.S. territory).[13] Webb noted that the McKinley Administration, feeling that "the price was too high," declined to enter the bidding for Spain's last possessions in the Pacific.[14]

Germany's commercial involvements in Micronesia, begun in the Marshalls with the Adolph Cappelle Company—a trading concern—as early as the 1860s, accelerated once the Germans had legal possession of the whole of Micronesia. Interestingly, the Cappelle Company, which had as one of the joint owners José DeBrum, a Portuguese (and an ancestor of Oscar DeBrum, the District Administrator of the Marshall Islands in 1977), failed. The company had acquired the atoll of Likiep, northeast of Kwajalein, where its plantation operations were satisfactory.

Introduction

However, the widespread trading efforts by the Cappelle Company did not succeed. Later, several of the German traders formed the Jaluit-Gesellschaft operation, which enjoyed "a commercial monopoly in the islands after 1901."[15] Also, "in 1912, the future looked bright for the *Deutsche Südsee-Phosphat-Aktien-Gesellschaft,* which had special rights to mine phosphate on Angaur [in the Palaus]. Just as the Germans seemed to be making some progress, their activities were terminated by World War I."[16]

The German Administration in Micronesia seemed to be characterized by a "no-nonsense" approach to matters. Neas tells that when the German officials approached foreigners who were in the islands, and apparently there were quite a few at the time the Spanish departed, the German administrators would immediately inquire as to where the foreigners were working, how they obtained the land they were using, and what their assets were. People without any financial means—those whom one might stereotype as the "adventurer-beachcomber" type—were banished, or shipped out, immediately.

Father Arnold says that the "big migration" to Saipan came during the German times, from about 1900 to 1911, especially. He says that the Germans wanted to develop the northern Marianas for the production of copra; thus, they initiated a program of enticing, or inviting, the people to come up to Saipan, with the promise of land and materials to build homes and water catchments. However, copra remained a major cash crop only in the Marshalls and Carolines.

The Germans required the Micronesians throughout the vast area to work on "public projects" over specified annual periods. Such service was credited to the islanders in lieu of paying taxes.[17]

To govern the islands, the German Administration used a minimum of personnel. Father Arnold remembers that possibly nine officials were sent to the northern Marianas. The Germans also brought in policemen from the Fiji Islands at the beginning. After realizing that those law enforcement officers would not be needed, they were sent home. In the northern Marianas, there was some friction between the German governor and the church at first. The governor was replaced. After that, relations between the clergy and the government were amiable. The clergy at that time was composed of German priests, the German Capuchins, who replaced the Spanish clergy when Spain withdrew from the Pacific in 1898.

The German approach to "capital punishment" was direct and uncomplicated. First, the death penalty was at the discretion of the governor, "to be accomplished either by hanging or shooting." An example of this practice being instituted under the Germans was uncovered by the Lands and Surveys Division in the Trust Territory Government a few years ago, when one of that division's personnel researched in the archives of the National University in Canberra, Australia. It seems a group of islanders in the Sokehs District of Ponape rebelled, in 1910, killing their German governor, several of his staff and then took over the administration of the island for a time. They "timed" their revolt to be during the absence of any German vessels. When a German ship did come back, the Ponapean rebels were subdued in the attack which commenced. The German officials shot the ringleaders—all 25 of them—and banished the others to a muncipality on the westside of Babelthuap Island, in Palau, presumably "for life." The rebels' land was taken away from them and the islanders from other areas—Mokil, Pingelap, Ngatik, and the Mortlock Islands (now in the Truk District) — were moved in and given deeds to that land. The policy outlining the resolution of the "Sokehs Rebellion"—including the carrying out of the death penalty and resettlement to Babelthuap and provisions for others to occupy the Sokehs area—consumed but *one* page in the German documents.

Perhaps the greatest accomplishment under the German Period was the concern shown with regard to land matters. The Germans refused to permit the "alienation of land" in Micronesia. In other words, they would not even allow their own traders to purchase land in the islands; rather, the officials would say to the inquiring traders, or other alien businessmen: "You want to be here, on this place? Okay. Now, here are your boundaries." Then, according to Neas, the German Administration would approach the Micronesians and negotiate for the land in their (the German Government's) name. The trader or businessman would, by permit or lease, occupy the land and pay a fee and taxes to the German Administration. Neas says that the German officials introduced the concept of simple ownership of land for the Micronesians and a concomitant principle for aliens, namely, "Use it [the land] or lose it [the right to have a lease]!"

A thorn in the side of the German Administration was the American adventurer David O'Keefe, who founded his own empire in Yap. O'Keefe, who left Savannah, Georgia, on a vessel, was somehow shipwrecked in the western Carolines. It is supposed that he came ashore in Yap around 1870. Over the years, he set up a trading station there. By the time the Germans arrived in 1899, O'Keefe was well established on Yap and the surrounding islands. He even had a Chinese partner in Hong Kong. The "key" to O'Keefe's success with the Yapese came when he found out that they made periodic canoe trips to a small island near Babelthuap, in Palau, to quarry a certain limestone highly prized by them. Those large, circular discs with a hole in the middle became the famed "Yap money." So, O'Keefe offered to transport the Yapese laborers and their precious stones (some of which might stand eight feet in diameter) aboard his ship. In turn, he negotiated with the Palauans so that the Yapese could continue their quarrying project. As a repayment for his services,

Introduction 9

the Yapese produced copra and whatever else O'Keefe wanted in his trading enterprise. It is estimated that O'Keefe—who disappeared at sea with his two sons by his second wife, a Yapese (he maintained his American wife back in Savannah at the same time) shortly after 1900—left a fortune of close to $1.5 million.[18] It is presumed his ship was lost at sea.

Neas says that the German documents are filled with references to the "reprehensible O'Keefe." They could not stand him. Possibly, it was more jealousy and commercial rivalry than even his life style which the Germans hated.

Formal education for the Micronesians was first established by the Germans in the Marshall Islands (in 1888) and then in the Marianas and the Carolines (in 1899). The subjects taught included the German language, world history, geography, arithmetic, music, and an emphasis on religion. Attendance was obligatory for all children between the ages of seven and 13 years, with fines imposed for nonattenders. Ramarui writes that the educational system under the Germans was more highly developed in the Marianas than the other districts, that, "in most districts, the German Administration stressed economic development while schools were left in the hands of missionaries. Perhaps Christianization was the main theme for which schools were established."[19]

Father Hezel adds that the first public school during the German Period was opened in 1905, with the stress on the "acquisition of the characteristically teutonic virtues of thrift and industry." Father Hezel quotes a German Government report of 1900, which offered the following "definition" of purpose: "Our task as regards the education of the natives is clear—they must be trained to work; they must be encouraged to earn and save money."[20]

The German Administration was more tolerant of religion than the Spanish had been. Whereas the Protestant missionaries experienced numerous disagreements with the Spanish officials, the German Government immediately, in 1899, let it be known that *all* religious sects were welcomed; however, such groups could stay only so long as they obeyed the German laws. There was no financial support for religion from the German Administration or official recognition of one church group over another. The Germans, Neas says, were very outspoken with regard to the "freedom of religion" and, at the same time, the need for the religious organizations to "support themselves."

In summary, the German Period (beginning, officially, in 1899 throughout the entirety of Micronesia except in Guam, which was a U.S. territory) was one of firmness in purpose and exactitude in performance. The commercial trading accelerated; education included the first public schools (in 1905); religious differences between Catholics and Protestants were tolerated, with no groups receiving official support from the German Administration; and, as in the earlier Spanish Era, the

Micronesians did not participate in the political offices of government. The land laws under the Germans excluded aliens from purchasing land during that time.

Perhaps a contrasting comment by an American official married to a Saipanese (Chamorro) is apropos. He says that when he speaks with his father-in-law, an octogenarian, the conversation is in German; with the mother-in-law, who is in her seventies, it is Spanish. When asked why, that official replied, "Because he [his father-in-law] liked the Germans. They were disciplinarians, and they were strict. They got things done in an orderly way!"

THE JAPANESE PERIOD (1914-45)

Japanese traders were found throughout the Micronesian islands in the decade prior to the German Administration. However, the Germans attempted to put a very tight lid on the Japanese involvement after 1899. All of this changed with the outbreak of World War I. Japan declared war on Germany, and the Japanese Navy seized the Micronesian islands in October, 1914. Less known is the role of the British in Japan's occupancy of the islands. It appears that Japan and Great Britain had an "under-the-table" agreement that the U.K. would take all of the German island possessions *south* of the equator and that Japan would occupy and control all of the islands (meaning, Micronesia) *north* of the equator.

Accordingly, British ships were present in Micronesia as the Japanese took control of those islands without resistance from the German authorities. Neas tells of an incident during the evacuation of the Germans which occurred in Yap. It seems a British man-of-war came to Yap. The Germans had established a cable station and a radio station there. The location of the radio station towers was well known to the British captain, who sent a message to the radio station that, "[in so many] minutes from now, we'll [the British man-of-war] destroy this thing [the station complex]. And if you want out of there, you better get out!" The Germans took the British commander at his word, and the Englishman was as good as his word: he lobbed shells into the station area and stopped the communications. Eventually, the Japanese Navy came by, taking the Germans off the islands of Yap. The Germans throughout Micronesia were shipped to Japan, from where they filtered back to their homeland.

Japan retained its military rule in Micronesia from the outset of World War I until the end of 1920, when the Council of the League of Nations confirmed Japan as the mandatory power over all of the former German islands north of the equator. Thus, Japan was assigned a class

Introduction

"C" mandate, obligated to promote "to the utmost" the material and moral well-being and social progress of those islanders. Japan was prohibited from building any fortifications or military installations under its mandate from the League. Micronesia formally, on December 17, 1920, was designated as the Japanese Mandated Islands.[21]

Did the Japanese *reverse* the trend of their predecessors, the Spanish and Germans, with regard to the noninvolvement of Micronesians in the governmental organizations throughout the islands? Opinions differ on this. Van Cleve wrote of the "total lack of Micronesian participation in political processes" under the Mandate Period.[22] Professor Moos indicated that the Japanese Government employed the indigenous population in some leadership positions:

> In addition to the local Japanese authorities, the South Seas Bureau employed islanders as government officials. In October, 1922, the Bureau established a system of local government in which there were four types of native officials: the villages of most islands were presided over by the *sosonchō* (a general village chieftain), and the *sonchō* (a village chieftain). The villages of the chamorro . . . [in the northern Marianas] were headed by a *kuchō* and the *joyakū*.[23]

Turning to the views of two Micronesians who lived during the Mandate Years, we find Dr. Ngas Kansou, Deputy Director of Health Services for the Trust Territory Government, a Trukese, recalling his experiences: "I think that the Japanese were trying to develop our place for themselves, not for us. They did not have any intention to develop the [Micronesian] people to run their own government and affairs." Manuel S. (M. S.) Villagomez, a successful entrepreneur on Saipan, remembers the constabulary (the civilian police) as an outstanding feature during the Japanese Days. Villagomez served as an interpreter for the Japanese Government when Guam was conquered in the week following the attack on Pearl Harbor.

The Japanese selected Koror, in the Palau District, as their administrative center for the Mandate. The *Nanyo-cho* Government, as the Japanese were called in the islands, was able to be self-sufficient without having to rely on financing from Tokyo. This was due mainly to the ability of that government's *Nanyo Kohatsu Kaisha* (the South Seas Development Company, to which Moos referred in the above), in which the *Nanyo-cho* Government held the majority stock.[24]

However, Japan's invasion of Manchuria, in 1931, appeared to change the emphasis regarding the conduct of affairs in Micronesia. Rumors began cropping up that the Japanese were fortifying those islands, notably Truk, as early as 1932, in violation of the mandate.[25] Commander Richard wrote that "between the years 1934 and 1941, the Japanese had built a chain of airfields and seaplane bases stretching from Saipan to the Palaus and from Truk to Wotje [east of Kwajalein, in the Marshalls]. The militarization of Truk and the Marshalls had been begun more than a year before the attack on Pearl Harbor."[26] The Japanese Government denied all such rumors. Nevertheless, Japan formally withdrew from the League of Nations in 1935.

The *Nanyo Kohatsu Kaisha* was formed in 1936, representing amalgamations of earlier commercial interests. Neas says that these companies were concerned primarily with land development for sugar and exploitation of the natural resources such as phosphate, bauxite, copper, and other materials indigenous to the islands. Whereas the Germans earlier (during 1899-1914) had deeded some 3,000 hectares of land to the local people during their Administration, the *Nanyo-cho* Government permitted Japanese citizens in Micronesia, after 1931, to buy land from the islanders. Kuribayashi indicated the six main areas in which the *Nanyo Kohatsu Kaisha* involved itself from 1936 until the end of the war. (*Note:* The "Value" was cumulative, from 1936-42; however, the yen and dollar conversions are as of mid-1977.)

Industry	Production	Yen Conversion (in Billions)	Dollar Conversion (in Millions)
(1) Sugar	50,000-60,000 tons	67.1	$223.5
(2) Alcoholic Beverages	5,772 litres	15.4	51.5
(3) Katsuo-bushi, Seasoning (Dried Skipjack)	1,905 tons	13.3	44.2
(4) Arafura Pearling	4,200 tons	9.4	31.5
(5) Fisheries (Skipjack)	11,545 tons	7.3	24.3
(6) Molasses	11,218 tons	6.3	21.1
TOTAL VALUE (1977)		¥118.8 bil.	$396.1 mil.

In addition to the above six main economic endeavors by the *Nanyo Kohatsu Kaisha,* Kuribayashi told Zeder that the company also operated stevedoring, shipping, and trading. The annual profits (of which the sugar industry was over 50 percent) amounted to between ¥14 billion-¥20 billion (or, $50 million-$70 million in mid-1977 dollars).[27]

To what extent did the *Nanyo Kohatsu Kaisha* employ Micronesians in the various enterprises during the 31 years of the Mandate Period? Purcell noted that the *Nanyo-cho* Government purchased from Germany, in 1922, the mining rights, buildings, and equipment on Angaur (in the Palau District) as well as on three other islands: Fais, Peleliu, and Togobai. The height of employment for the islanders during the period from 1922-38 in mining operations on the above four islands occurred in 1938, when, out of a total of 743 "mine labourers," 401 of them were Micronesian. The remaining 342 were Japanese that year with the

Introduction 13

exception of two Chinese workers.[28] Working conditions in the mines for the islanders were arduous: Purcell said that the workers (excluding the Japanese, who were considered "supervisors" or "equipment operators") were "treated as peons," receiving a *maximum* pay of less than 23¢ daily (in pre-World War II rates) during that 16-year period (1922-1938).[29]

Dwight Heine, Special Consultant to the High Commissioner in the Trust Territory Government, and a Marshallese, recalls the Japanese Mandate Years as not "too bad" when the civilian government was in charge (prior to World War I), and how things shifted as the military gained ascendancy in the islands:

> They [the *Nanyo-cho* Government] were interested in economic development, . . . except in the Marshall District, [where] we were fortunate because we were the only one who could make copra—the only thing that the district exported in great quantity, and exports [during the Mandate and at present] more than all the rest of Micronesia put together. And then we're [the Marshallese] the one with good eye. Whereas in the Carolines [Ponape, Kusaie, Truk, Yap, and Palau] the type of agriculture they practice here the Japanese were far better than the Micronesian people, so they [the Japanese] took over in many places, like here in Saipan, the sugar industry, and so on in Palau and Ponape and so on. But I remember the [Japanese] military start moving in in the '30's—'36, I remember that in '36—they start moving in, and now things begin to change. And it was rough for both the Japanese and the Micronesian people, but especially the Micronesians. We were recruited to work on these fortifications, and you cannot say no. It was labor. They pay you something, but, and they feed you, but you cannot decline, and it was then ordered when the military took over. That's when we began to feel how hard it was for us.

Did the Micronesians have the opportunity to participate as businessmen during the Japanese Mandate Period? José C. (JoeTen) Tenorio, considered one of the most successful Micronesian entrepreneurs since World War II, remembers his own experiences in the final decade of the Mandate: "I was a farmer growing sugarcane, sugar plantation with my brother. All I know is almost everything is controlled by Japanese—economic, political, and just everything." In response to a question on how many Micronesians had their own businesses, JoeTen said: "Most of the businesses were Japanese, with the exception of a few—I could remember there's a few, a grocery store in the locale [of Saipan]; it's just a 'mama and a papa' type [of store], very small." Ramarui, a Palauan, confirms the "lack of Micronesian businesses" extended to his home area: "They [the businesses in Koror] were all Japanese. There was no Micronesian store—not a single one on Koror. There were Micronesian stores outside of Koror, but on Koror, itself, I can well remember that there was no Palauan store there. I mean, no store in Koror was owned by a Palauan." Richard noted that the pre-War Japanese population in the Palau District totaled some 20,000, most of whom resided on Koror, the capital of the *Nanyo-cho* Government. At the same time, the islander population in Palau was about 6,500, of whom 1,200 were on Koror and 3,400 on Babelthuap.[30]

By the close of World War II, in mid-1945, there were over three aliens for every Micronesian (e.g., about 147,000 Orientals—Japanese, Okinawans, Koreans, Chinese, and Formosans—vis-à-vis some 45,000 indigenes).[31] How well did the islanders perform as laborers under the Japanese managers? Masao Kuwano, Manager of the California First Bank (a subsidiary of the Bank of Tokyo) on Saipan, and a nisei, comments about what the Saipanese people have shared with him concerning the pre-1945 days: "They [the Saipanese] were taught to work. And many [Saipanese] people saying that when they work, they [the Japanese] buy you liquor, rice that they wanted to eat, and, you know, they used to get whatever they work for, for their living; and so long as you work, and they support you, and just enough money for savings—to save up. This is what they [the Saipanese] are really interested in."

Kuwano adds that the Saipanese would save about one-third of their pay checks, working six days a week (Sundays excepted). "But," Kuwano says, "most of the Saipanese during that [Japanese Mandate] time, they work about eight months to nine months, and they don't work any more [than that], because they've got enough money to be saved."

Ramarui became a carpenter in Palau during the Mandate Period. Whereas the average Micronesian was receiving between 20 and 30 yen a month, Ramarui earned as much as 150 yen a month. "I don't quite consider that [150 yen per month, or about $37 in pre-1945 rates to be economically a very good one except that the prices were so low that I think everybody was happy," Ramarui says. "There was always, despite the wages, the Japanese were much higher and the Micronesians much lower [in the economic and social standings]." A comment by an American official during the post-War era (1947-51, in particular) reflects back on the "close supervision" the Japanese had to place on many of the Micronesian workers:

> We have men who are excellent carpenters, cement constructors and others who worked with the Japanese for years, but they require constant supervision. For example, we have men laying a concrete foundation for a Quonset. If they require one additional board to complete the form, they will sit there until someone comes and tells them where, when, and how to get it. The Japanese always had someone there to do this [supervising].[32]

Dwight Heine tells of an abortive attempt on the part of a group of Marshallese to form a "co-op" during the Mandate Period:

> We begin to form co-op [in the Marshalls], and they [the Japanese] know if we will be very effective, because we will ship our copra to Japan

Introduction

by passenger [ships], and then we'll order our own goods, and that will kill their business, so they pass a law that no natives can have a business. And that wasn't very good. I think they should have let us do it so that we show them how clumsy we were and [we have to then] invite them in. (Laugh.)

Senator Olympio T. Borja, of the Northern Marianas Legislature, and a Saipanese, while not noticing any islander proprietorships or local entrepreneurs on Saipan during the Mandate Period, did say that some of the indigenes joined with Okinawans "in terms of fishery or in terms of farming" endeavors.

What of the life styles of the Micronesians during the Mandate decades? Were they much affected by the tremendous influx of aliens, most of whom were from Japan? Saipan, Toland wrote, had become "a little Tokyo" at the time of the attack on Pearl Harbor, with the sugarcane fields covering 70 percent of that relatively small island (only 85 square miles). The peak alien population on Saipan prior to the close of the War was some 30,000, with fewer than 4,000 Chamorros.[33] Dr. Kansou, a Trukese, recounts the *dual* "medical programs" available in his home area under the *Nanyo-cho* Government:

> There was a health service that was provided to the Trukese during Japanese time, . . . a medical care system that existed. . . . We had two system: one Japanese go to, and one for the Trukese people. I don't know about [the other] districts. I'm sure they have a similar setup. So, the medical care that they [the Japanese] provide, I think, I would say it is sufficient when you compare with the level of medicine everywhere in the world. I mean, the way they practice medicine at that time, the drugs are available: like, treatment of yaws [a venereal disease]; treatment of other things. Antibiotics was not used at that time. There were other things that they use, so the Trukese received that. They perform surgeries, they perform obstetrics, but it was very insufficient. In other words, it doesn't reach all the people—only people that closer by, and live within the so-called, we would call it "district center" there at that time.[34]

Unfortunately, the Japanese Government trained only a handful of Micronesians to be "native practitioners and corpsmen:" one Saipanese and five Marshallese. A "bonus" for the Kusaiens came when Arobati Hicking, a British (Tarawa-Suva) trained medical practitioner (and a member of the Gilbert and Ellice Colony Medical Service) was transferred—along with several hundred Ocean Island inhabitants—by the Japanese Navy to Kusaie early in the War.[35]

Before discussing the plight of Christian missionaries in the islands as the Mandate Period entered the World War II years, it would be well to recall that the Japanese, as a people, traditionally have been little affected by Christianity. While the present and future interests of Japan with regard to the Trust Territory of the Pacific Islands will be evaluated in chapter 5 herein, suffice it to say that Japan's primordial religion is Shintoism, which was used by the Tojo Government to create a fanatic patriotism in the 1930s and 1940s. Buddhism at present has its largest number of adherents in Japan; Confucianism is the smallest of these three. It is not uncommon today to see a Shinto shrine and a Buddhist temple within close proximity of each other throughout the prefectures (or counties) of Japan. As Forbis observed, the Japanese usually "marry in a Shinto ceremony because it stresses purification, live by Confucian ethics, and go to the grave in a Buddhist rite because this guarantees that one will be remembered for a few generations."[36] There are fewer than one million Christians in Japan, one-third of whom are Catholics, in a population approaching 115 million by mid-1977.

Dwight Heine, a Marshallese who for many years has been active in the functions of the Saipan Community Church (see chapter 3), recalls that the "[Christian] missionaries' activities [under the Japanese] was very much curtailed. . . . The Japanese came, and they untie those things. . . . The Japanese assassinated many of their [the islanders'] elder statesmen. . . . So they [the Japanese] didn't like anything Christianity or anything [such as that]." Heine further says that the German clergy (both Catholic and Protestant) were unable to remain in Micronesia after the defeat in World War I; however, Spanish Jesuits (the Society of the Jesuits) were permitted to return to the islands. "But," Heine observes, "they're [the Jesuits are] not as dynamic as their predecessors, the Germans. They just stay in their, where they stayed, and when people showed up, then they had services—Masses. If they don't show up, . . . [the Jesuits] don't go around and pick them up."

Richard recorded that the *Nango Dendo Dan*, a Japanese Christian group which was affiliated with the American Board of Commissioners for Foreign Missions, directed the work of the German Liebenzeller Mission (Protestant missionaries primarily in the western Carolines) between 1919 and up to the start of the Second World War. The Spanish Jesuit missions in the Carolines and northern Marianas during that time were organized into a vicariate under the jurisdiction of the Bishop in Truk.[37] However, by the outbreak of the War in 1941, all foreign missionaries had left the Marshalls. That meant the indigenous ministers, trained at the Boston Mission School on Kusaie, "continued to hold services and Sunday School, often secretly to escape punishment by the Japanese. The tolerance which the Japanese administrators had usually shown toward the practice of Christianity by the natives disappeared when the invasion of the islands became a possibility." Richard further commented that no religious services were permitted on Kwajalein after June, 1943.[38] In Palau, the foreign missionaries were all resettled by the Japanese military on the island of Babelthuap for the duration of the War; thus, the Palauans, mostly of the Catholic faith, were without

Introduction

authorized Christian services until the arrival of the American Armed Forces in 1944-45.[39]

Christian missionaries on Guam also faced resettlement during the War. Father Arnold, a Capuchin Franciscan, first arrived in the western Pacific in 1941, with his initial assignment in the Marianas being on Guam. Within a few months, he was taken prisoner by the Japanese (the fall of Guam occurring on December 10 of that year). The missionaries at first were in a prisoner-of-war camp on Guam with American military personnel. Then, on January 10, 1942, the clergy—with the military and other U.S. citizens—were taken to Japan. After two or three weeks in Japan, the missionaries and the other civilians were separated from the military prisoners and remained in their own respective camps until the War's end. Father Arnold returned to Guam in March, 1946.

How well did the islanders get along with the Japanese and other Asians who actually became the majority population in Micronesia by the latter part of the 1930s? The general consensus appears to be that relations were quite amiable under the *Nanyo-cho* Government when the civilians were in charge of the islands; however, the exigencies of the immediate pre-War and the actual Wartime operations under the Japanese military officers made things extremely hard for the Micronesians. When "discrimination" is mentioned, it is well to differentiate between the various "classes" of people found in Micronesia under the Mandate Period.

For example, Michael F. Caldwell, Chairperson of the Division of Curriculum and Instruction in the Department of Special Education, University of Guam, who also previously lived in Palau as an official of the Trust Territory Government's Department of Education, believes that those Micronesians over the age of 45 years who hold "fond memories" of when the Japanese controlled the islands constitute "a certain class, or a particular group of Micronesians, and those [islanders] are the ones to whom the Japanese talked, because those with whom the Japanese didn't deal during that [Mandate] time are not fluent [in Japanese] and don't have those fond remembrances." Caldwell continues by referring to "positive" reinforcement vis-à-vis "negative" reinforcement under the Japanese:

> Those who were *positively* reinforced by Japanese come forward when Japanese are present. Those who were *negatively* reinforced, [do not]. . . . If you stop to think about it, who's going to visit with the Japanese when they [the latter] come? Not those who had bad experiences with them, right? It's going to be those who had positive [experiences]. And so those are the ones that come forward. I know in Palau, when Japanese came—the first really Japanese that came into Palau were in the late '60s—after, you know, subsequent to the War, and they were very warmly received by many old Japanese families. [The late] Mitch Solang, . . . [who] was the Community

Development Officer in Palau, . . . [his] wife's father was Japanese. So, Mitch . . . [and his wife] had fond memories. The father had come back to visit them. So, there were relationships like that, I think, which were very *positive*. Whether there were *negative* relationships or not, those [things] are not talked about.

JoeTen, on Saipan, believes that the reason why the Micronesians his age (over 45 years) liked the Japanese was the availability of material goods and the willingness of the indigenes to work hard, at least in the northern Marianas:

> The majority of the people—the reason why they liked Japanese, especially my age, eh?—I'm thinking about during the Japanese time—is, everything you could find, I mean, everything that what you want you could find, because it's many enterprises going on within the Japanese [Period]. Like, for instance, you know, even wood—firewood—you can sell. Anything you got, you can get, you could sell. Maybe that's the reason why, and there was a lot of employment that if you wants to go, you can get a job. Maybe that's the reason why they like it. But other than that, I think it's almost everybody got to have a hard work, it's got to be hard work.

JoeTen also recalls that "the highest position of the locals or indigenous that they have is about policeman. The rest is only their [the Japanese'] store clerk or delivery boy. That's most I can think [recall under the Mandate]."

Ramarui, from Palau, categorizes "*four* classes" of citizenship when the Japanese were in Micronesia, so far as "discrimination" was concerned:

> It's difficult to judge now, because now I know the American system. I have a mixed feeling. But at the time I was under the Japanese, I think I felt things went just natural and okay. I know what you now term "discrimination" existed then. But, at that time, you didn't think things could be discrimination. We thought that, and led, perhaps we were led to believe that they [the Japanese] were *first*-rate citizens, and, of course, the Okinawans and the Koreans and the Micronesians [in that order] at the bottom. But we were led to believe that that was how things would be. . . . Micronesians were *fourth*. We don't normally hold up the file to be telling them [the Japanese]; we only say they were first-rate position and we were second. But, in my observation, there were those [the Okinawans and Koreans] in between us [the Japanese and Micronesians]. But when it comes to schools, we have only two school systems. One system for the Japanese, Okinawans, and Koreans; the other was for Micronesians.

Dr. Kansou, a Trukese, agrees with Ramarui, above, respecting the existence of discrimination against the Micronesians during the Mandate Period: "Oh, yes, definitely. There was no hidden thing at that time. We certainly know that you [the islander] are below, and they [the

Introduction 19

Japanese] would force you and they would tell you, too. In the school system, itself, we cannot talk in the Trukese in the school [which was for Trukese students only]."

Neas recounts the respect which a "Mr. Tanaka," a police officer stationed at Jaluit, in the Marshalls, received from the Marshallese, and adds that "corporal punishment" was a fact of life under Japanese Rule:

> The Japanese provided a minimum of social benefits to the people of Micronesia, but there was employment. And there was also a clear understanding of what the purpose of the Japanese was, and how to get along with them. A typical example of the "understanding" that the Japanese and the Micronesians had is a case over in the Marshall District [involving Mr. Tanaka].... And the story—if it isn't true, it could have been—Mr. Tanaka was on Majuro, and there was a Marshallese on Majuro that lived on Arno, a neighboring atoll. And this fellow, the Marshallese, was trying to get some point over to Mr. Tanaka, and Tanaka listened imperturbably until he [the islander] was fairly well finished, and was fairly irritated, apparently. Tanaka took the cigarette out of his [own] mouth, and ground it out on his [the Marshallese's] forehead, and he says, "Now, look! This is just a *sample*! You get back to Arno and *stay* there. I don't want to see or hear of you being around here anymore!" The fellow took him at his word and left. Tanaka was a *highly* respected person. It's amazing that the people, many of the people, ran afoul of the Japanese, and some of them *lost* fingers. If they were stealing public property or taking it without the Japanese consent, it was sort of a *gradual* losing of the joints of the fingers. It was no question about it. Corporal punishment was used, and whether it was abused or not, it's hard to say. But there is a terrific show of affection and feeling, *good* feeling, among the older Micronesians and many of the Japanese that are seen in the Territory now, that were here as officials with the trading company, the *Nanyo Boeki Kaisha*, [which company] had a virtual monopoly on trading all over the present Trust Territory [during the Mandate Period].[40]

A sanction even more severe than "corporal" punishment was apparently evident, at least in the minds of some of the islanders, once the military began arriving in the islands during the latter half of the 1930s. Neas recalls the following conversation he had with a Trukese male in the late 1960s with regard to the Japanese military fortifying the island of Moen, in the Truk Lagoon, on the eve of World War II:

> *Neas:* Why were these [Japanese] guns placed up on this hill? Did you talk to them [the Japanese military who installed that artillery]?
> *Trukese:* No.
> *Neas:* Well, when they started off-loading guns and took them up the hill, you didn't say anything to them?
> *Trukese:* No.
> *Neas:* Did they say anything to you?
> *Trukese:* No.
> *Neas:* What if you *had* said anything to them?
> *Trukese:* We'd probably have got our head cut off or [been] shot if we tried to argue with them!

An older driver for the Hafadai Beach Hotel, on Saipan, when asked if he remembered what things were like under the Japanese Mandate Years, said: "As they [the Japanese] were losing the War, they were very bad to us. But before they were losing the War, we were happy." Jesus Ilo, another driver for that Saipan hotel in the northern Marianas, recalls the "forced child labor" and other living conditions experienced on Saipan once the War involvement became more intense. In particular, Ilo remembers that "some Japanese were good to natives, but when Japanese soldiers came, even Saipanese school children were pulled out of school to work as laborers on airstrips or as stevedores unloading cargo from ships. The Japanese civilians on Saipan would *not* do such work." Ilo also notes that, as more Japanese military personnel were stationed on Saipan, they would come to the natives' homes and tell them to move out so that the soldiers would then have housing. Many of the Saipanese thus had to resettle on farms, to the east and north of the populous villages along the west coastal area. The islanders used bicycles as their mode of transportation. The only cars available to them were taxis, which ran between the villages of Chalan Kanoa and Tanapag (just north of Garapan).

C. S. Cruz, a Security Officer at the Trust Territory Headquarters on Capitol Hill, Saipan, said that, during the War, the Japanese were "very mean" to the Saipanese. When asked if things were better prior to the outbreak of the Second World War, Cruz reflected: "Well, there was many discriminations. We were treated like third-class citizens. We didn't want to be a master race, but we wanted to be treated better." If Cruz's observations appear somewhat hard on the treatment the islanders received from the Japanese in the northern Marianas, it should be noted that his brother was one of the hostages the Japanese military used at the end of the War. His brother was killed. Ironically, Cruz was employed by the Japanese Imperial Navy during the War.

Dwight Heine, a Marshallese, recounts that the Japanese "became very, very different after the war in China. Then you begin to see a *new* breed. They really—I don't know how to put it—but the *worst* in men came out to the surface." Heine recalls why the invasion of Manchuria in 1931 was to have an effect on those officials and businessmen who came to Micronesia as World War II approached:

> Later on [after 1931], when they [the Japanese] were fortifying this place, more and more people came out from there, who served in China, and some of these, they were out of uniform, but they served maybe as a storekeeper or working in a big company, but they served, and the Army—the Japanese Army—they left the Japanese Army but the Japanese Army, in them, stayed *with* them. And they showed the way they acted. *Military*-type feelings. For instance, if you [an islander] do not bow to him, then he slap you around, and so on. Things like that.

Introduction

21

Senator Borja believes that the *Nanyo-cho* Government was democratic "up to 1938," but that, as World War II closed in, and the islanders' homes were confiscated by the military to quarter the soldiers, "there's no due process of law." Force was used against the Micronesians.

Izumi Kobayashi, Secretary General of the Japan Micronesia Association, Asia Center of Japan, graciously interviewed two senior Japanese citizens for the author, one of whom is now in his sixty-eighth year (and had lived in Truk during the 1939-42 period as a member of *Nanyo Takushoku Kaisha*), and the other, sixty-five years of age (who had lived in Palau and the Marianas during the Mandate Years as a member of a fishing company). Kobayashi summarized the views of those two former officials who had spent periods of time in Micronesia under the Japanese, as follows:

> The Japanese had a very good relationship with Micronesian. They [the two senior Japanese] told the successful reason—
> A large number of the Japanese, except the military who had lived in Micronesia, were Okinawas [Okinawans]. Some Japanese had a discrimination consciousness against Okinawas so that as a behind phenomenon, the Okinawas' discrimination consciousness against islanders was stronger than Japanese'.
> Generally, Japanese, officials and businessmen, were not only diligence but also courteous. The Japanese life attitude was good enough to get their respect.
> The islanders' school was different from the Japanese's one, they received Japanese education of the Empire thought, and also received modern techniques for agriculture, house building, etc., and they knew the value of labor. Particularly the school teachers had served them faithfully in order to raise up the cultural standard of the people.
> Japanese Government planned to rule Micronesia over a long time, and the people also thought to live in there continuously so that they had been attentive of good relation with islanders. In those days, generally Japanese were not so rich, so a standard of living of Japanese was within the limits of islanders sympathetic feeling. But such a good relationship between the Japanese and Micronesian would be broken when the military arrived at Micronesia.

Kuwano, the nisei banker on Saipan, feels that, from his conversations with Saipanese, the islanders had more affinity for the Okinawans and Koreans than the ruling Japanese, at least so far as the Micronesians who worked for the *Nanyo Kohatsu Kaisha* sugar factory are concerned: "The island people don't like this 'top class' [in the sugar factory management], because, you know, they [the Japanese executives] want to be a big man and all that, so they pushed the 'bottom people' around, too. A lot. But Okinawa labor or Korean labor came in, and they mingled with Saipanese people a lot."

Kuekazu Hamanaka, Consul General of Japan in Agana, Guam, confirms that "most [Micronesian] people, aged 45, can speak Japanese very well." The Consul General sees the nostalgia for Japan since tourism opened in Micronesia in 1968, on the part of the islanders, as being an acknowledgment of what many Micronesians have told him, namely, that "Japan did very good business in Micronesia, and Japanese people taught Micronesian people how to earn money, see? ... And when Japanese Government governed, Japanese people taught Micronesian people that human kind must work, and to keep room on their earnings, see?"[41]

The earlier observation by Caldwell, concerning intermarriage between some of the Japanese and the islanders, is evident in various parts of Micronesia. For example, Pedro T. (Pete) Nakatsukasa, the Political Affairs Officer in the Government of the Northern Marianas (and, at the same time, Commissioner for District 6, San Antonio Village on Saipan), is the son of a Japanese official who married a Chamorro back in the Mandate Days; and a Mr. Mirashita, in Palau, with whom Consul General Hamanaka visited in Palau (in 1976), has a Japanese father who was working in that lower district prior to the War. The father wanted to stay in Palau, permanently, "but," Hamanaka observes, "during the War he [the Japanese father] was forced to go back to Japan. Now, he is permanently in Palau."

Van Cleve wrote that the Guamanians "remained resolutely pro-American throughout the [Japanese] occupation, many engaging in acts of great heroism, many losing their lives while doing so, and almost all suffering substantial privations."[42] Emilie G. Johnston, Curator of the Micronesian Area Research Center (MARC) at the University of Guam, tells of the experience her husband's family (Guamanian) had during World War II. Generally, Johnston recalls, the Guamanians "got along fairly well with the Japanese in the beginning. The military people that came in, in the beginning, were rather friendly. They expected to stay and were setting up things so that they would have things the way they wanted them." However, she continues, her father-in-law "was taken prisoner-of-war because he was one of the U.S.-born residents at that time. He was no longer with the [American] military, but he worked for the Navy. Members of his family—although they were U.S. citizens—were not taken prisoner; they were allowed to remain here [on Guam]." Thus, the father-in-law of Johnston was taken prisoner along with a number of other Guamanians, confined locally on Guam temporarily, then shipped to Japan for the duration of the War along with American military personnel and members of the clergy, such as Father Arnold, mentioned earlier, in the first month of 1942. Johnston confirms Van Cleve's comments, above, concerning "privations" on Guam once the War began. Thus, although the inhabitants of Guam were treated quite well at the outset of the War, as the tide of battle turned in the Pacific and the

Japanese realized that things were going against them, they began to be "more cautious, and that's when the atrocities that you hear of were beginning to happen [on Guam], so that when they [the Japanese military] felt that the American return was imminent, the people were collected and put in areas—concentration camps—back away from the capital city [of Agana]."

The final area to be considered under this introductory section on the Japanese Mandate Period involves education. Ramarui, who was schooled in the elementary grades by the Japanese and later received higher education under the American Administration (and now is the Director of Education for the Trust Territory Government), wrote that "the first school system established under the Japanese Naval Administration [in 1914] was for three years and was called native school or islanders' school."[43] Later, with the advent of the civil government, the system of education was changed to "public school with three years compulsory education and with two additional years optional education, and with emphasis on boys over girls. A territory-wide vocational school was established in Koror, Palau, in 1927, mainly for training in carpentry."[44]

Father Hezel affirmed that "the fundamental object of the Japanese-run public school in Micronesia was 'the bestowal of moral education as well as of knowledge and capabilities as are indispensable to the advancement and improvement of their (Micronesians') lives.' "[45] Thus, Hezel indicated, "Not surprisingly, the first and most important step towards the 'advancement' of the native children was felt to be knowledge of the Japanese language, and fully half of the native students' class time was spent learning to speak and read Japanese."[46]

Dwight Heine, a Marshallese, remembers the three years of compulsory education he received during the Japanese Mandate Years, and indicates that those Micronesians who were good students did receive two more years, "and, following that, then a few, they go to Palau for a school in carpentry and other subjects [such as auto mechanics, electronics, and surveying]. Mainly, Japanese language and industrial arts, and working with your hands and create little things" constituted the elementary school's curriculum.

Senator Borja, a Saipanese, recalls that, during his education under the Japanese, "our opportunity of school was very limited. The Japanese, of course, have the feeling and belief that limited education was provided up to sixth grade, and those people only with Japanese blood will like to see them full education opportunity be intermediate school [beyond the elementary grades]." M. S. Villagomez, a father of 12 children, feels that the five years of schooling he received on Saipan from the Japanese enabled him to "know as much" in the fifth grade then as his boy in the 12th grade (during the 1976-77 school year) "knows today" under the American Administration. JoeTen remembers that the compulsory schooling on Saipan began at the age of eight years until the fifth grade (or through that grade): "That's the compulsory, and that's all we [the Saipanese] have with the exception of anybody who wants to go farther in education, they can enter the Japanese school. And the [latter] school, the military school, is different between the local and the Japanese, separate." Ilo says that after his five years of schooling on Saipan under the Japanese, that he was sent to Maug (an island north of Saipan) and used in communications work for the Japanese Imperial Navy.

Dr. Kansou recalls that his Trukese schooling was interrupted after four years due to the War: "The fifth year sort of fouled up because of the War reached out here, so the school just stop and we were just working." Kansou also says that the schools were segregated between the Japanese and Trukese children. Richard noted that the education provided to the Marshallese during the Japanese Period was "unequaled" in Micronesia at that time, but not so much due to the few public schools established by the Japanese Government as the long experience under American missionaries:

> The Japanese had provided four public schools for selected natives [in the Marshalls] and the Boston Missionary Society had, during its 90 years of work among the people, established church schools on 22 of the atolls. The main objective of the church schools was the teaching of religious subjects but the native preachers who conducted the schools gave some instruction in arithmetic, geography, and music. Until 1935 the Japanese had allowed attendance at the church schools to be substituted for public school training; after that date attendance at the public schools was required of a stated quota of children in the immediate vicinity of the [four] Japanese-directed schools and the church schools were allowed to provide *supplementary* education. The Japanese schools ceased to function shortly before World War II began and only in isolated instances were native teachers able to continue instruction of the children. No schools were in existence when American forces landed on the islands [in 1944].[47] (Italics mine.)

Ramarui, a Palauan, completed the three compulsory grades on Babelthuap, then received two additional years at the larger five-year elementary school on Koror. He was fortunate in being selected for the only vocational school in Micronesia, which was located on Koror, as mentioned earlier. Thus, he "majored in carpentry and general woodwork." Asked what the Japanese school system was like, Ramarui responded:

> It was an *authoritarian*-type of system where you're indoctrinated much more than assisted to learn and study. Maybe I'm exaggerating, but under the system in that primitive situation is—perhaps the best possible word to use [is "primitive"] to describe the situation. During my fourth and fifth grade in Koror, I was in a classroom of *84* students in *one* classroom, with

Introduction
25

> *one* teacher teaching every course: Japanese language, reading, writing, arithmetic, science, gardening. . . . We did have a course in geography, and we did learn world geography as well, within even, as early as second grade, . . . with emphasis in Japanese. There was a question period. Most of the time we open the book up to certain chapter, and we all read [or repeat] after the teacher and then after we read the pages, we begin to ask questions, and the teacher answer question. But length of class was 45 or 50 minutes, so, naturally, not all [of the 84] students could ask questions.

Alfonso R. Oiterong, also of Palau, was one of the few Micronesians to be sent to Tokyo for his three years of vocational training, where he studied electronics and mechanics. Oiterong, now Director of Education for the Palau District, said in a radio interview that, "in their system, the Japanese educated us to become Japanese, sort of."[48] Ramarui agrees with Oiterong's conclusion, and adds:

> Whether the Japanese intended to destroy the local language and custom, I cannot say; but maybe some facts can verify that, in school, you were told *not* to speak our own language. Not only in school, but even outside of the school. The only time you're allowed to speak our language was when we spoke to older people who could not speak Japanese. In school, when we were caught speaking our language, we were severely punished by *beating*. . . . But [I] can't indicate that the Japanese wanted to really, eventually, destroy the [Palauan] language.

Dr. Kansou says that the "main emphasis" in Truk was also to learn the Japanese language "so that we could communicate with the Japanese. That was their most important thing." Kansou further indicates that the Trukese school curriculum under the Japanese contained "very little in math, science, and things like that. They did not teach us social science, although they try to give us vocational type of thing like carpentry, and a little bit about mechanics, in case, so that the people could be useful to them [the Japanese], not for themselves [the Trukese]." Similar approaches were found in Yap and Ponape.

The Chamorro children in the U.S. territory of Guam also were taught in Japanese during the War years. Johnston says that her husband, who was supposed to attend school but managed to work, instead—not in the fields or on the airstrip, but eventually was able to take over one of the businesses his family owned and make soap during the War—"learned a little bit of the Japanese language, but only enough to confuse words, and often got into trouble because he didn't use quite the right word." For those Chamorros in school, they were required to speak in Japanese; however, they were allowed, "at least on the streets, to use Chamorro." English—the official language of the American Government on Guam since 1898—was forbidden.

Summarizing the thirty-one year period of the Japanese in Micronesia (from 1914-45), one may say that the Micronesians were subjected to a tight governmental control over their lives. The economic development accomplished two noteworthy goals: to be self-sufficient (for the *Nanyocho* Government), not having to depend upon subsidies from Japan (up to the World War II period), and to employ the islanders, instilling in them the necessity of hard work. Socially speaking, the indigenes were able to maintain their traditional ways except in the area of language, with Japanese becoming the *lingua franca* through the school system—which segregated the Japanese and other Oriental aliens from the Micronesians—and in the commercial business sector, which was almost wholly Japanese owned and controlled. The military involvement, beginning with the fortifying of the islands in the mid-1930s—in violation of the League of Nations Mandate which the Japanese had been granted in 1920—changed the direction of the administration. Privations occurred as the Americans turned the tide of the War in the Pacific: No church services were held as the foreign missionaries were either banished from the islands or resettled by the Japanese Government; and public schools also were closed as the War was winding down. Still, the Japanese Mandate Period is recalled as one of tremendous economic development of the islands. A chief weakness was in the lack of bringing Micronesians into the political process other than as minor, local officials throughout the islands.

THE TRUSTEESHIP AGREEMENT OF 1947

The islands of Micronesia faced a fourth successive occupying power in 1945 as the Japanese military was defeated by the American forces. Beginning with their incursion in the Marshalls (in early-1944), the United States completed its occupation with a sweep through the northern Marianas (by mid-1944). Thus, the Spanish, Germans, and Japanese were followed by an interim U.S. Naval Administration in 1944-45 which was to last until 1951 for most of Micronesia. The remainder of this chapter will detail the coming forth of the Trusteeship Agreement between the U.N. Security Council and the United States in 1947. (The Navy Period, from 1944, will be considered as part of the overall American Administration in Micronesia from 1947 in the following chapters.)

That the Japanese Mandated Islands, as well as other possessions of Japan in the Pacific Basin—outside of the four main islands of Japan proper—should be taken from the Japanese following the end of World War II was a subject agreed upon initially at Cairo, in 1943 (when President Roosevelt, Prime Minister Churchill, and Generalissimo Chiang Kai-shek met for the first of a series of tripartite Wartime conferences),[49] and later affirmed at Potsdam (with President Truman, Churchill, and Premier Stalin) in 1945.[50]

Within a week following President Roosevelt's death in April, 1945, his successor, Harry S. Truman, received the U.S. Delegation (previously appointed by Roosevelt) which was preparing to attend the United Nation's charter-structuring conference in San Francisco, beginning on April 25. Senator Arthur H. Vandenberg of Michigan, the ranking minority delegate, recorded in his diary that the Government appeared "sharply divided" on what should be done with the Japanese Mandated Islands. Thus, Vandenberg wrote that those officials present in the White House on April 17, 1945, heard the Army and Navy view that the United States "must *keep* full control of most of the Pacific bases taken from the Japs"; while Vandenberg indicated that "the State Department is afraid this [military control] will set a bad example to the other great powers [i.e., Russia, Great Britain, France, and China]."[51]

More specifically, Secretary of War Stimson believed that the formerly Japanese Mandated Islands should *not* be placed under a United Nations trusteeship, for such trusteeships[52] were associated with colonialism, large populations, and extensive economic resources. Stimson expressed his view in a memorandum to Secretary of State Edward R. Stettinius as follows:

> Acquisition of . . . [Micronesia] by the United States does not represent an attempt at colonization or exploitation. Instead, it is merely the acquisition by the United States of the necessary bases for the defense of the security of the Pacific for the future world. To serve such a purpose they must belong to the United States with absolute power to rule and fortify them. They are not colonies; they are outposts, and their acquisition is appropriate under the general doctrine of self-defense by the power which guarantees the safety of that area of the world.[53]

The State Department countered with the argument that, should Micronesia be exempted from the new Trusteeship System, such would lead "to reservations of other nations until the non-aggrandizement plan of the Atlantic Charter would become a mockery."[54] Thus, the State Department proposed that "America's best interests lay in wholehearted support of the United Nations, and that any reservations to such a commitment meant subverting the chances of maintaining peace through that organization."[55]

Against this background of controversy between the then War Department and the State Department, it became President Truman's responsibility, ultimately, to decide the American position for the post-War status of the Pacific Islands (beyond the interim administration by the U.S. Navy of those islands since the 1944-45 occupational period). Truman announced his decision on November 6, 1946, when he said that the United States was "prepared to place under trusteeship, with the United States as the administering authority, the Japanese Mandated Islands . . . for which it assumes responsibilities as a result of the Second World War," and that a "draft trusteeship agreement" would be formally submitted to the U.N. Security Council for that body's approval "at an early date."[56]

Surprisingly, the Soviet Union, which originally felt that the U.S. should not enter into a trusteeship for Micronesia before a Japanese peace treaty was signed, supported the American position and said, in a note to the American Secretary of State dated February 20, 1947, that "it is not worthwhile to postpone the question about the former mandated islands of Japan and . . . the decision of this question comes within the competency of the Security Council"; and further, that it would be "entirely fair to transfer to the trusteeship of the United States the former mandated islands," for "the armed might of the U.S.A. played a decisive role in the matter of victory over Japan, and . . . bore incomparably greater sacrifices than the other allied governments" in the Pacific warfare.[57] Warren R. Austin, the U.S. Representative to the U.N., formally submitted the above-mentioned draft trusteeship agreement to the Security Council on February 26, 1947. The other members of the Security Council were also to consent, unanimously, to the American draft proposal with but four minor amendments.[58]

In discussing the legal status of the Trust Territory of the Pacific Islands, and the obligations of the American Government under terms of the Trusteeship Agreement of 1947, the question may arise: *why* was this a "strategic" trusteeship? First, the responsibility to the United Nations is between the United States and the Security Council rather than to the General Assembly. The implications of this are that the U.S. is protected by the veto power which it can exercise in the Security Council over any proposed change in status.[59] Much importance was attached to this protective factor at the time the Trusteeship Agreement was negotiated; however, subsequently, as the question of terminating the Trusteeship has moved to the fore (especially since 1967), the question of whether or not this protection may not prove to be something of a hindrance has become more obvious.

Two articles of the Trusteeship Agreement, in particular, grant the United States, as the "administering authority," a *broad* mandate of power over the Trust Territory of the Pacific Islands: Articles 3 and 5. In the former article, the United States

> shall have full powers of administration, legislation, and jurisdiction over the territory, subject to the provisions of this agreement, and may apply to the trust territory, subject to any modifications which the administering authority may consider desirable such of the laws of the United States as it may deem appropriate to local conditions and requirements.

Introduction

Article 5 of that 1947 Agreement gives the American Government, in order to "ensure that the trust territory shall play its part, in accordance with the Charter of the United Nations (Articles 76[a] and 84 therein), in the maintenance of international peace and security," the following entitlements:

1. to establish naval, military and air bases and to erect fortifications in the trust territory;
2. to station and employ armed forces in the territory; and
3. to make use of volunteer forces, facilities and assistance from the trust territory in carrying out the obligations towards the Security Council undertaken in this regard by the administering authority, as well as for the local defense and the maintenance of law and order within the territory.

Also as a "strategic" trusteeship, Micronesia may be subjected to the presence of large numbers of American military forces and installations, and parts, or all of the Trust Territory, *closed* for "security reasons" in keeping with Article 13 of the Trusteeship Agreement.

Article 15 of the 1947 Agreement reminds the United Nations, as well as the Micronesians and any others who may be interested, that "the terms of the . . . agreement shall not be altered, amended or terminated without the consent of the administering authority." This provision would appear to be a stumbling block to "future status" negotiations *if* the United States so chose to exercise a domination over the Micronesian leaders in such talks (which have continued, with intermittent pauses, since 1968).

Article 6 of the Trusteeship Agreement of 1947 contains the "four major goals" for the United States to pursue in Micronesia. These goals—the attainment of which will be the focus in the following chapters—are, as follows:

> [*First*, to] *foster the development of such political institutions* as are suited to the trust territory and . . . [to] promote the development of the inhabitants . . . toward self-government or independence as may be appropriate to the particular circumstances of the trust territory and its people and the freely expressed wishes of the peoples concerned; and to this end . . . give to the inhabitants . . . a progressively increasing share in the administrative services in the territory; and . . . take other appropriate measures towards these ends;
> [*Second*, to] *promote the economic advancement and self-sufficiency* of the inhabitants, and to this end . . . regulate the use of natural resources; encourage the development of fisheries, agriculture, and industries; protect the inhabitants against the loss of their lands and resources; and improve the means of transportation and communication;
> [*Third*, to] *promote the social advancement* of the inhabitants and to this end . . . protect the rights and fundamental freedoms of all elements of the population without discrimination; protect the health of the inhabi-

tants; control the traffic in arms and ammunition, opium and other dangerous drugs, and alcoholic and other spiritous beverages; and institute such other regulations as may be necessary to protect the inhabitants against social abuses; and

[*Fourth,* to] *promote the educational advancement* of the inhabitants, and to this end . . . take steps toward the establishment of a general system of elementary education; facilitate the vocational and cultural advancement of the population; and . . . encourage qualified students to pursue higher education, including training on the professional level. (Italics mine.)

Thus, the following chapters will evaluate how well the United States has fulfilled its commitments under each of the above four goals as expressed in Article 6 of the Trusteeship Agreement, which became effective on July 18, 1947, when President Truman signed a joint resolution (H.J. Res. 233) adopted earlier that day by the U.S. Congress. That resolution authorized Truman to approve the Trusteeship Agreement between the U.N. Security Council and the United States, earlier accepted by that council on April 2, 1947.

NOTES FOR INTRODUCTION

1. The most recent official census for the Trust Territory of the Pacific Islands, or Micronesia, as the present six administrative districts (the Marshall Islands, Ponape, Kosrae, Truk, Yap, and Palau) and the interim Government of the Northern Marianas are called, was conducted in 1973. At that time, there were 110,805 Trust Territory citizens (the indigenous population) and 4,168 non-Trust Territory citizens (mainly, tourists, expatriate workers, and dependents). The *Five-Year Indicative Development Plan,* compiled by the Congress of Micronesia in 1976, projected that the Micronesian population by 1978 would be about 125,600; hence, the 120,000 estimate for mid-1977. (Guam, although in the northern Marianas, is not part of the Government of the Northern Marianas; rather, Guam is an unincorporated territory of the United States, originally ceded to the Americans by the Spanish at the Treaty of Paris in 1898, after the Spanish-American War. Guam's population in 1977 was estimated at about 110,000.)
2. For a concise overview of the three pre-American administrations in Micronesia, see Daniel T. Hughes and Sherwood G. Lingenfelter, eds., *Political Development in Micronesia* (Columbus, Ohio: Ohio State University Press, 1974), p. 19ff.
3. See William A. Lessa, *Ulithi: A Micronesian Design for Living* (New York: Holt, Rhinehart and Winston, 1966), p. 5. Not all

Spanish missionaries were well received in their efforts to convert the natives to Christianity: "In 1710, a patache, the *Santissima Trinidad,* succeeded in putting some [Jesuit] missionaries ashore at Sonsorol [an island in the Palau District], but they were killed by the natives while the vessel was away in the course of discovering the Palaus." *Ibid.,* p. 6.

4. As indicated earlier in the Preface, Neas is a long-time observer of developments in the western and central Pacific. William H. Stewart, Deputy Director of the Department of Resources and Development in the Trust Territory Government, refers to Neas as "probably the leading historian on the Trust Territory, and a researcher par excellence." Should the reader visit on Guam, the Micronesian Area Research Center (MARC), housed in the University of Guam Library, has the most extensive collection of documents relating to Guam and the Trust Territory of the Pacific Islands. The Western Association of Schools and Colleges, in its 1974 accreditation team report on MARC, said, in part: "Since its establishment in 1967, MARC's primary activities have been in acquiring and cataloguing of books, documents, photographs, and any other printed materials. Extensive searches have been done in libraries and archives in Spain, Italy, Germany, Mexico, and the Philippines. The result is a multi-lingual library that must be the world's most extensive collection of materials on Guam and Micronesia."

5. See David C. Purcell, Jr., "The Economics of Exploitation," *The Journal of Pacific History,* XI (3-4, 1976), 189. This article concentrates on the Japanese economic development during 1915-40 in Micronesia.

6. See David Ramarui, "Education in Micronesia: Its Past, Present, and Future," *Micronesian Reporter,* XXIV, 1 (First Quarter, 1976), 9. Ramarui is the Director of Education in the Trust Territory Government.

7. Ruth G. Van Cleve, *The Office of Territorial Affairs* (New York: Praeger Publishers, 1974), p. 83.

8. Francis X. Hezel, S.J., "In Search of a Home: Colonial Education in Micronesia," an unpublished article, n.d. [1977], pp. 9 and 10. Father Hezel is the Director of Xavier High School, Moen, Truk, and also the Executive Secretary of the Micronesian Seminar, which is the organization of the Catholic Church in the Vicariate of the Caroline and Marshall Islands concerned with stimulating discussion on contemporary social issues in Micronesia.

9. David S. Boyer, "Micronesia: The Americanization of Eden," *National Geographic* (May, 1967), p. 743. Boyer commented that "reminders" of the New England whalers' visits to Kusaie "survive in today's Caucasian faces" on that island.

10. Willard Price, *America's Paradise Lost* (New York: The John Day Company, 1966), p. 149. The Protestant missionaries apparently encouraged the Kusaiens and others in the eastern Carolines and the Marshall Islands to "cover" themselves, in the case of the women, through the introduction in the isles of the so-called "mother hubbard"—a one-piece, loose-fitting dress covering the woman from her neck to her ankles. While that style of dress was popular in Hawaii and Polynesia, as well as in the eastern parts of Micronesia, the "mother hubbard" was not adopted, apparently, in the Yap Islands; at least Lessa, in commenting on dress in Ulithi, said that "the incipient use of clothing was not at all inspired by growing modesty, for the [Catholic, and later, Protestant] missionaries had never deprecated the native dress and certainly not encouraged the belief that it was indecent for women to expose their upper bodies." (See William A. Lessa, "The Social Effects of Typhoon Ophelia [1960] on Ulithi," in Andrew P. Vayda, ed., *Peoples and Cultures of the Pacific* [Garden City, New York: The Natural History Press, 1968], pp. 354-55.)
11. See Hughes and Lingenfelter, *op. cit.*
12. Francis X. Hezel, S.J., "Spanish Capuchins in the Carolines," *Micronesian Reporter,* XIX (Second Quarter, 1971), 37,
13. Van Cleve, *op. cit.,* p. 127.
14. James H. Webb, Jr., *Micronesia and U.S. Pacific Strategy: A Blueprint for the 1980s* (New York: Praeger Publishers, 1974), p. 88.
15. Purcell, *op. cit.*
16. *Ibid.*
17. Dorothy E. Richard, Cdr., USNR, *United States Naval Administration of the Trust Territory of the Pacific Islands* (Vol. II; Washington, D.C.: Government Printing Office, 1957), p. 483.
18. Neas indicates that one of the daughters of O'Keefe approached the Trust Territory Government in the early 1970s, inquiring whether she could get possession of one of the islands, Tarang Island, in the Yap Lagoon harbor area, where O'Keefe's home and trading station were located. Her request was denied.
19. See Ramarui, *op. cit.,* pp. 9 and 10.
20. See Hezel, "In Search of a Home . . . ," pp. 10 and 11.
21. For an authoritative account by a then State Department official who dealt with the background of bringing the former Japanese Mandated Islands into the strategic trusteeship of 1947, see Robert R. Robbins, "United States Trusteeship for the Territory of the Pacific Islands" (*State Department Bulletin* of May 4, 1947), pp. 783-90.
22. Van Cleve, *op. cit.,* p. 128.
23. From the verbatim transcript of the remarks of Felix Moos at the symposium, "Political Development in Micronesia," American

Introduction

Anthropological Association annual meeting, New York City, November 18, 1971. See also Professor Moos' article, "The Old and the New: Japan and the United States in the Pacific," which appears as Chapter 15 in Hughes and Lingenfelter, *op. cit.*, pp. 278-98.

24. This was mentioned in a personal letter from Tokuichi Kuribayashi, Tokyo, to Fred M. Zeder II, then Director of the Office of Territorial Affairs (DOTA), Washington, D.C., July 21, 1976. Kuribayashi headed the *Nanyo Kohatsu Kaisha* in Micronesia from 1938 until the end of World War II.
25. Robbins, *op. cit.*, p. 785.
26. Richard, *op. cit.*, I, 101.
27. Kuribayashi, *op. cit.* This letter also told of the *Nanyo Kohatsu Kaisha's* involvement in other parts of the Pacific, including the following: "Cotton cultivation in the old Dutch New Guinea (Momi and Salumi areas), 1,560 ha. [hectares]; Sisal Fiber farm (Momi and Salumi areas), 500 ha.; Damar resin harvesting (Nabire area), 31,000 ha.; Corn, Coffee and Cacao farms in Timor, [and] Coconuts Plantation and Copra trades in Celebes."
28. Purcell, *op. cit.*, pp. 191-92. He compiled the employment figures from several Japanese documents, including two annual reports to the League of Nations (for 1937 and 1938). See his footnote (p. 192 therein).
29. *Ibid.*, pp. 209, 193, 194. The Japanese mining management rationalized the *low* Micronesian pay scale on the basis that the islanders "were unskilled and lazy." (See p. 194.)
30. Richard, *op. cit.*, I, 623.
31. *Ibid.*, II, 26.
32. *Ibid.*, III, 641.
33. See John Toland, *The Rising Sun* (Vol. II; New York: Random House, 1970), p. 609.
34. The "district center" to which Kansou referred is Dublon, an island near Moen in the Truk Lagoon.
35. Richard, *op. cit.*, II, 349. Hicking, incidentally, decided to remain on Kusaie after the American forces arrived at the close of the Second World War.
36. See William H. Forbis, *Japan Today* (New York: Harper & Row, Publishers, 1975), p. 107.
37. Richard, *op. cit.*, II, 392-93.
38. *Ibid.*, I, 400-401.
39. *Ibid.*, I, 635.
40. The *Nanyo Boeki Kaisha* (or "South Seas Trading Company") was formed in 1906 and took over the assets of the German Jaluit Company in 1914, when the Germans were forced out of the islands. For a fuller account of this episode, as well as others dating back to the

Spanish Era, see William A. McGrath, "Resolving the Land Dilemma," *Micronesian Reporter,* XIX (First Quarter, 1971), 9-16.
41. Parenthetically, Consul General Hamanaka said that "the main complaint" from all the aged Micronesian people with whom he has conversed on this topic has been that the later U.S. Administration "didn't, [or] haven't teached them how to earn money."
42. Van Cleve, *op. cit.,* p. 85.
43. Ramarui, *op. cit.,* p. 10.
44. *Ibid.*
45. Hezel, *op. cit.,* p. 11.
46. *Ibid.,* pp. 11 and 12.
47. Richard, *op. cit.,* I, 395.
48. From the verbatim transcript of a live broadcast interview, featuring Alfonso R. Oiterong, Director of Education, Palau District, Radio Station WMPL, Hancock, Michigan, September 27, 1971. Oiterong also said in that context: "In the American system, we were educated to be ourselves, so there was a difference in education systems there [between the Japanese and American approaches]."
49. Specifically, that Japan "would be stripped of all territories seized from the Chinese, all islands occupied since 1914, and 'all other territories taken by violence and greed.'" See John C. Campbell, *The United States in World Affairs, 1945-1947* (2d ed.; New York: Harper & Brothers, 1947), pp. 12 and 254.
50. Robbins, *op. cit.,* p. 786.
51. See Arthur H. Vandenberg, Jr., ed., *The Private Papers of Senator Vandenberg* (Boston: Houghton Mifflin Company, 1952), p. 169. Senator Vandenberg identified the two military spokesmen at that meeting as being Secretary of War Henry L. Stimson and Navy Secretary James V. Forrestal; while Harold E. Stassen and Dr. Isaiah Bowman, as advisers, "insisted that, while we *must* follow War and Navy advice, we must also make it plain that we seek no right of social or economic exploitation in respect to any of these [island] peoples."
52. In addition to the Trust Territory of the Pacific Islands, administered by the U.S. on behalf of the U.N. Security Council beginning in 1947, there were 11 other trusteeships—all of which were under the direction of the General Assembly of the U.N. Those others (with the administering authorities shown in parentheses) were: Tanganyika (Britain), Ruanda-Urundi (Belgium), Cameroons (Britain), Cameroons (France), Somaliland (Italy), New Guinea (Australia), Togoland (Britain), Togoland (France), Western Samoa (New Zealand), Nauru (Australia, on behalf of itself, Britain, and New Zealand), and West New Guinea U.N. Temporary Executive Authority, or UNTEA, for some seven months ending May 1, 1963).

Introduction 35

See United Nations, Office of Public Information, *Everyman's United Nations* (8th ed.; United Nations Publication E.67.I.5, 1968), pp. 20, 124, and 125; also see Philip E. Jacob, Alexine L. Atherton, and Arthur M. Wallenstein, *The Dynamics of International Organization* (rev. ed.; Homewood, Illinois: The Dorsey Press, 1972), pp. 298, 508-12, and 535. Each of the other 11 trusteeships has now been dissolved, Papua New Guinea becoming independent most recently (in 1975).

53. Henry L. Stimson and McGeorge Bundy, *On Active Service in Peace and War* (New York: Harper & Brothers, 1948), pp. 599-600.
54. Arthur Krock, *New York Times* (April 19, 1945), as quoted in Jack W. and James W. Peltason (eds.), *Functions and Policies of American Government* (Englewood Cliffs, New Jersey: Prentice-Hall, Inc., 1958), p. 82.
55. James N. Murray, Jr., "Foreign Policy," in Peltason, *Functions and Policies*, p. 83.
56. Robbins, *op. cit.* The manner in which the late President carried out this responsibility is common knowledge, but recorded, in the original, in File 85-L of the Harry S. Truman Library, Independence, Missouri.
57. *Foreign Relations of the United States, 1947* (Vol. I; Washington, D.C.: Government Printing Office, 1973), pp. 264-65.
58. For the various transmittals between the Security Council members —some of which were "classified" (as "Restricted" or "Secret") until 1973—see "Negotiation of the Trusteeship Agreement for the Former Japanese-Mandated Islands in the Pacific Concluded between the United States and the Security Council of the United Nations, April 2, 1947," in *Foreign Relations of the United States, 1947*, Vol. I, pp. 258-78.
59. The three applicable chapters in the U.N. Charter are: XI ("Declaration Regarding Non-Self Governing Territories"), XII ("International Trusteeship System") and XIII ("The Trusteeship Council"). The 1947 Trusteeship Agreement is officially entitled "Trusteeship Agreement for the Former Japanese Mandated Islands." These documents are contained in *Trust Territory Code*, edited by John Richard Steincipher (Vol. I: Seattle, Washington: Book Publishing Company, 1970). Preface, pp. 11-21.

Chapter 1

"To Foster the Development of Political Institutions..."

Before considering American efforts to fulfill the above *first* "goal" of Article 6 in the Trusteeship Agreement of 1947 in the *fuller* commitment of *involving the islanders* in the political processes as well as in the fulfillment of the other three "goals" (to be discussed in chapters 2 through 4, respectively), some background on the initial administration of the U.S. Navy in Micronesia (which began during the War), followed by the "political warfare" in Washington, D.C., over whether a military *or* a civilian administration should be in charge of Micronesia once the trusteeship would become effective (in mid-1947), is necessary.

THE NAVY'S INITIAL ADMINISTRATION (1944-47)

Commander Richard, in her first of three volumes on the U.S. Naval Administration in Micronesia, used the term "The Wartime Military Government Period (1942-1945)" to indicate the Navy's initial involvement with those islands in the central and western Pacific. Technically, the Navy was not "officially" given authority by President Truman to administer the whole of Micronesia until a few weeks after the Japanese surrendered aboard the U.S.S. *Missouri,* in September, 1945. At that time, Truman stressed such Naval rule was an "interim arrangement pending study and recommendations by the State, War, and Navy Departments."[1] Still, no one questions the presence of Naval forces in the waters of Micronesia as early as February, 1942, less than two months following the Japanese attack on Pearl Harbor, when assaults were made on the Marshall and Gilbert Islands. Two years were to elapse, however, before the Navy occupied islands in the Marshalls and then, later, in the Carolines and Marianas, including Guam.[2]

That President Truman would designate the U.S. Navy to administer the islands of Micronesia, even on a "temporary" basis, should not be surprising (although that assignment was desired by the Army). The Navy's first experience with dependent peoples involved Alaskan Indians for a year (1879-80), with creditable efforts expended;[3] and the Navy was also in charge of the temporary occupation of Vera Cruz, Mexico (in 1914), but that brief stay produced no rehabilitation measures.[4] Probably, the Navy is best known as an administrator for its nearly 50-year involvement with Guam and American Samoa, beginning around the turn of the twentieth century.[5]

Both the Army and the Navy began preparing, as early as 1942, for expected administrative responsibilities in the Pacific areas once the American occupations would occur. The first training school for Army's "military government officers" was established at the University of Virginia (in May, 1942); the Navy's counterpart school began at Columbia University three months later.[6] (As the Navy was eventually chosen by Truman to administer Micronesia, only that service's preparations in this regard will be discussed hereafter.)

Stringent standards of selection were imposed by the Navy on those civilians who applied for the School of Military Government, conducted at Columbia. Basically, the candidate was expected to meet the same physical and educational requirements needed for appointment in the Naval Reserve, including being between the ages of 28 and 45. Additionally, the candidate was expected to possess *one* of the following: (a) knowledge of the customs, language, and character of the people in one of the specific areas of the Pacific; (b) administrative experience of an important nature, either domestic or foreign; (c) educational experience such as that of a university administrator or faculty member; (d) engineering experience involving construction of public works, utilities, or transportation; or (e) legal training and experience, with a recognized standing in the legal profession.[7]

A total of eight classes, involving 347 officers, was completed at Columbia between the initial class in August, 1942, and the last one in December, 1944. Originally, the course was 10 months; however, the final two were only six months each. Sixty-six of the officers (the candidates being commissioned into the Naval Reserve) received M.A. degrees for their efforts. Rank for these civilians-turned-Reserve officers ranged between ensign and captain, with the average individual being a lieutenant. A second training school was established at Princeton University. The Princeton experience differed from that at Columbia in that the former involved military instructors. Overall, Columbia and Princeton produced 1,333 of the 1,414 Naval officers formally trained for "military government duty" in the Pacific.[8]

In addition to the above formal courses offered to prepare Naval officers for expected assignments in the Pacific areas, the Navy became involved as early as 1941 in compiling "military handbooks" from existing published works or unedited manuscripts. Neas says that examples of these materials included Spanish documents, German books, and Japanese *Annual Reports* to the League of Nations. For Micronesia, four such "handbooks" were produced: for the west Caroline Islands, east Carolines, the Marshalls, and the Mariana Islands. Neas feels that those "handbooks" were "a very, very well done piece of work." A civil affairs unit—composed in large measure of the graduates of the two schools mentioned above—was attached to each invasion force. The ideal plan was to have people trained in civil government to take over administration of the captured areas after the combat stage was completed. The worth of the "military handbooks" may be seen in an expenditure by the U.S. Navy in 1948: $125,000 to produce an updated "School of Naval Administration Handbook" for Micronesia.[9]

Unfortunately, all the formal courses and handbooks combined cannot make discretionary decisions for Naval commanders, especially when those who are sent to such schools and read such handbooks are the Reserve officers in staff (or advisory) positions to the commanders. A case in point is what presumably happened on the island of Dublon, in the Truk Lagoon, at the time the U.S. Navy occupied that area when hostilities ceased toward the end of the War. Dublon was Truk's urban center when the Japanese military was there. The lagoon at Truk was the center port for the Japanese Imperial Navy. Photographs of Dublon during the War show paved roads, complete water systems, and power lines—all of which were capable of supporting 20,000 Japanese. The island, itself, was not badly damaged, for the American aerial attacks from Naval carriers were primarily aimed at the shipping, oil storage, and depots.

What happened to the Japanese infrastructure on Dublon when the U.S. Navy arrived is not found in Richard's three volumes or such sources as Van Cleve's book. However, Jeffrey J. White, an American traveler (and later, a U.S. contract teacher at the Marianas High School, on Saipan) spent some time in Truk and alluded to this episode. An American official in the Trust Territory Government confirmed it for the author as being a "legend"—although the evidence would seem to place credence in such happening. As the "legend" goes, the U.S. Naval commander (an admiral) who was in charge of the occupational forces in Truk instructed his bulldozer operators: "Everything standing that's Japanese *goes down!*" So, the Navy construction workers proceeded to raze the whole island of Dublon. Perhaps two minor Japanese structures—stuck back in the jungle—remain there. As White believes: "If the Americans [the Navy] had some foresight, . . . instead of rejecting it [the Japanese infrastructure on Dublon] and moving to another island [Moen], if they would've chosen Dublon as the island to develop, and to maintain a district center on, it would've been easy, really. The Japanese even had airstrips there, too."[10]

The first contacts between the U.S. Navy and the Micronesians actually occurred before the occupation began. Dwight Heine tells of some Marshallese acting as spies for the American military in his home islands (during late 1943 and early 1944). When the Japanese determined that subversive activities were being conducted, they rounded up a group of the islanders and executed, in one instance, Heine's grandfather. However, the spy in that case was not the grandfather but his grandson, Dwight, then in his mid-twenties.

Richard writes that the Naval or Marine Corps occupational forces charged with administering the islands of Micronesia as area after area was taken in the closing stages of the War, beginning in the eastern portion with the Marshalls, respected the tribal chiefs or clan leaders in contacting the indigenes, and concluded:

> In no instance were local officials bypassed. During the first months of occupation and reconnaissance, when emphasis of military government had to be upon providing the people with the barest necessities of life and establishing an economic system that eventually would make them self-supporting, local affairs were regulated in accordance with custom, tradition, and the prestige of certain individuals. In almost all cases former officials on each atoll were authorized to continue in their official capacities with respect to the military government in accordance with the proclamations [of the Navy]. The people were informed that this arrangement depended upon the good behavior of their officials.[11]

The American forces found a chaotic condition throughout Micronesia when the series of occupations concluded (during 1944-45). No law was in effect, for the Japanese, during their nearly 31 years in the islands, had extended, with only "necessary modifications," the basic laws of Japan to the Mandated Islands. Richard noted that "practically all law enforcement had been in the hands of the Japanese and no indigenous system of law and law enforcement, other than that of custom, had ever been developed by the Micronesians"; thus, with the almost immediate evacuation of Japanese governmental officials and employees to Japan and, at the discretion of the military commander, the rest of the inhabitants who were Japanese nationals were segregated into camps and treated as prisoners of war under the Geneva Convention of 1929. Some exceptions were made, again at the discretion of the military governor, to permit Japanese nationals to conduct "minor governmental functions" among the Japanese in their segregated areas. The highly efficient Japanese police forces were replaced, after some training by U.S. officers, by an indigenous force. Military courts generally replaced the Japanese courts, with "summary judicial powers exercised by native chiefs and headmen in the area over minor offenses committed by natives," but those islanders exercising such authority were not permitted to impose sentences with a punishment "in excess of one year's imprisonment or a fine of more than one hundred dollars" until approval was received from the military governor in that island district.[12]

The Micronesians were utilized in a variety of helpful roles for the U.S. Navy, especially in the first year or so. M. S. Villagomez, an entrepreneur on Saipan who earlier, under the Japanese, had been an interpreter on Guam during the War, later was a member of a group of 50 Saipanese selected after the occupation of Saipan by the Americans (in mid-1944) to help clear the northern islands (i.e., those north of Saipan). These Chamorros and Carolinians received Marine training, including how to use weapons, although they were not to fight. Their mission was simply to show the American military where the Japanese were. Villagomez has a photo in his office which shows four rows of Japanese soldiers who had surrendered in the northern islands as a result, in part, of the Saipanese paramilitary force efforts. C. S. Cruz, a Security Officer at the Trust Territory Headquarters on Capitol Hill in Saipan, was also a part of that Saipanese complement. Both Villagomez and Cruz spent a number of years as police officers in the constabulary (the former for 12 years, the latter, 32 years before joining the Trust Territory Government in 1971).

A number of Micronesians who had some proficiency in English were used initially as interpreters for the U.S. Navy. Dwight Heine was one of those. He began as an "Interpreter Second Class" in the Marshalls even while the War was still winding down in parts of the islands. Then he became "Interpreter First Class," the difference being $10 a month (beginning at $40 per month). Later, Heine became an "adviser" (at $75 a month) for the government. Added to the salary were "all of meals, housing, clothing, all were issued, so it wasn't too bad. Could I use the money? I don't know what it is for [then] (Laugh.)"

Did the formal schooling and use of handbooks by the military government officers bring a high level of efficiency to Micronesia during the initial period of 1944-47? Dwight Heine was impressed. In comparing Navy with the Interior Department involvement, which was to begin in 1951, he says:

> [Navy's] more, they do things in a more, are better organized, and they do things in an organized matter. No, they're not sloppy. Things are bang, bang, bang. But this same highly organized thing can be contrary to civilians' desire (laugh), because you've got to do it *their* [the Navy's] way. And one [Naval] officer told me one time, "It's not a right way or a wrong, it's the *Navy* way. So, *do* it the *Navy* way! You got it now?" (Laugh.) So, I think he put it very clearly. Don't ask if there's a right way or a wrong way.

The opinion above by Heine regarding Naval efficiency is shared by Lazarus Salii, a long-time senator (1965-77) from Palau and, more recently, Director of the Office of Planning and Statistics (a Cabinet-level position in the Trust Territory Government). After acknowledging that the Micronesians "were not a factor in those [Navy] days," that they "weren't involved in the decisions, especially basic ones," Salii recalls:

> I think, in retrospect [in more recent years], the people [islanders] began to think that the Navy was better [than Interior]. I think there was some truth to this. I think a lot of it was simply a way of criticizing the Department of the Interior. "Gee whiz, the *old* days of the Navy are *better* than under the Interior [since 1951]!" This type [of thinking]. But the Navy, I think, was a little more efficient, because they had been more prepared. A lot of the advisers—a lot of the people who became the district administrators or political affairs people—knew enough, knew something about what they were doing. They had some clear ideas of what they were doing. They were to immediately put the level of education number one, to organize some governments, health. And they were well picked, and there was very little bureaucracy. There may have been but as real, pour out the listening end of this work, I don't know of any bureaucratic hassle they may have had in the U.S. And the Navy moved *fast!* And they could scrounge.

The initial period (up to the Trusteeship Agreement in 1947) for the Navy was not one of establishing or chartering municipalities; such was to be done later. Caldwell remembers the Navy "wasn't in the political ball game of establishing self-government. . . . I don't think they made strong moves in that direction, from what little I can tell." Dr. Kansou, from Truk, recalls the Naval efforts, including the "Island Affairs" section of government. In answer to the question, "Did the Navy make a lot of things, goods, available to the Trukese?" Kansou responds:

> Yes, that's the one thing I know during the time I was in Truk [up to 1948, when he left home to pursue his secondary education]. There were many changes [from the Japanese Mandate days], of course. First, they give free food when they first came in. Then, later, they trying to develop a government by Navy. They have the Education Section, they have the Health Section, and maybe there will be a Public Affairs at that time, but they call it "Island Affairs," which deals with political thing with developing government, and things like that.

The *quality* of Naval personnel assigned in those first three years is seen in part by the several officials who later served in Micronesia under the Interior Department. An example is Alan MacQuarrie, presently on a special assignment as Liaison Officer between the Trust Territory Government's High Commissioner and the Resident Commissioner for the Government of the Northern Marianas. MacQuarrie was a lieutenant in the Navy's military government in the northern Marianas during the War and served in several positions during the Navy Administration's seven years in the islands (from 1944-51). He left Micronesia when the Navy exited the islands in 1951 (in all but the northern Marianas), returning to Saipan in 1962 to assist in the transfer from the Navy (in the Marianas) to Interior. Continuing his long association in Micronesia, MacQuarrie was appointed as Assistant District Administrator in the Mariana Islands (until 1966), then he became the District Administrator in Truk for two more years. MacQuarrie, in the opinion of Neas, "is one of the really top scholars of the T.T.P.I. [Trust Territory of the Pacific Islands]." In addition to his liaison duties, he was, in mid-1977, engaged in combing the High Commissioner's files on Saipan to glean out historical material to be microfilmed.

Other products of the Naval Period are Cmdr. Edward P. Furber, U.S.-N.R., Attorney General during the Naval Period and later long-time and distinguished Chief Justice of the T.T.P.I., and Dr. Norman Meller, Professor Emeritus of Political Science at the University of Hawaii. Professor Meller participated in the invasion of Micronesia and in 1945 served on Saipan in the Navy's military government. Twenty years later, Meller, considered a leading scholar on Pacific area developments, teamed with Tom Dinell (then Director of the Hawaii Legislative Reference Bureau) and former U.S. Congressman Thomas P. Gill, in presenting a two-week "pre-session workshop" which was conducted to "equip the freshman [Micronesian] legislators with the parliamentary knowledge and skills necessary for the functioning of the new legislative body [the Congress of Micronesia]," which held its First Session on Saipan in July, 1965.[13]

Two other Naval officers who continued at later points to serve in Micronesia were the late Roy T. Gallemore, a former District Administrator in three different districts during the decade of 1955-65 (in Truk, Yap, and the Marianas), who retired as a captain in the U.S. Navy; and the late Percy D. (Red) Steele, who, during 1954-61, first was an Assistant District Administrator under Maynard Neas in the Marshalls, then an Assistant District Administrator (and, for several months in 1960, Acting District Administrator) in Truk, who retired as a commander in the Naval Reserve. Thus, the Department of the Interior was to reap the benefits of a number of experienced military officers or scholars from the War and immediate post-War years.

"POLITICAL WARFARE" INVOLVING 1947 TRUSTEESHIP DECISION

As mentioned in the Introduction, there was a *strong* difference of opinion between the Departments of State and War with regard to what the future disposition of the formerly Japanese Mandated Islands should be. Concurrent with that dispute over a "trusteeship" vs. "annexation" was whether there should be a continuing military administration (such as under the U.S. Navy from 1944) or a change to civilian control (say, under Interior). The trusteeship question was settled by the signing of the Trusteeship Agreement in 1947. The who-should-administer question began in 1945 and was a bitter struggle among the departments through the remainder of the 1940s until President Truman definitely assigned Micronesia to the Interior Department, effective in mid-1951.

An early example of the differences of opinion over who should be named as administrating authority in Micronesia occurred in 1945, when Secretary of the Interior Harold L. Ickes "strongly supported the idea that his Department should administer the islands as soon as the war was over." Legislation was introduced in the U.S. House of Representatives to that effect on January 6, 1945, by Representative W. Sterling Cole, of New York, who was a member of the post-War Military Policy Committee. That bill, which was defeated, called for a civilian agency to handle the "civil affairs" in Micronesia, that agency, in turn, responsible to an Assistant Secretary of the Navy. When Secretary of the Navy James V. Forrestal was asked in one of President Roosevelt's last Cabinet sessions to comment on that proposed legislation, Forrestal replied that the Navy's suggestion was that "Mr. Ickes be made king of Polynesia, Micronesia, and the Pacific Ocean Area."[14]

Not only was the Navy aligned against the Departments of State and Interior at various points in the immediate post-War era, but there was a dispute with a sister service, the Army. The Army Chief of Staff disagreed in December, 1945, that it was necessary for the Navy to be the administrator in Micronesia. The Army, he stressed, "because of maneuver, training, and local defense requirements involving localities throughout the [Micronesian] islands not normally included in military reserves, needed close cooperation between the civil authorities and the Army command."[15]

Ickes, mentioned above, resigned from his post as Secretary of the Interior in March, 1946, setting a longevity record for such service (13 years) which has not been equaled to date.[16] He continued his opposition to the Navy remaining in Micronesia. Strik Yoma, Director of Public Affairs in the Trust Territory Government, and a Ponapean, recalls that Ickes would visit U.S. college campuses and expound on how things should be done in Micronesia. Less than three months after leaving office, Ickes spoke before the Institute of Ethnic Affairs and the Institute of Pacific Relations, meeting jointly in Washington, D.C., on May 29, 1946. In his remarks, entitled "Meet the Navy," the former Interior Secretary severely criticized past Naval administrations in Guam and American Samoa, accusing the Navy of running those islands like a battleship: "A rule of authority, color distinction and the ignoring of the problems of and striving toward democratic living." He further said that the Navy wanted the trusteeship in Micronesia to be "strategic" so that it could maintain a "top secret" classification on its administration of dependent peoples.[17]

John Collier, President of the Institute of Ethnic Affairs and the publisher of a popular biweekly magazine bearing his name, submitted an article to the *Honolulu Advertiser* (a daily newspaper) on December 18, 1946, in which Collier closed with the warning: "Beware of Admirals in Sheep's Clothing"; however, the *Advertiser* declined to print that story. Meanwhile, Ickes used his own syndicated newspaper column to arouse anti-Navy opinion with regard to administering in Micronesia beyond the initial period which began in 1944 and was approaching 1947.[18]

The "pro" and "con" side of continued Naval administration for Micronesia was articulated in the U.S. Congress by two members, in particular, who had visited the islands on an "inspection" trip in December, 1946, one month after President Truman announced publicly that the U.S. would be willing to enter into a trusteeship agreement for the formerly Japanese Mandated Islands. In favor of the continuance of the U.S. Navy as the administering authority in Micronesia was the then U.S. senator from Montana, Mike Mansfield, who was later to support House Joint Resolution 233 (which called for the setting up of a "strategic trusteeship" for those islands). Mansfield, however, "qualified" his support as follows:

> Personally, I would rather have a civilian administration over the mandates, but, in view of practical and realistic considerations, I am forced to the conclusion that the Navy would be the best administrator [in Micronesia]. It [the Navy] would have the best and only means of maintaining liaison between the various islands and it would have the only trained personnel to carry out the job of administration.[19]

To "counter" Senator Mansfield's Navy position, above, was the late California Representative Clair Engle, who also was in favor of the draft trusteeship agreement but *not* under U.S. Naval administration. Thus, he took to the House floor to denounce, in part, the "Army-Navy dominated" State Department—implying that "neither the Congress nor any civilian agency of the Government [except the State Department] . . . had a hand in the drafting of the trusteeship agreement," and exclaimed:

> It has been stated that the trust agreement makes ample provision for the political, economic, social, and educational development of the inhabitants of the islands. I would like to say right here and now that pious platitudes in a trusteeship agreement will not provide [that] development. . . . They are goals which are best achieved under enlightened and democratic practices. In my opinion they can only be achieved under civilian administration along democratic, American lines.[20]

Engle concluded his opposition to the Navy in the islands by referring to the above tour of Micronesia in late-1946. He expressed "utter and complete shock" with what he termed the "absolute and undemocratic" approach to government in two of the U.S. possessions, Guam and American Samoa, and hoped that such would not be thrust upon the Micronesians. He pointed to the lack of "local self-government in the various island communities" of Micronesia under the Navy, and stressed: "We owe them more in the way of government than a Guam-Samoa type of naval civil government. . . . I, for one, want to see the Congress . . . enact organic legislation for these islands without delay. . . . I want to see civilian administration for the trust territory—and I want to see it before the end of the Eightieth Congress [i.e., by January, 1949]."[21]

The same day that Truman signed the Trusteeship Agreement (on July 18, 1947), thereby bringing it into force, he also issued Executive Order 9875, which had the effect of terminating the military rule of the former Japanese Mandated Islands. Civil administration was again placed in the hands of the Navy Department, on an "interim" basis. What happened to Congressman Engle's strong demand for "organic legislation" for those Pacific Islands "before the end of the Eightieth Congress"? An entry in the *Annual Report* of the Secretary of the Interior, for 1948, answered that question:

> The Department of State, pursuant to a report submitted to the President in June, 1947, by the Secretaries of State, War, Navy, and Interior, prepared draft organic legislation for the Trust Territory. This was submitted to Congress on May 10, 1948, but Congress took no action with respect to it. . . . It appeared likely that all draft organic legislation for the Pacific islands submitted by executive departments of the Government would be shelved by Congress in favor of legislation drafted by congressional committees.[22]

The ideal, following World War II, was that organic legislation would be forthcoming shortly for the U.S. territories of Guam and American Samoa, as well as the Trust Territory of the Pacific Islands (or, Micronesia). It is interesting that Guam received its organic legislation within three years following Truman's executive order (No. 9875 of 1947), while in the late 1970s organic legislation for the Trust Territory, as a whole, remained to be established. (Guam came under the supervision of the Department of the Interior in 1950, and, by a further organic act of that year, the inhabitants of Guam became U.S. citizens. Meanwhile, American Samoa and the Trust Territory were to remain under the Navy Department until July 1, 1951, the inhabitants continuing as U.S. nationals [in American Samoa] and citizens of the Trust Territory of the Pacific Islands [in Micronesia].)

THE NAVY'S INTERIM RULE IN MICRONESIA (1947-51)

The Navy Department realized in mid-1947 that its continuation as the administering authority in Micronesia was strictly on an "interim" basis. President Truman seven months later, in a letter dated February 11, 1948, directed the Interior Department to "proceed to make plans for the administration of the Pacific islands," and he stated that it was his intention to "transfer responsibility for such administration to the Department [of the Interior] upon the enactment of organic legislation." The Committee of four Secretaries—those of State, War, Navy, and Interior—had recommended to Truman that "transfer of administration be made at the earliest practicable date."[23]

(Why the objectives of President Truman, as outlined in his letter, above, have *not* been fulfilled is tantamount, in large measure, to reciting the history of political development in American Samoa and the Trust Territory since his administration. While the status of Guam was developed as an unincorporated territory of the United States, and its inhabitants became U.S. citizens in 1950, as mentioned above, the status of the inhabitants of American Samoa and the Trust Territory has remained unchanged as of mid-1977 except in the case of the northern Marianas, which is petitioning to become a commonwealth of the United States.)

Admiral Carlton H. Wright, designated as the Deputy High Commissioner in the new Trust Territory of the Pacific Islands (or simply "Trust Territory") Government which came into being on July 18, 1947, while satisfied that the Navy was experienced (almost 50 years on Guam and American Samoa as administrator) and had competent personnel (several of the key staff members having been schooled during the War at either Columbia or Princeton, as noted earlier), did feel that the Naval Administration had "two strikes" on it at that point: the "interim" status of Navy's role in Micronesia from mid-1947 on, and the difficulty of persuading Naval officers to apply for assignment to an area (the Trust Territory) which would have no Naval future, so far as the professional advancement of such career officers would be concerned.[24]

The "security" nature of the trusteeship was uppermost in the plans and concern of the Naval Administration throughout its seven-year term in Micronesia. The U.S. Ambassador to the U.N., Warren R. Austin, succinctly expressed that continuing responsibility in unequivocal terms on February 26, 1947—some six months before the Trusteeship Agreement was to become operational—when he said that "security is the overriding consideration in a strategic area [meaning, Micronesia]," and Austin continued: "These islands constitute an integrated strategic physical complex vital to the security of the United States. . . . Our purpose is to defend the security of these islands in a manner that will contribute to the building up of genuine, effective, and enforceable collective security for all members of the United Nations."[25]

There were a number of events in the 1947-51 period which made the Navy ever conscious of the "strategic" trust reposing upon it: the establishing of atomic weapons proving grounds in the Marshalls; the instability in the Far East, which was to culminate with the outbreak of hostilities in South Korea on June 25, 1950; and the announced transfer of the trusteeship from the Navy to the Department of the Interior, which would mean replacing U.S. military personnel with civilian employees. In that day when "push-button" warfare had not yet arrived, the location of the Trust Territory Government Headquarters at Pearl Harbor instead of within Micronesia proper, or at least on neighboring Guam, would seem to be a handicap. However, the Navy apparently felt differently, and could point to the fact that the Headquarters of the Pacific Command was also in Hawaii, so any time lag in possible "strategic" military actions might not be a hindrance.

Regarding the nuclear testing program in the Marshall Islands, which drew considerable worldwide publicity once the destruction of Bikini Island occurred, Neas recalls the start of that program in 1946 and the establishment of the field headquarters at Enewetok (the complex called the Enewetok Proving Ground), in late 1947. Those tests continued in the Marshalls until the program ended in 1958.

Once the Trusteeship Period began in mid-1947, the Navy used "civil administration units" for each of the six districts: the Mariana Islands, Yap, Palau, Truk, Ponape, and the Marshall Islands. To each such unit was assigned a corps of 12 Naval officers and 50 enlisted personnel, with one of the officers appointed as the civil administrator and another as his subordinate (or deputy). Those units represented the command structure in each district, the High Commissioner (a flag officer) having his headquarters at Pearl Harbor.[26]

Did the Navy systematically bring Micronesians into various governmental leadership positions? A Naval directive, "Municipal Governments and Local Taxation," was promulgated in May, 1947, which allowed each municipality to "make such local rules as it [the municipality] desired, subject to the approval of military government."[27] By 1948, the Navy permitted the forming of 118 municipalities throughout Micronesia. American anthropologists Hughes and Lingenfelter referred to the coming forth of those municipalities as "the first step in the democratization of Micronesia" by the Navy, and explained how such local units were supposed to operate:

> These municipalities were to be the basic political units of the territorial government. As far as possible, they corresponded to the traditional Micronesian sociopolitical units. The chief executive official in each munic-

ipality was called the municipal magistrate. At first, these officials could be either chosen by popular election or appointed by the district administrator [the Naval civil administrator]. Although elections were preferred by the administration, in many cases the district administrator followed the simpler course of appointing traditional chiefs as magistrates. Later, the administration instituted a program of chartering the municipalities, . . . [which] charters also established a legislative council of elected members in each municipality. Thus, the executive and legislative powers were split between the magistrate and the council.[28]

Dr. Kansou, a Trukese, remembers the setting up of municipal governments under the direction of the "Island Affairs" section of the Naval Administration. In Truk, he recalls that only the traditional chiefs were chosen at first to be the magistrates, then, "as the time goes on, this traditional chief had to find it difficult, a system that they [the Navy] try to institute at that time which is, of course, by election." Kansou says that the late Chief Petrus Mailo, in Truk, was "a prominent" leader, being "one of those that hang onto the chieftain thing—uses his influence as a means of [later] being elected as a mayor, elected as a congressman, and that sort of thing."

Andon Amaraich, a former senator from Truk and more recently the Chairman of the Commission on Future Political Status and Transition (since 1976), looks back on the Navy Period and feels that things were somewhat disorganized, especially with the absence of district legislatures throughout Micronesia. Actually, Professor Meller traces the antecedents for such legislative bodies back as early as 1947 in Palau (the elected Palau Congress), and in 1950 in the Marshalls (a bicameral Marshall Islands Congress).[29]

Father Arnold, on Saipan, reflects on the final years of the Navy in the Marianas just prior to the transfer to the Interior Department (in mid-1951), feeling that "the Navy had much more resources at their disposal at that time, and the programs were, I wouldn't say were more programs, but they did a much better service to the northern islands [those north of Saipan] and also to the people here [on Saipan]." Part of such "resources" by the Navy was to be passed on to Interior: experienced personnel. On April 3, 1950—some 15 months before that transfer was to be effected—the Naval High Commissioner, Admiral Arthur W. Radford, from Hawaii instructed his civil administrators in Micronesia to conduct a survey to determine how many Naval and civilian personnel then assigned in the six districts of the Trust Territory would be willing to remain during the final year of the Naval Administration. Meanwhile, "in order to assist the new [Interior Department] administration, both officers and men were given the opportunity to leave the Navy and accept employment with . . . Interior."[30] Thus, the civil administration of the Interior Department was to begin in mid-1951

"*To Foster the Development of Political Institutions...*" 49

with an orderly transfer from the Navy Period and a goodly number of experienced personnel, as mentioned earlier, to help fill governmental positions throughout the Trust Territory.

INTERIOR DEPARTMENT
BEGINS CIVILIAN RULE, EXCEPT . . .

The Department of the Interior replaced the U.S. Navy in Micronesia on July 1, 1951, a transfer which went smoothly, as mentioned earlier, in large measure due to the Navy's cooperative attitude. However, some behind-the-scenes "lobbying" apparently was conducted by Navy interests over a 16-month period (from the signing of the original executive order, in June, 1951, effecting the transfer, until November, 1952) to see that the islands of Saipan and Tinian, in the northern Marianas, would be returned to Naval jurisdiction. Van Cleve quoted a former Director of the Office of Territories, James P. Davis, as referring to Navy's successful campaign to influence President Truman to make the reversion "the worst end run in the history of the United States Government," and Van Cleve added: "The Interior officials first learned of [the reversion] . . . when they read the executive order [of November 10, 1952] the next day in the Federal Register. Military facilities existed on those two islands, and there was thus some reason for the action."[31]

The above-mentioned change—giving Navy renewed control over Saipan and its closest neighbor to the south, Tinian—became effective on January 1, 1953. This left Interior in the awkward position of trying to administer Rota (south of Tinian) and the small scattered (and uninhabited) islands north of Saipan. Interior petitioned the new President, Dwight D. Eisenhower, for relief in that situation. Eisenhower accordingly, in mid-1953, placed the whole of the northern Marianas under Naval jurisdiction. Dwight Heine says that, for a two-year period (1951-53), Rota and those 10 islands north of Saipan thus became the smallest of the six administrative districts in the Trust Territory Government administered by the Interior Department.

Van Cleve, above, referred to "military facilities" on Saipan and Tinian as a possible justification for Navy's desire to maintain the northern Marianas in the 1950s, and added that the Navy allegedly was "smarting under its loss of jurisdiction in Guam, [American] Samoa, and the Trust Territory."[32] The reasons behind the return of Saipan and Tinian to Naval control (in 1953) constituted in the early days a very finely kept secret. Subsequently, such became a rather widely revealed one. The consensus of opinion on this subject at present is that the U.S. Government spent about $28 million for the construction of a site on Saipan where Chinese Nationalists were trained, primarily, followed in the early 1960s by South Vietnamese advisers. The *New York Times*, in its fourth article exposing the "Pentagon Papers," on July 1, 1971, referred to May, 1961, as the time when President Kennedy "ordered the start of clandestine warfare against North Viet Nam, conducted by South Vietnamese agents directed and trained by the . . . [CIA]."[33] That the existence of the CIA on Saipan was known to the Saipanese, at least, seems attested to by conversations with those islanders in more recent years. For instance, C. S. Cruz, a Security Officer at the Trust Territory Headquarters on Saipan, says that the main headquarters building on Capitol Hill was constructed for the CIA in 1955; and numerous Micronesian officials there refer to their building complex as "formerly occupied by the CIA."

Were conditions comparable to earlier times when the Navy returned to the northern Marianas in 1953? Francisco C. Ada, Executive Officer to the Resident Commissioner of the Government of the Northern Marianas since the start of that interim government in the spring of 1976, and formerly the District Administrator for the Mariana Islands (from 1969), refers to the so-called "security restriction" which existed in the northern Marianas in that decade of 1953-62. That meant everyone traveling to those islands "had to undergo a certain kind of security pass" when arriving on Guam (the entry point to Saipan). No tourists were permitted. Ada concludes: "Even the level of so-called uplift of development was rather fragmented. In the early '50's, we [on Saipan] did have a municipal administration with an elected mayor and an elected municipal council." Did the *political* separation of the northern Marianas from the rest of the Trust Territory appear to have an adverse effect on interdistrict relations of the islanders during the decade of 1953-62? Ada observes: "I didn't have any strange feelings then, nor do we have any commonality with each other as well. It's sort of like a peaceful coexistent kind of an atmosphere—be friendly to each other, talk to each other, but there was no commonality between the districts."

The Interior Department's first decade in Micronesia was frustrating from several standpoints, all of which seemed to focus on the *lack* of funds to run the programs and maintain the governmental infrastructure. This problem was stated in the Interior's 1953 *Annual Report:*

> The Trust Territory was somewhat handicapped in its operations by restrictions placed in the Interior Department Appropriation Act, 1953, and by lack of funds to replace public buildings and utilities which have outlived their usefulness. The replacement of these buildings and utilities is becoming increasingly urgent.[34]

Professor Robbins explained the shortage of funds, and the relationship of this to Interior's slowness in developing programs and efficient management in the Trust Territory during the 1950s, as the *price* it was

"*To Foster the Development of Political Institutions . . .*" 51

obliged to pay for the outcome of "political warfare" which accompanied the advent of the Department of the Interior's responsibility in Micronesia (as discussed earlier in this chapter). Robbins said that Interior indicated it could handle the same administering responsibilities in the Trust Territory which the Navy had performed (from 1944-51) "for the same amount of money with economies that the Navy spent; . . . and, having said this, Interior for a long time was stuck with this low figure [i.e., an annual budget of $4-7 million] which . . . wasn't raised—it became regressive . . . and lasted down to the Kennedy Administration."[35]

J. Boyd Mackenzie, who in recent years has served, respectively, as a Special Consultant to the High Commissioner, Deputy and Acting High Commissioner in the Trust Teritory, first came to Micronesia with the Atomic Energy Commission on Enewetok in the Marshall Islands (in 1954), later remaining as a district administrator there and serving similarly in three other districts, in responding to the question, "Was the Navy a little better in working with smaller sums than Interior could do?" is emphatic is correcting such an impression of "small budgets" under the Navy Period:

> No, no, no. This is a fallacy. We [the Interior] got what the Navy got as a budget [from the U.S. Congress], but, remember, the Navy used money in training. They used millions of dollars in training, which did not show as budget items. You see, all of their planes out there, their military [sea]-planes out there that did all of the flying between islands—and they had LST's [amphibious landing barges] that went between islands which did not come under the Trust Territory Budget—so-called Trust Territory budgets; this was paid by U.S. military funds. Now for the people, themselves, yes, you had a very small budget; but the things that went towards the support of the military was not included in the budget. So, if you had a $4.5 million budget, this does not include all of the transportation that went with it. So, you see, there's a big difference now if you consider the "training" aspect—and I believe it's what the Navy considered it . . . in which the LST's were provided, [and] planes were provided. . . . There was quite a bit of scrounging of materials. . . . Quite a bit of it. And so the military was able to operate. And they could never have operated on a $4.5 million [only].

Some officials in the Trust Territory Government believe that a more correct *annual* expenditure by the Navy during its seven-year administration in Micronesia was probably in the neighborhood of $25-30 million.

Mackenzie also remembers the kinds of officials Interior sent out during that first decade as being, in many cases "highly dedicated," with several either retired or former Naval officers who transferred over to Interior: "There was a small nucleus of people, and I found that, when I first came out, that there were quite a few very dedicated people that were out here. . . . And, in many cases—a lot of them—did quite a bit of heavy drinking, which is normal, I guess, in the Trust Territory, . . . because of the limited recreation facilities that are provided out here." Neas recalls that he knew nearly all of the early district administrators and their deputies personally as well as professionally, and he was impressed with their varied abilities: "Some [of them] were more capable than I am in one field, I'm more capable than they [in another]. But, essentially, we were a pretty homogeneous group of people in practically anything that you want to take: education, dedication to professional ethics, and application to the job."

Whereas the Naval Administration maintained its Trust Territory Government headquarters (during 1947-51) at Pearl Harbor, Interior moved its headquarters from Hawaii to Guam in 1954, at the same time relocating some of the executive departments to points throughout Micronesia: the Department of Public Health to Ponape; Education, to Truk; and the Fiscal and Supply Office, to Guam. Hope was still held out for "organic legislation" for the Trust Territory by 1960 with the announcement of the Congressional Enabling Act of 1954, which extended governmental authorization in the Pacific Islands until 1960, by which time it was "anticipated that suitable organic legislation for the territory will have been adopted."[36] Although Guam is not part of the six administrative districts of Micronesia, as mentioned earlier, that relocation of the Trust Territory Government headquarters to the western Pacific must have been viewed as a progressive step by the islanders.

Were programs instituted by Interior in Micronesia to bring the Micronesians into positions of responsibility during the decade of 1951-60? In 1955, the Palau Congress was granted a charter, and, as an early "Micronization" effort, an islander was finally chosen for a top-level district post: "In the education department, a Micronesian replaced an American as District Education Administrator. This is the first instance of a Micronesian assuming full charge of a district department."[37] Interior's 1956 *Annual Report,* without mentioning the specific position involved, indicated that "another islander has become a top district official. While the process is necessarily a slow one, a major administrative goal in the Department is the appointment of Micronesians to government positions as rapidly as they can be trained to take over such responsibilities."[38] Professor Robbins referred to such easing in of the indigenes as one of an "enlightened gradualism" on the part of the Trust Territory Government during President Eisenhower's two terms (1953-61), which "satisfied the United Nations remarkably well each year" as the High Commissioner would make his oral report to the Trusteeship Council in New York City. Robbins concluded: "The process of developing local responsibility and institutions to achieve the avowed ultimate goal of 'a full measure of self-government' moved ahead during this period."[39]

"To Foster the Development of Political Institutions . . ."   53

About the same time Interior was pursuing its political goal of "enlightened gradualism," the U.S. Navy, in the northern Marianas, was attempting to instill sound accounting procedures. Terry L. Garrett, present Director of Finance in the Trust Territory Government, recalls seeing "an old accounting manual [of] 1954 that was very reasonable and had a lot of good accounting policies and procedures in it. I asked what had happened to these, and no one [in his department] seemed to know, except that they had nothing but bad words for Navy Administration." Garrett adds that he, personally, thinks that "perhaps if the Navy [accounting] system had been allowed to remain, that we'd [the Trust Territory Government] have been a lot better off."

The granting of a charter for the Palau Congress, in 1955, "marked the integration of newly acquired democratic concepts with traditional Palauan institutions. This was a step in the direction of self-government toward which the Palauan people and their Congress have been working for many years"; and that year's Interior *Report* indicated the powers vested in the Palau Congress, including assisting in the drawing up of the district budget and the collection of taxes and fees, would permit those indigenous legislators "to formulate laws which will be submitted to the High Commissioner for approval."[40]

Local government in the islands also made advances in the mid-1950s when the village of Kolonia, in Ponape, became the "first chartered town in all of Micronesia." At the district level, the Palau Congress, in addition to "implementing the collection of taxes and fees," mentioned earlier, established a district budget. In Truk, an annual Magistrates' Conference, for the first time, approved a district-wide budget. The entire Trust Territory Budget for the 1957 Fiscal Year was announced as $6,250,000.[41] The most significant political development during the 1956-57 period in the Trust Territory was "the establishment of basic plans for the incorporation of municipalities and the completion of the chartering of district congresses [or legislatures]," in which Micronesian leaders—mostly selected by the local district congresses—participated in a convention on Guam, contributing to "a broader understanding of the political problems of the islands."[42]

Emphasis on local government continued in the Trust Territory in the remaining years of the 1950s. The *Annual Report* in 1959 referred to such focus in rather glowing terms:

> In the field of government, the most dramatic progress [among the noncontiguous territories of Interior] has occurred in the Trust Territory. In this far-flung territory, first emphasis is placed on the local level. During the fiscal year [1959] . . . charters were issued to 20 municipalities, while one island-group congress [i.e., Yap] received a charter. . . . Increasing numbers of Micronesians are being placed in top positions in such diverse fields as education, finance, public health, and the judiciary.[43]

Growth in the programs of "chartering municipalities" and the placement of Micronesians in high-level positions seemed to gain momentum as the Trust Territory moved into the decade of the 1960s. The *Annual Report* for 1960, for example, credited the "diligent efforts of Micronesians on district staffs" for the chartering endeavors locally. Those staffs, according to that report, "visited outlying communities in teams to explain and answer questions on functions and procedures of chartered municipal government." Within the Trust Territory Government's Office of the High Commissioner (the headquarters of the Government, on Capitol Hill, Saipan), "three Micronesians were promoted to newly established positions of administrative work"; and the report also stressed that, "throughout the districts and [executive] departments, Micronesians have been advanced to higher grades." Micronesian leaders also met for consultation in what was termed an "Inter-District Advisory Committee" in 1960, which had become an annual conference four years earlier, on Guam.[44]

Dwight Heine is not as impressed with the "municipal chartering" efforts of the Interior Department in the 1950s, feeling that such was a "bastardization" of the indigenous approach to government:

> They [Interior] said, "Let's go out and charter out the municipalities." And we [the Micronesians] didn't see any point in it, because the municipalities are governments that will exist ever since the Micronesian people arrived in these islands. They have their own way of handling things. And that's what's not the urgency there. As a matter of fact, after they [Interior] charter them, they become a problem, because now people expect that to be ruled not in kind but in money. (Laugh.) They become, you know, a problem because it's no longer Micronesian but it's bastardized form of government, because the old folks cannot openly transform to an American-type of government; and what's more, how can we pay them [the indigenous employees to be hired under the charters]?

How did the islanders express themselves, politically, during the decade of the 1950s? Peter T. Coleman, a Samoan who retired in February, 1977, as the Acting High Commissioner (having previosuly been Deputy High Commissioner and, before that, a District Administrator for the Marianas), reminded the U.N. Trusteeship Council, in his remarks of June, 1976, that "the very earliest petitions to the United Nations from the [inhabitants of the] Trust Territory . . . [dated] as far back as April 1950," and dealt with the subject of "war claims" (to be discussed in chapter 3, herein).[45] Micronesia was visited by a U.N. Mission from the Trusteeship Council during February and March of 1953—the first of such tours to be held every three years (the most recent, in 1976). Again, the subject of "war claims" against both Japan and the United States "for combat and noncombat damage . . . [and]

land claims" were complaints by some of the islanders who submitted "petitions" to that visiting team.

The Trust Territory delegation to the U.N. Trusteeship Council's annual session in mid-1953 included two Micronesians—making the United States "one of the first nations to include local advisers on its official delegation . . . when annual reports [from the trusteeships] are being considered."[46] The Micronesian spokesman to the council meeting the following year objected to the use of islands in the Marshalls for "nuclear testing," and Van Cleve wrote that "the protest was polite, and the fact that it was made at all was viewed by most in Washington as a kind of aberration."[47] Criticisms from the U.N. Trusteeship Council were not to be felt by the Administering Authority in Micronesia, in Professor Robbins' view, until about 1960 or 1961, when most of the other trusteeships (principally, in Africa) had terminated and that council's members could thus turn their eyes more fully on the United States' stewardship.[48]

Mackenzie recalls the political development of Micronesia under Interior during 1950s from a number of perspectives. While the physical facilities were hampered by a lack of sufficient yearly funding by the U.S. Congress, Mackenzie "measures" the development of the Micronesians as follows:

> The development was with the people [the islanders], themselves. I would say political development, for instance: freedom of speech—things that they were never used to, under the Japanese. And how do you measure this growth in the population, itself? This is the first time they were able to express themselves; this is the first time they were able to vote; this is the first time they had any kind of councils; this is the first time that they were able to have something to say about what little, even if it was just a little—of what their future would be. But they were developing politically much faster than any other area [such as medically]. . . . But physically, there was practically no development because there were no [adequate] funds available.

THE "MICRONESIA CLUB" TAKES THE INITIATIVE

The foregoing pages in this chapter should have led the reader to a very basic conclusion with regard to "political development" in Micronesia during the first 15 years of American rule (or, from 1945-60) under the successive administrations of the U.S. Navy and the Department of the Interior (except, as also noted earlier, in the northern Marianas): namely, that *decisions* made were usually those of the Administering Authority in response to *initiatives* invariably put forth by the American officials. Lazarus Salii recalls possibly the first effort by the future leaders of Micronesia to take the initiative on their own, without the overt or covert promptings of "outsiders." Salii recalls that, by the mid-1950s, his generation was reaching adulthood, graduating from high school and beginning to work in the district governments. As those young Micronesians saw the neglect in the maintenance of the infrastructure, the relatively poor transportation services available, and the lagging economy in their respective home islands and district centers, they began to evaluate the overall situation in the Trust Territory. He recounts the formation of the "Micronesia Club" around 1959 for those islanders who were attending the University of Hawaii, and the conclusions they, as a group, reached:

> The [Micronesian student] group in Hawaii was really the group that was evaluating the Trust Territory from a review of the Trusteeship Agreement [of 1947]. . . . And, I think when that group returned [to the islands], we really began to needle the Administration. Article 6, this [from the Agreement] we began to pull out. . . . That generation of Micronesians, my group: Dwight Heine, Alfonso Oiterong, David Travari, Tosiwo Nakayama, Oscar DeBrum, Leo Falcam, Bailey Olter, Bethwel Henry.[49] And there was a consensus in the group that thinks we're not moving fast enough [as of the early-1960s], that there was really a serious neglect of obligations under the Trusteeship. So, I'd say in late 1961, '62, when I just started working with public administration, on public questions, I was asked to contribute in every district [i.e., his ideas on such questions].

There were two other gestures made by members of the "Micronesia Club" in the early 1960s to let the U.S. Government know how they felt. First, some of them actively campaigned for John F. Kennedy in his 1960 Presidential race. Salii remembers that he personally campaigned for the Democratic nominee as part of a government course assignment at the university, adding: "I don't think any Micronesians in those days could have been described as 'radicals,' but we were 'liberals' in a sense. I think if you took a poll in those days, every Micronesian would say he was a Democrat rather than a Republican." (That observation by Salii is noteworthy inasmuch as the Republicans had controlled the White House, and thus the Interior Department, for the eight years beginning in 1953. The U.S. Congress was Republican only during 1953-55 of Eisenhower's two terms.)

The second effort made by the "Micronesia Club" came after Kennedy was sworn in and had selected a Democrat, M. Wilfred Goding, to replace the Republican Delmas H. Nucker as High Commissioner for the Trust Territory. (Nucker had served in that capacity since 1956.) Again, in Salii's view, there were Micronesian student initiatives which resulted in Goding stopping off at Honolulu to meet with that club's members en route to his new assignment in the islands:

"*To Foster the Development of Political Institutions* . . ." 57

    I think he [Goding] was aware that there was a big Micronesian group in Hawaii that is the future of these islands [of Micronesia]. I do suspect that he would have stopped on his own, but there was a combination of factors. We made it known, as I recall, that we had a Micronesia Club. But we wanted to see the new High Commissioner, and we asked for him, that's why he came. We did ask as a club—the Micronesia Club—the Micronesian students. And we asked him what he planned to do. We didn't the first time; in coming the High Commissioner was questioned: What are you going to do about [economic] recovery? What are you going to do about projects for recovery? That was the first time he informed us that the [annual] budget wasn't enough, that he was going to ask a group of experts—most likely from Harvard and Yale—to come and look at the situation [in the Trust Territory], and give him a recommendation of what to do. The group eventually came: it's the Solomon Task Force [of 1963].

Dwight Heine recalls the above happenings with regard to the new High Commissioner, Goding, arriving in Micronesia. However, Heine had already finished college and was employed by the Trust Territory Government. He adds that the whole matter of the "Micronesia Club" approaching the High Commissioner in 1961 "was not very famous [or publicized]. We sort of went by word of mouth. . . . It was not one of those things that there's so much talk that everybody heard about it." Strik Yoma, who attended the University of Hawaii after 1961 and was to serve as President of the "Micronesia Club," remembers that Goding's visit with the students was just before the summer of 1961.

Salii, who graduated from the University of Hawaii in June, 1961 (majoring in political science, as most Micronesians did during the 1960s), took the opportunity between the time of Goding's Honolulu visit and his own graduation that June to write a letter to the new High Commissioner, suggesting that "the district legislatures, the Council of Micronesia, and the High Commissioner begin to discuss about the [future political] status." Goding's response to the Salii letter? Again, in the words of Salii, who eventually (from 1967-76) was to chair (or co-chair) the various Micronesian delegations on the "future political status" question, "he [Goding] didn't respond. He distributed the letter throughout Micronesia. I think that at that time the idea of developing the Congress of Micronesia was already being discussed [in 1961]. I don't think he could have responded, anyway. I think this basically was a Micronesian decision."

THE "SOLOMON MISSION" IN 1963

President Kennedy, in the year before his death, selected a "mission" to visit the Trust Territory. The findings and recommendations of that mission to Micronesia in 1963 were compiled in the "Solomon Report" (so named after the team's chairman, Anthony M. Solomon, then a professor in the Harvard Business School, and later Assistant Secretary of State for Economic Affairs). This entire report was initially "classified," the first part dealing with the team's mission and a discussion of the political future for the Trust Territory. The remaining two parts were concerned primarily with the social, educational, and economic development (to be discussed in the following chapters).

Dr. Harlan Cleveland, who retired as President of the University of Hawaii in 1976, was Assistant Secretary of State for International Organizations in 1963 when the Solomon Mission was chosen. He indicated in an interview in mid-1971 that he was the one who organized the 1963 Mission, although he only nominated one of its members (Professor Gerald Mangone, from the Maxwell School at Syracuse University).[50] Cleveland also described the situation existing at the time of the Solomon Mission as "the classic Washington battle between big departments, the White House and Congress." He appeared to indict the Interior Department for being "bent on preserving the status quo" in Micronesia, as evidenced by Interior striving to keep the annual budget for the Trust Territory at a low amount (averaging less than $7 million). The Defense Department, in Cleveland's hindsight of 1971, was "naturally . . . interested in defense considerations," although he supported the military view by emphasizing that the civilian leadership in the Pentagon "was also interested in improving the situation in Micronesia because, from the long-term strategic view, they wanted to deny the Trust Territory to other major powers and figured, in effect, that 'unless we treat them [the Micronesians] better, there will be trouble.' "[51]

There appears to be controversy over the "classified" nature of the 1963 Solomon Report. Initially, all portions of it were "classified;" however, the present Director of Territorial Affairs (DOTA), Ruth G. Van Cleve, indicated in a personal letter to the author (in June, 1977) that, when she was previously DOTA (during 1964-69), "we undertook [in the mid-1960s] to declassify Volumes II and III, and following very tedious and protracted negotiations with the State Department, plus some 'sanitizing' (as they say) by them, those Volumes were declassified. I immediately made them available to whoever wanted to see them, and that included a reporter for a Honolulu newspaper." Van Cleve went on to say that, "as for Volume I, it has never been declassified."

That pivotal Volume I (or Part I) of the Solomon Report of 1963 has been reproduced by a number of groups, beginning in 1971 with the *Young Micronesian,* an islander student publication during the 1970-71 school year at the University of Hawaii. The editor of that paper, Francisco Uludong, a Palauan, in a "Dear Readers" article of the March 1, 1971, edition, claimed to have obtained the "Introduction and Summary" of the Solomon Report (Volume I), stating that "the key first

"*To Foster the Development of Political Institutions...*"   59

part [having] remained until now [1971] confidential and has been seen by only [a] handful of Americans." In mid-1971, the *Micronitor* (now, *Micronesian Independent*), a weekly newspaper published at Majuro, in the Marshalls, ran a special edition (on July 10, 1971) which reproduced the *Young Micronesian* exposé; the "Friends of Micronesia," an American independence-for-Micronesia group in the early-1970s, also reproduced portions of the Part I revelations from the Micronesian student newspaper, above; and most recently, Dr. Donald F. McHenry, formerly with the State Department (from 1963-73) and a member of the Carnegie Endowment for International Peace, published *Micronesia: Trust Betrayed* (in 1975), in which he included excerpts from the Solomon Report's Part I as an appendix. McHenry reportedly told Washington officials that he obtained that classified portion through the good offices of some Micronesian students at the University of Hawaii.

What is basically contained in Part I of the Solomon Report of 1963 which has raised the ire of at least some Micronesians and Americans concerned with the future political status of the islanders? The "Introduction and Summary" section lists the "major objectives and considerations" addressed in Parts I-III, respectively, giving that for Part I in the form of a *question* first, then the Mission's *findings and recommendations* as follows:

> [*Question:*] What are the elements to consider in the preparation for organization, timing and favorable outcome of a plebiscite in Micronesia, and how will this action affect the long-run problem that Micronesia, after affiliation, will pose for the United States?
> [*Findings and Recommendations:*] Winning the plebiscite and making Micronesia a United States territory under circumstances which will: (1) satisfy somewhat conflicting interests of the Micronesians, the United Nations and the United States along lines satisfactory to the [U.S.] Congress; (2) be appropriate to the present political and other capabilities of the Micronesians; and (3) provide sufficient flexibility in government structure to accommodate to whatever measure of local self-government the Congress might grant to Micronesia in later years.[52]

Maynard Neas, who was the District Administrator in Ponape at the time the Solomon Mission toured in Micronesia, recalls that he worked with those team members during the period they were in Ponape. He was impressed by their dedication: "They were a very hard-working bunch of men, intelligent, and knew what they were doing. They were gathering information to mount quite a jump in funds to administer the Territory, and it was no secret what they were doing, who they were talking with, and there was nothing hidden about it." Parenthetically, Neas says that the Solomon Mission members "were answering, in a way, the request that fellow [district] administrators—Americans in the [Trust Territory] Administration—had asked for for years: more money to do some of the things that we felt should be done to answer the physical needs of the people, for better health care, for better education, for better opportunities in roads and shipping and communications."

After the Solomon Report was compiled in mid-1963, prior to its submission to Kennedy in October (one month before the President's assassination), High Commissioner Goding had his six district administrators meet on Saipan for four or five days to discuss how the Solomon Report's recommendations could be implemented. One of those volumes was sent to the district administrators before their conference at the High Commissioner's Office on Capitol Hill, and the others were made available to them when they arrived. Aside from discussing the economic and educational aspects (to be mentioned in succeeding chapters), Neas remembers that "we [the district administrators] did make comments to the High Commissioner on this [Solomon] report, and when we went home, to our home districts, we took the reports [the volumes] with us, and soon we were instructed to return them to headquarters." Does that mean that those district administrators—all Americans at the time—were accordingly told by Goding that the Solomon Report was *then* to be treated as "classified" material? Neas recollects: "My understanding was that they [the volumes] were withdrawn from circulation, . . . but we [the district administrators] were never enjoined to shut our mouth about what we had talked about here in Saipan, or what we had read." Again, Neas points to the feelings of those U.S. administrators in the six districts at that time: "None of my fellow workers that I know of considered them [the volumes] as anything except a plan that probably was a little bit in the nature of getting a favorable plebiscite. . . . It certainly wasn't doing anything that we hadn't asked to be done for years."

The subject of "annexation" in the Solomon Report was discussed among the district administrators at the above conference in 1963. Neas recalls there being mentioned among them and other American officials in the Trust Territory that the Solomon Report recommendations might result in some kind of "post-political ties" with the United States. Neas concludes that "annexation" was always thought of as being possible, but he feels that there was never any attempt to *push* "annexation" as the answer to such future relations: "I think I would have been about as sensitive to it ["annexation"] as anyone else, if anyone had hinted that that's what they [the Administering Authority] wanted us to be doing, was to slant our attention and our activities to that end, [but] I was never under that kind of pressure, and I don't think any of the other people in the Territory were." The Interior Department, in Neas' view, was trying to bring the Micronesians "up to the level of where they could make an informed decision of their own."

Salii feels at present that Dr. Solomon's team saw the situation in Micronesia rather clearly, and adds his own puzzlement that the United

"To Foster the Development of Political Institutions..." 61

States did not push for a lasting association with the Micronesians at that early moment:

> In retrospect, I think that there was a conflict that soon developed with the Solomon recommendation [in 1963] calling for a plan of "annexation": wrap it up quick. And it would have been a very different ball game here if that recommendation had been adopted. For some reason, it's been very interesting to me why the United States has been so conscious of the Trusteeship Agreement for Micronesia. I suppose . . . the United States developed those obligations in Article 6, really. But, my God, Micronesians were not politically conscious in those days! They didn't care, really. They didn't have any kind of national pride. Any kind of political initiative had really been killed in the 30 years of Japanese Administration. And I don't think, outside of the small group in Hawaii [the "Micronesia Club" members], the population in Micronesia would have raised a resistance. I think they really would have liked for the United States to possess Micronesia. I don't think in those days the U.N. would have had much ground to object. That would have been the best solution for the United States. In terms of cost, I think it would have been cheaper to end this way [i.e., "annexation"]. . . . So, this insignificant agreement [the 1947 Trusteeship Agreement], something bothers me. I think Dr. Solomon saw the situation [in Micronesia] as it was in those days, and what he really tried to do was, "Let's do it now before these people [the islanders] wake up. We're sending them to school [college] and we're not giving them any restrictions—unlike the Japanese [did]. We're sending them en masse. And we can look at them now [in 1963]: they're all going into political science or education. They're mixing with students from Southeast Asia, from Africa. It's bound to affect their view of things!" And it did.

The estimated cost to the U.S. Government for the expenses of the Solomon Mission and the resultant three-volume report was $300,000.[53] Cleveland said that the Solomon Report, when completed, was sent directly to President Kennedy; however, "the White House lost interest" in that report after Kennedy's death.[54]

THE CONGRESS OF MICRONESIA: AN ELECTED LEGISLATURE

Kurt Ludwig, an American who served as an Assistant Political Affairs Officer in the Trust Territory Government for more than four years (1964-69), reminisced over his impressions of political development in Micronesia and viewed the coming forth of the Congress of Micronesia in the mid-1960s as more of a culminating event than a catalyst in the islanders' participation in territorial legislative activities:

> The most significant factor in helping to develop territorial unity has been the Congress of Micronesia. And this influence did not start with the establishment of the Congress in 1965, or its coming into being, but stretches back to its immediate predecessor, the Council of Micronesia, and

further than that, the Inter-District Advisory Committee, which functioned in the 1950s. These were the first moves in territorial political development, leading toward the establishment of a territorial legislature. Although not much unity was visible in the '50's, . . . at least these sessions of the Inter-District Advisory Committee did give leading Micronesians from each district the opportunity to begin to think in terms of territorial problems, and see each other's problems.[55]

Strik Yoma, a Ponapean who also became an Assistant Political Affairs Officer for the Trust Territory Headquarters in 1964, recalls that the initiative for a Congress of Micronesia came from a series of cables and correspondence between Washington, D.C., and the High Commissioner's Office, on Saipan, that year, and Yoma clarifies the roles played by the United Nations and the earlier Council of Micronesia (the later name for the Inter-District Advisory Committee dating back to 1956):

> Just prior to the summer of '64, the last meeting of what they called the Inter-District Conference [the Council of Micronesia], advisory committee to the High Commissioner, which was a predecessor of the Congress of Micronesia, was held. This group was first established in '56, I believe, by High Commissioner [Frank H.] Midkiff, and they served the function of advising the High Commissioner on policy matters and programs in the Trust Territory. And various [U.N.] Visiting Missions had taken interest in the work of this group and made recommendations that perhaps this group could be upgraded to a de facto legislative body of the Government of Micronesia. Of course, if you recall, prior to the Congress of Micronesia, the High Commissioner had both the executive and the legislative authority of the Government of the Trust Territory. And so the last recommendation made—we have to go back to [Delmas H.] Nucker [High Commissioner during 1956-61] now, he made the same recommendation that this be done—and so in the U.N. [Trusteeship Council] hearing, in 1964, there was some discussion on some of this subject, and so, on September 28, '64, the [Department of Interior] Secretarial Order 2882 was issued, establishing the Congress of Micronesia and investing in this body the legislative authority for the Government of the Trust Territory.

Dwight Heine, who was Chairman of the Council of Micronesia, differs with Yoma, above, with regard to the *initiative* for developing the Congress of Micronesia in 1965. He believes that the push to develop political institutions in the islands came from *both* the American officials and the Micronesians, adding that "we'd [the islanders had] been agitating about this thing" as early as the mid-1950s.

The Council of Micronesia's most important meeting occurred in 1963, when two representatives from each of the six administrative districts met "to consider and advise upon the creation of a Territory-wide legislative body with legislative powers."[56] Van Cleve wrote that the most taxing problem facing that council was whether the proposed Congress of Micronesia should be a single-chamber body (unicameral) or have two houses (bicameralism), and commented on why U.S. officials generally favored the former type:

> Council [of Micronesia] members were urged by most of their non-Micronesian advisers to recommend a unicameral legislature—partly on the usual grounds of economy and efficiency, but partly too because of the fear, which some candidly expressed, that hereditary chiefs would dominate the upper house and thereby contribute undue conservatism. [American] Samoa was the cited example. But the Council concluded that it had a different preference: first, a bicameral legislature, with the lower house based upon population, the upper house on equal representation per district; second, a unicameral legislature, with equal representation from each district; and only last, the theoretician's preference, a unicameral legislature based upon population. The Secretary of Interior's order [No. 2882], issued in September '64, adopted the Council's first preference.[57]

The determined size of the Congress of Micronesia—12 senators (two from each district) and 21 representatives (somewhat based on population)—would allow more Micronesians to participate in a territorial legislature than was experienced in the two predecessor bodies, the Council of Micronesia and the Inter-District Advisory Committee. The election for the First Congress of Micronesia was held in January, 1965. At the request of Raymond Ulochong and Strik Yoma, in the Political Affairs Office of the Headquarters, both of whom were impressed with the background of Professor Norman Meller at the University of Hawaii (mentioned in this chapter), High Commissioner Goding contracted to have a three-man team from the Institute for Technical Interchange at the University of Hawaii come to Saipan and hold a two-week workshop for the newly elected legislators. Those three men (Meller, Dinell, and Gill) decided on multiple objectives which they felt would "encourage a sense of identity sufficient to permit the Micronesian congressmen to manage their own affairs." The workshop also allowed "ample opportunity for the members-elect to assay the competence, articulateness, and interest of potential officers and committee chairmen, as well as occasion for them to meet in informal caucus."[58] Without exception, the present and former congressmen who participated in that workshop told this author that such was a *most* worthwhile experience, especially for those with no prior legislative background.

Originally, the Congress of Micronesia's two houses were titled the House of Delegates (later, the Senate) and the General Assembly (then, the House of Representatives afterward). Lazarus Salii says that the reason why the Micronesian legislators chose to rename those two bodies was simple: "We [the congressmen] couldn't really explain [to their district constituents] what a 'delegate' was, and 'assemblyman.' They were alien terms and they tended to confuse us in terms of our relationship with the Administration. So the change was natural and there was no objection from the Administration."

For the first Legislative Counsel of the Congress of Micronesia, provision was made through a Secretarial Order to hire someone with expertise who could guide the Micronesians elected to be territorial legislators. The choice was Professor Robert R. Robbins, then Chairman of the Department of Government at Tufts University, Medford, Massachusetts (and a former State Department official, mentioned earlier). Salii remarks on the wisdom in that appointment, which was to last the length of the first session of the Congress of Micronesia in 1965:

> I think he [Robbins] was well liked and highly respected by everybody. There's a lot of respect for age in Micronesia. He was already an old man [in his mid-'50's] when he came. He was a professional type of man. He'd never held any position with the Trust Territory. . . . I think people in the Congress [of Micronesia] immediately knew that this was not a spy for the Administration, but this was a man who really was ready to get the job done. For the first session of Congress, nothing much was required in the Administration. There were a few bills. . . . People knew that he wasn't here for a very long time. He was destined to spend available time with the congressmen. In general, I say he was and is very highly regarded by those of us who knew him when he came here. . . . I think now if they [the Administering Authority] had brought a younger lawyer-contract type, [or the] Peace Corps [volunteer lawyer type], it wouldn't have worked out and Congress may have taken a different character in the earlier days. He never interfered. He let us really define our role, scope of work.

Salii's opinion of Robbins as a Legislative Counsel to help the Congress of Micronesia operate smoothly at the outset is also shared by others. One rather humorous experience is related by Andon Amaraich, a former senator from Truk. Amaraich recalls chairing the first Credentials Committee in 1965, and receiving the moral support of the Legislative Counsel in a difficult—and almost physical!—encounter over whether to seat a representative-elect who had a criminal record: "Bob Robbins and I sat behind this small, narrow table. There was a dispute about a representative elected from Saipan, and the opposing attorneys [seated on either end] could reach across the table and grab one another. (Laugh.) I wish the table had been wider!" That representative, incidentally, was seated but with the reservation that the action should not constitute a precedent.

That the members of the Congress of Micronesia, meeting for the first time as a legislative body on Monday, July 12, 1965—"the day to be remembered"[59]—were to carry over some of the "political maneuvering" tactics discussed in the pre-session workshop, mentioned earlier, may be seen in the following anecdote involving the first General Assembly (later, House of Representatives) Speaker, Heine, as recalled by Robbins:

"To Foster the Development of Political Institutions . . ." 65

There's probably some advantage in running a legislature in Micronesia if you can't be heard. (Laughter.) You can just preside. Dwight Heine [the Speaker] found this out in the First Congress of Micronesia [in the July-August, 1965, sessions], in using the late Chief Petrus Mailo, from Truk. When he [Heine] got into a political bind with the lower house, he would have a "diplomatic" sore throat and let Chief Petrus take over. Then you got the proceedings operating on the basis of respect, rather than what was said.⁶⁰

FUTURE POLITICAL STATUS INITIATIVES BY MICRONESIANS

President Lyndon B. Johnson proposed to the U.S. Congress, in 1967, that a "status commission"—composed of eight members presidentially appointed—be authorized. The ultimate objective would be to hold a "plebiscite" among the Micronesians within the following five-year period (or "by June 30, 1972"). The U.S. Senate seemed agreeable to the commission idea, adding that eight U.S. Congressional members should be included. The U.S. House of Representatives, with Congressman Jonathan B. Bingham as sponsor, proposed H.J. Res. 594, in May of 1967, calling for a nine-member commission;⁶¹ however, in the words of former Congresswoman Mink, "the measure languished in the House."⁶² The Congress of Micronesia's first Legislative Counsel considered the U.S. Congress' failure to act on President Johnson's commission proposal as a *second* "major mistake" by the United States with regard to the Pacific Islands in the post-War period (the *first* mistake being the "political warfare" between Navy and Interior leading up to 1951, discussed earlier).

While the American Congress appeared to be dragging its feet over the formation of a "status commission" as requested by President Johnson in 1967, a U.N. Visiting Mission toured Micronesia that year and later, in its report to the Trusteeship Council, while lauding the development of the Congress of Micronesia since the latter's inception in 1965, stated that the "hope" expressed by the previous Visiting Mission (in 1964)— that changing the Council of Micronesia into a "full-scale legislative body . . . would bring about a radical change in the outlook for political development in Micronesia"—was "not misplaced." That 1967 report continued: "Micronesia now has a central body to speak for it, to legislate for it in the best interests of the whole, and to provide a focus for loyalties which are beginning to instil a growing unity among members of the [island] public."⁶³ The 1967 U.N. Visiting Mission also made a suggestion to the United States that the Administering Authority in Micronesia ought to create a "cabinet-type body" to aid the High Commissioner in his decision-making process. The advantage of such a "formal consultative body on the lines of an executive council or cabinet," especially if "outstanding Micronesians" were members thereof, would be that "government policy could be publicly seen to be determined not by the High Commissioner alone, or by the Secretary of the Interior alone, but by the joint effort and deliberation and with the joint advice of those appointed to this high council."[64]

The High Commissioners since 1967 have not heeded the U.N.'s advice with regard to a "cabinet-type body" to aid them in their decision-making; however, the islanders since that time have been progressively placed in key positions both on the High Commissioner's headquarters staff and in the districts. As of mid-1977, all six district administrators were Micronesian, and the Executive Branch officers were all islanders with the exception of the High Commissioner and three of his department heads: the Attorney General, and the Directors of Finance and Transportation/Communications. A fourth key official—the Programs and Budget Officer—has also remained an American.

The U.N. Report of 1967 also noted that "this is the first year the Congress of Micronesia has selected the advisers" to serve on the U.S. Delegation to the Trusteeship Council's annual meeting in New York City.[65]

The first meeting of the Future Political Status Commission of the Congress of Micronesia, which commission was formed at the initiative of the Micronesian Congressional leaders, took place in November, 1967, on Saipan, with Lazarus Salii being elected chairman of that six-man group. Salii's election was deemed highly appropriate, for this senator from Palau had been a prime mover of Micronesian overtures regarding future political status. (Interestingly, and not untypically of life in the political arena, Senator Salii was to exclaim some 18 months later, in May, 1969, that he would be leaving politics at the end of that term, in January, 1973. " 'This decision is irrevocable,' said Salii. He emphasized that, through the remainder of his term as senator and Chairman of the Political Status Commission, he would feel free to act without regard for political considerations."[66] However, Salii was to stand successfully for reelection in November, 1972, retiring in January, 1977, having been appointed as Territorial Planner for the Trust Territory Government in December, 1976.)

William R. Norwood, the High Commissioner during the formative period of the above Micronesian status commission, testified before the U.N. Trusteeship Council, in the spring of 1968, that the Congress of Micronesia had proceeded to establish its own status group at the Third Regular session of that Congress (during July-August, 1967), and had held a series of "meetings and hearings and . . . decided to establish contact with representatives of various agencies, territories and nations whose experience is relevant to Micronesia." Norwood appeared some-

"To Foster the Development of Political Institutions . . ."

what pessimistic as to what the United States might do by way of "cooperating" with the Micronesians in the seeking for a suitable political future: "The [Future Political] Status Commission also plans to establish liaison with the United States Status Commission if and when the latter is authorized and appointed."[67]

Ironically, Congresswoman Mink, in an official visit to Micronesia in 1968, reportedly found the islanders "objecting strenuously" to the possible passage of legislation in the U.S. Congress which might establish the "Presidential Commission" earlier requested (in 1967). According to Mink, the Micronesians "were themselves unsure what route they wanted to take and did not want outsiders to decide their future."[68] Johnson's proposed "Presidential Commission" would *not* have included any Micronesians within its membership, or even as ex-officio members thereof.

If the United States had behaved differently in the middle 1960s, it could have worked greater cooperation from the Micronesians. What *might* have been is footless speculation; however, many have theorized as to what might have been *if* the United States had been more dynamic, imaginative, and sensitive to Micronesian aspirations in the period of 1967-69 than was the case. Previously, U.S. Senators Hiram L. Fong, of Hawaii, Ernest Gruening, of Alaska, and Ralph W. Yarborough, of Texas, co-sponsored a concurrent resolution on August 18, 1965, which called for the inclusion of the Trust Territory in the state of Hawaii, contingent on a "referendum" to determine if the peoples of both Hawaii and Micronesia would approve of that merger.[69]

The Micronesian congressman who accompanied High Commissioner Norwood to the Trusteeship Council session in 1968 was Jacob Sawaichi, of Palau, who, in addressing that body, expressed in rather succinct phrases what the *aspirations* of the Micronesian legislators appeared to be at that point:

> [In 1967,] there were three remaining territories under the Trusteeship arrangement. Today, with Nauru having gained its independence, two territories remain, namely, New Guinea [which was to become independent in 1975] and our Pacific Trust Territory. The need, therefore, to reexamine our rate of progress towards self-determination has gained a new dimension of urgency. We are anxious to get on with the job of nation building.[70]

Also in 1968, the Future Political Status Commission of the Congress of Micronesia released its "interim report," which, in 125 pages, gave an indication of the extent to which some of the commission members were willing to travel in their search for political future "options" for Micronesia. Thus, note is made in that report of two of those members—Chairman Salii and Senator Bailey Olter—who, after visiting the U.N. in May, 1968, proceeded to Puerto Rico and the Virgin Islands (the former, a "commonwealth," the latter, a "territory").⁷¹ The Second Congress of Micronesia, after hearing the above "interim report" of its own status commission in the summer of 1968, decided to extend the life of the latter group, feeling that "the scope of this [future political] study requires that a substantial amount of additional consideration be given to it by the members of the Future Political Status Commissioner"; therefore, the commission was charged, through a House Joint Resolution, to "continue to conduct a study and investigation as to the range of alternatives open to Micronesians."⁷²

(At this juncture, the discussion will return to an evaluation of the Congress of Micronesia. Suffice it to say that the Micronesian "status commissions" were to meet with U.S. delegations for *eight* "rounds of negotiations" between 1969-76, during which sessions various "options" were discussed. Reference will be made at a later point in this chapter with respect to those "options" and the more recent meeting of representatives from Micronesia and the United States in Honolulu during May 18-21, 1977.)

SOME "CONFLICTS OF INTEREST" RESOLVED

Several of the original members of the Congress of Micronesia were obligated to make a choice between either staying in the Congress or resigning their seats. This was prompted by "dual employment" of a number of those legislators. For example, Dwight Heine recalls that, "at that time [1965], it didn't matter if you were in both the Executive Branch and the Legislative Branch, so I was also Educational Administrator for the Marshalls at the same time when I was a Speaker [of the House]." Heine just happened to be a one-termer who left the Congress after two years to be appointed as the first Micronesian district administrator (for the Marshalls, 1966-69). Lazarus Salii was employed as a management specialist in the Personnel Department of the Trust Territory Government when initially elected to the House in 1965. As Salii remembers, "at that time, most of us in the Congress were also employees of the Executive Branch.... I think it was in 1968 that we had to make a choice: either to stay with the House [or Senate] or to retire and stay with the Executive Branch. I chose to stay with the Congress." David Ramarui, from Palau, was also a district educational administrator while serving in the Congress, and agrees with Salii that "it was made very clear that in 1968, I believe, was the time when we had to decide whether to remain in the Executive Branch of the Government or resign and remain in the Legislative Branch. And that's the time when I agreed, I decided to terminate [from the Executive]." (Ramarui later left the

Senate to become the Deputy Director of Education for the Trust Territory in 1971, then, Director after two more years.)

Two other legislators who had to make a choice—and there was a considerable group involved—were Andon Amaraich, from Truk, and Luke Tman, a Yapese. Amaraich was an assistant district administrator for public affairs at the time of his election to the Congress in 1965 and he retained that former position until forced to choose between the two jobs. Amaraich recalls that the Administration was surprised so many "dual" employees chose to remain in the Congress and resign from the Executive Branch. Tman was employed in the Public Affairs Office of the Trust Territory Government and simultaneously served as a congressman in the House. Tman was one of the relatively few to opt for the Executive Branch, although four years later (in 1972) he resigned his Executive position and was reelected to the House from Yap.

Other "conflicts" remain to be resolved for the Congress of Micronesia, not unlike similar situations found in the U.S. Congress or the state legislatures. Dr. Kansou, from Truk, summarized this dilemma and blamed the "foreign" nature of such a territorial legislature for part of the problem:

> Even in the Congress of Micronesia . . . they [the legislators] think that they are trying to put together, the area together. I don't feel that they do. Because the way they do things, in there, make the people [and] the Congress going far apart, or even when the people in the districts who knew what they were doing, it makes them [feel separate]. Now, an example for this. Each of the congressman—and also let me say before I say this—that I think this Congress is a foreign idea that comes to us, so we are doing it and it is the best for everybody. Yes, maybe so; but, it's too early for the Micronesians. Now, getting back to what I was trying to say, that Congress thought that they are doing, forcing the Micronesians to come to, not forcing, but they thought that they were bringing them together, but they are not. When we observe it, each of them is a constituent. Every congressman [has] his own constituents. And he . . . has to please them. . . . One fellow from Palau do not have constituents in Truk. And another fellow but do not have constituents in Marshalls. I mean, each of these congressmen came from a certain group which was isolated for a long, long time, who knows nobody else but themselves except through Japanese Administration and now American Administration. And when these representatives come, and they start fighting over money and over things for their own constituents, which is their own islands.

Kansou says that he is not opposed to unity; he hopes that the Micronesians will find a way in which they can unite all of their districts together, that someone will have the solution to do so. While he agrees that it is well to have a Congress, he questions whether the political development may not have come a little too quickly for the Micronesians: "It's still too early. Many of our island neighbors have been under certain administration and, like Fiji, like Samoans, for hundreds of years before they become now independent, and before they now know that they are a unit." In other words, Kansou believes that there is *no* need to "rush things" in Micronesia's political development: "I don't see what's the hurry!"

Boyd Mackenzie adds two other elements on the Congress of Micronesia to Dr. Kansou's analysis in posing a rhetorical question, "Would Micronesia be as far ahead—as far advanced as they are right now—in their political thinking [if not under American rule since 1945]?"

> They [the islanders] have a Congress that first took its seat in 1965. And nowhere in the Pacific can you point to another nation in so short a period of time that they had their own governing body, their political party put together, called the Congress of Micronesia. Nowhere in the Pacific has this ever happened before. The British, the French, have all been here for hundreds of years. They're [in other developing Pacific areas] only now beginning to develop political [institutions]. . . . And these are the kind of things that I think people forget about, and they look strictly from the viewpoint of "How many buildings do you have?" . . . Are these things [i.e., the number and type of buildings] really important in a development of an emerging nation? . . . Your young [Micronesian] man coming back from college. Look at the people that, you can have over 2,000 people away at school—over 2,000 [from the Trust Territory]—and we have, the Congress of Micronesia's a very good example. Sixty percent of the [Micronesian legislative] body in 1965 were college graduates. The doctors . . . [and] dentists went to school in Suva. These are the people you also have in the Congress. But they have an education; they have some type of education that many of your legislative bodies throughout the Pacific don't have. New Guinea [Papua New Guinea], for instance, . . . [with] some 200 dialects.

Strik Yoma, the Director of Public Affairs in the Trust Territory Government, was one of the three principal officials in the 1965 Congress of Micronesia (serving as the first Clerk of the Senate while Frank Ada—later the District Administrator in the Marianas—was the Clerk of the House and Dr. Robbins was the Legislative Counsel). Yoma characterizes that legislative body as originally having a "strong feeling" for unity in the Trust Territory which was felt "from the Marshalls all the way to Palau." He continues: "If you were to read the speeches which were made by the various delegations in '65, and compare with the speeches that we hear, say, 7-8 years later, it's fantastic how the thing has completely turned around." Yoma *excepted* the Mariana Islands in this "pro-unity" stance. Yoma describes what caused a change in congressmen's thinking during the early 1970s, and differentiates between the "haves" and "have nots:"

"To Foster the Development of Political Institutions..." 71

I would say early '70's, to be precise, there was this beginning of wanting to pull away. The districts throughout were already realizing their potentials, beginning to show unwillingness to share. The "haves" [i.e., the Marshalls, Palau, and the Marianas] are beginning to show an unwillingness to share their wealth with the "have nots" [i.e., Yap, Truk, and Ponape]. . . . It is very fantastic, to me, it is just amazing how, in '65, you can read their speeches. . . . And you come back and read their speeches 10 years later, and it's amazing. I don't know what went wrong.

One of the earliest criticisms of "unity" as seen on the part of the Congress of Micronesia came from Carl Heine, formerly a Clerk of the House and more recently Deputy Director of Public Affairs under Yoma. From 1971-73, Heine was the Staff Director for the Joint Committee on Future Status, working for Senator Salii. In 1974, he became the first Micronesian to write a book on the political development in Micronesia, entitled *Micronesia at the Crossroads: A Reappraisal of the Micronesian Political Dilemma* (1974). Heine, in a "position paper," stated a rather *negative* "impact" of the Congress of Micronesia during its first six years (1965-71):

Much has been made of the fact that the Congress . . . is a "unifying force" in Micronesia. This statement, while it may be true, needs to be qualified. The Congress . . . is a highly respected institution in Micronesia, but its record does not justify what some observers have come to view as a unifying force. It can be stated that [the] Congress has a "united front," a false sense of unity, it seems, only because it has a common foe—the presence of the American Administering Authority. However, once that adversary is removed, the united front may fade away, and the inherent feelings of rivalry and regionalism will resurface as they did in the summer of 1967 when a resolution was about to be introduced [in the Micronesian Congress], the essence of which was to divide up the whole territory into two regions, East and West.[73]

Yoma has mixed feelings over Heine's analysis, above, saying: "I was not at that time [the early 1970s] able [to], and I still can't, say that the Congress of Micronesia was responsible for disunity now. Carl [Heine] may be right; perhaps we overplayed [the] Congress of Micronesia, the fact that it is a unifying factor." The Director of Public Affairs concludes that there are a number of "unresolved issues" facing the Congress of Micronesia at present:

Several things have happened since [1971], . . . and, in a way, maybe it's part of growing up—becoming mature, politically—that one has to go through this period of stress and strain; one has to really address, forthrightly and directly, these issues that, I guess over the years we sort of slipped under the rock and hoped that they would go away. But we can't just keep on doing that. I think the issue[s] of taxation . . . and the distribution of revenue [have] . . . to come about; and I think when they begin to address these issues, and then that's when the "haves" are saying [to the "have nots"], "Well, I don't think we'll have to give you this," you know. (Laugh.) Well, the districts are not that generous with their money. Understandably, maybe so. It's an unfair distribution of their rightful [revenue]. . . .

Salii, who retired from the Congress in 1977 after 12 years, believes that Carl Heine was frustrated over that legislature's failure to do *more* to unify the six administrative districts into thinking as a *single* entity, and the former senator adds his own analysis of Congress' contributions to unity:

> He [Heine] expected more out of the Congress. Sure, I don't think he's denying that it was a unifying force, but that the narrow-mindedness of the members of the Congress, their overriding concern to get as much money for their own districts. Not enough within the Congress to speak of Micronesia. That's what he was attacking. . . . I think he was speaking out of frustration. He worked with me [during 1971-73]. . . . We discussed this problem. . . . Now, Congress is not really a force of unity. When the revenues was more, people were talking about Micronesia, until revenues became a factor. . . . Well, really, the Congress, in general, I feel sure, was becoming a national force. But in 10 years, it developed, really, the sense of Micronesia unity developed. There's no denying that. I think Congress was—and is—really [has] been the only factor for unity in Micronesia.

(The matter of "revenue"—either through appropriations of the U.S. Congress, the manifold federal grants-in-aid programs extended to the Trust Territory, or taxation within the islands—is a subject to be discussed in chapter 2, which focuses on the economic development and self-sufficiency goal.)

The inhabitants of the Mariana Islands District did not share the delight in seeing a Congress of Micronesia formed in 1965. Frank Ada, Executive Officer in the Government of the Northern Marianas (mentioned earlier), recalls writing a 12-page report in 1964 or early 1965 for the then District Administrator of the Marianas, in which he analyzed the "reaction" of the people of that district to Secretary of the Interior Udall's issuing of the Secretarial Order (No. 2882 in September, 1964, amended by No. 2918 in December, 1968), which created that Congress, and indicated that the people of the Marianas had "separatist" intentions even in 1965:

> There was a tremendous amount of, not necessarily surprise, but anger, expressed by the people in the Secretary [Udall] creating a Congress of Micronesia. The fear is that we will be locked in perpetually with the rest of Micronesia [the Trust Territory], and that there is no way in which we could obtain our recently acquired status [i.e., to become a common-

wealth in the northern Marianas]. In certain parts of that report, . . . I mentioned that the people didn't realize that the creation of the Congress of Micronesia will facilitate the desire of the people of this district to obtain a separate status. And, true enough, in 1973 . . . the Marianas Delegation to the Joint Commission on Future Political Status requested for a separate talk [with the U.S. Delegation], and they [the Micronesian status commission] accepted.

JoeTen, the Saipanese businessman, while feeling the Congress "is great," expresses criticism of that body for the extensive travel of its legislators: "It's . . . going around too much in a conference, . . . and running around in three million square miles of water is not easy, you know, like you're running from west coast to east coast in the U.S. It costs money, running back and forth, and almost all the money that we have [for the Congress] it disappear on their [trips]."

A number of Americans have observed the Congress of Micronesia from different vantage points. For instance, Dennis L. Duncan, Vice President-Administration for the Bank of America's Asia Division, headquartered in Tokyo, has been in Asia since 1969 (except for two years in the United States, 1973-75), and visits Micronesia quarterly (in addition to such other areas as India and Australia). Dennis' candid appraisal of the Micronesian legislature follows:

> I've attended a couple of sessions just as an observer of the Congress of Micronesia, and it does not appear to be as well structured as it should be. A lot of time appears to be wasted on bills that really have no important effect on Micronesia; they tend to be much more localized problems that are raised by a senator from X island, and his talk will tie up three or four days on the floor.

N. Neiman Craley, Jr., Special Assistant to the Resident Commissioner of the Government of the Northern Marianas, and formerly Director of Public Affairs in the Trust Territory Government (1967-72), in addition to being a Special Assistant for Legislative Affairs to the High Commissioner (1972-76), was particularly close to the Congress of Micronesia, and felt a certain empathy for the islander legislators. Craley during 1965-67 was an American Congressman in the 89th Congress. Thus, his observations are particularly apropos in response to the query, "What would you say is your general impression of the work of the Micronesian congressmen over the years?"

> It's one of very, very mixed emotions. I dearly loved the Congress [of Micronesia]. Having been a legislator myself, there's a feeling that you get. You just can't help but relate to legislative types, to the legislative process. It's a process I feel very comfortable with, and one that I enjoyed and, as a consequence, I enjoyed working with the congressmen and with the Congress of Micronesia. I had great hopes for the Congress in the '60's

and even in the early '70's, because I felt that if there is ever going to be any possibility of Micronesia becoming truly self-governing, and, at the same time, truly responsible as it related to the people of Micronesia, the Congress was going to have to provide the leadership example. I have become somewhat disenchanted with the process, because I think that the Congress has, by and large, failed. It has failed to provide the leadership and the direction that I think was extremely—well, is extremely important, and was extremely critical several years ago when they had the chance, and I'm not convinced today that they have a chance anymore. I think that they've been left by the side of the road, and subsequent events have passed them by. The Marianas have split out, become a separate district [preparing for commonwealth status]. There's a good possibility of Palau splitting off at this point; the Marshalls have made noises about this—long and loud in the past; [and] we have a new district coming on board—Kusaie. I don't know what political aspirations they [the Kusaiens] might have.

Neas, whose knowledge of the Congress of Micronesia dates back to when he was a district administrator the year that legislature began (in 1965), and has increased as he moved to the Trust Territory Government headquarters in other Executive positions in the interim, says that he was "never very happy with the formation of the Congress," indicating that it has accomplished about what he expected to see: "practically nothing." Neas explains why he feels that the Congress has failed to succeed:

> It [the Congress of Micronesia] got off onto a tangent of being in opposition to the High Commissioner—you know, that "we're opponents." And too much of their effort was put into nothing except that—of being in opposition to anything that the Executive Branch [does, that] it's all bad. They never did, they never have, in my opinion, reached any maturity as far that they legislate. They still want to do the Executive part. They don't want to just make laws; they want to do the Administration. That's what they really want to do. And they have even suggested the British parliamentary system, where the Legislative Branch is also the Executive.

Neas adds that Andon Amaraich, the former senator from Truk, spoke before the U.N. Trusteeship Council a few years ago and said (in his capacity as a incumbent senator) that the only good things that have happened for the Micronesian people are those initiated by the Congress of Micronesia.

A fourth American to analyze the behavior of the Micronesian legislature is Thomas E. Tavares, Chief of Roads, Harbors, and Structures, and Airport Advisor in the Transportation Division of the Department of Transportation and Communications for the Trust Territory Government. Tavares, who has been in Micronesia since 1961, is frequently called to testify before Congressional committees. He sees "district

"*To Foster the Development of Political Institutions . . ."*   75

rivalry" when construction projects are discussed, followed by a "unity" posture as the situation may dictate territory-wide:

> Just about every session that they [the congressmen] have I go and testify on different projects. Since we're quite easy, and the Congress sympathizes with a lot of our projects, they try to work the problems out, and they know what's going on, I mean, as far as projects are concerned. They want to see the islands built. Some of the problems that we [in the Transportation and Communications Department] do have is that every district wants to take care of themselves first—I mean, the individual congressman. So the problem is who comes first and who's second, and they all want to be first. So it's a "give and take" to decide who gets what project when. . . . But, there's a lot of unity involved, also, when you have a Trust Territory-wide type of a program, and they're very much for it.

A final U.S. "critiquer" is Daniel J. High, Attorney General in the Trust Territory Government, who arrived on Saipan in mid-1976. His initial contact with the Micronesian Congress came during the special session of July-August, 1976, at which time the Senate Committee on Judiciary and Governmental Operations exercised its "advice and consent" role with regard to his appointment in the Executive Branch. High recalls his trip to the Ponape setting of the Congress:

> I was only down there [in Ponape], I think, five days. I did not actually view a lot being done. My attendance was special committee hearings, and I saw several sessions of the Senate. . . . The first real contact I've had with them [the senators], as far as trying to establish what our roles are, and how we get along, came during my confirmation hearings. And, again, I was dealing with a small portion of the Congress—the people on that particular committee. But, I found it refreshing. I went to the hearings not knowing what to expect. My Deputy, "Mo" [Mamoru Nakamura], went with me. And a good exchange of ideas. I tried to level with them and tell them, "I don't know all the answers, but I can assure you that you haven't got a guy on your hands that's going to do anything that he doesn't think is morally and legally right." . . . And they believed me.

(Other opinions on the Congress of Micronesia, its members, and achievements, will be discussed in succeeding chapters dealing with the economic, social, and educational development in the Trust Territory, respectively.)

MICRONIZATION, DECENTRALIZATION, AND THE HIGH COMMISSIONER

To bring the Micronesians to a point of "self-government," and to give those islanders "a progressively increasing share in the administrative services in the territory"—both of which are integral parts of the first

goal expressed in Article 6 of the Trusteeship Agreement of 1947—
requires money as well as experience gained either through formal schooling or on-the-job exposure. The doubling of the annual budget from the U.S. Congress in Fiscal Year 1963 (to $15 million) meant that funds would be available in the Trust Territory to hire more Micronesians and/or provide increased scholarships to send them abroad for college. The establishment of the Congress of Micronesia in the mid-1960s was one benefit of increased appropriations. The gradual "Micronization" process—one of bringing the islanders into the positions previously occupied by expatriates (meaning Americans employed through the Federal Civil Service, or later, on contract), began in the mid-1950s, as noted earlier in this chapter, and accelerated somewhat by the mid- to late 1960s. Dwight Heine became the District Administrator for the Marshalls in 1966; a number of college-educated young Micronesians found themselves being appointed to responsible positions in the Trust Territory Headquarters, such as a Deputy Director of Public Affairs (Strik Yoma, under Neiman Craley) or as the Political Affairs Officer (Raymond Ulochong). As will be discussed in the following chapters, appropriations concentrated during the 1960s in the areas of education (the hiring of American teachers and building of schools) and health services (increased numbers of dispensaries and some hospitals), although simply operating the Government was an enormous expenditure even as the annual appropriations from the U.S. Congress (with supplemental payment) rose to *over* $80 million by 1977.

Secretary of the Interior Walter J. Hickel, who visited Saipan in May, 1969, to install the then new High Commissioner, Edward E. Johnston, promised the more than 1,000 Micronesians and American officials assembled at the Mt. Carmel High School—including "nearly all members of the Congress of Micronesia, ... along with Speakers of the District Legislatures and Administration representatives from each district"[74]— that the Micronesian legislators would "be brought into the planning and decision processes as full and equal participants with American personnel," and he indicated that he had directed the new High Commissioner "to start within 90 days an active and imaginative program of training of Micronesians for positions of greater responsibility in the Administration."[75]

High Commissioner Johnston reported in 1970 that a number of the "key Micronesian officials" in the Trust Territory Headquarters on Saipan were mostly college graduates and that a number of those islanders were recently former members of the Congress of Micronesia, and he concluded: "We [the Administering Authority] are developing an executive branch and a legislative branch, each of which should have its own duties and its own powers. And if either one gets weak at the expense of the other, then we're in trouble."[76]

How well has the "Micronization" program succeeded by mid-1977? Podis Pedrus, a Ponapean who graduated from the University of Hawaii in 1966 (majoring in political science) and, after working his way up through the ranks first as a management intern in Headquarters Personnel on Saipan (later serving as a personnel administrator in the Truk District, then Supervisor of the Trust Territory Merit System prior to becoming the Deputy Director of Personnel under an American, Arthur Akina, of Hawaii), became the Director of Personnel for the Trust Territory Government in December, 1974. Pedrus believes that, "in most cases," the "Micronization" has been "a very good program." He does see some mistakes, however, as might be expected in a developing area:

> I think we have—the Trust Territory Government—has placed Micronesians to responsible, in positions which, of course, include district administrators and the directors up at headquarters [on Saipan]. And I think that the program is one that ought to continue and endure. Personally, I endorsed it very much, and we are for it and we would like to see it continue. Of course, in every program you find some in it, or some cases that should not have part of it, but that's expected. But, overall, I would say the program is one that ought to continue since we're moving toward Micronesians taking over, and assuming responsibilities and going toward self-government. You know, people say that maybe putting Micronesians too early might not give you the kind of effective service that you would like to have in a government, since some people believe that in replacing expatriates the quality of performance will go down. People have said that, if the Micronesians are going to remain without trying something—trying to do something—even if in the process make some mistakes. But still all right, because they are going to face every mistake they make and correct them if they want to correct them; otherwise, they will never learn, and they will never know how to handle responsibilities.

Yoma agrees with Pedrus, above, and comments that, unfortunately, "politics" in some cases entered into the "Micronization" process: "I think, over the years, in some cases, we have had to select someone to be in a position where, I think, perhaps, he was not quite ready yet, or perhaps someone else was, but was not selected." How would "politics" enter the "Micronization" selection process? This would vary according to whether approval (or consent) was required from the Congress of Micronesia. Where not required, the High Commissioner would make the choice at the headquarters level. (District-level selections—below the district administrator—would be made by that head.) Yoma also indicates that sometimes those selected for Executive positions show too much *loyalty* to their home districts vis-à-vis the welfare of the Trust Territory as a whole:

> Those [islanders] who were selected to top positions, because of their political experience, some of them—I noticed today—they haven't, they're so loyal to their own districts that, while one would expect it as an official

of the Government of the Territory, as a whole, he should, as much as possible, think in terms of districts. I see, unfortunately, I must say I see where a person's position and action is affected, to some extent, by his loyalty to his own district. . . . It is really unfortunate and really regrettable. Again, this is a fact of life which I can't ignore. But I wish that we could have more control over the selection of people, . . . because I don't think the selections which have been made were given enough kind of discussion among High Commissioner's staff and the High Commissioner.

Peter T. Coleman, a Samoan who retired from Federal Civil Service as the Acting High Commissioner in early 1977, as mentioned previously, responds to the question "Has Micronization as a program been successful?" with the following opinion: "The answer to this question is yes. I should like, however, to qualify that statement by saying that Micronization for its own sake does not serve the best interests of the Micronesian people." Coleman explains *why* his "qualification" in the above answer: "In some areas I think the timing and the selection of individuals were near perfect. In other areas we may have moved too fast or too slowly, but the concept itself as a mechanism to promote self-government is an excellent one and it is working."

That Micronesians would be placed in positions of responsibility— usually occupied by U.S. officials—has its limitations, especially in the legal field, where indigenous attorneys generally lack "trial work" experience. When High was flying to Saipan to become the Acting Attorney General for the Trust Territory Government in June, 1976, he recognized aboard the Air Micronesia flight one of the Micronesian senators from Truk. After introducing himself to that legislator, he proceeded to explain his own philosophy of wanting to bring "good attorneys" into his staff. High was encouraged by the Trukese senator's reply: "Get skilled people out here who know what they're doing in the area of trial work, as you fill these new slots, so that we just aren't a sitting duck, and so when we [the Congress of Micronesia] need good advice on how to proceed on laying claim matters, and on setting up a new district in Kusaie, that we have competent legal advice." Then the legislator continued: "You know that we need it [legal advice] just like a client in the states would need it, and you have to have good, solid attorneys to render that service." High was further told by the Senate Judiciary and Governmental Operations Committee, during the "confirmation hearings" on his position in the summer of 1976: "Congress told me that— and they said it in their official report on the hearings—that 'we're pleased that we got a lawyer [High] that's got a trial background, because right now it appears that's what we need out here.' "

Zeder, the then Director of Territorial Affairs (DOTA), informed the U.N. Trusteeship Council in June, 1976, that there were "over 700 people employed" in the Trust Territory Headquarters as of 1975, of whom "642 ... were Micronesians, and 95 were American civil service employees. It is estimated that when fully implemented the decentralization programme will eliminate as many as 500 of those positions." Zeder further indicated a "target date" for cutting the total size of the Headquarters complement: by the end of 1980. That would leave a skeletal organization of less than 300 personnel.[77]

What effect does the above announced "decentralization policy" by Zeder—which may be varied somewhat by Van Cleve once she has completed her evaluation of the direction the Office of Territorial Affairs should indicate for the Trust Territory—have upon those American officials presently employed by the Administering Authority? For William D. Jackson, Program Development Officer in the Community Development Division of the Office of Public Affairs, this is *not* a new problem. Originally a Peace Corps volunteer in Nigeria (in 1961), and trained for that earlier duty in the Virgin Islands, Jackson came to the Trust Territory in 1968. With the "Micronization" and "decentralization" programs operating in the interim, Jackson has been "frozen" in his Federal Civil Service grade, and he understands that, eventually, he will be replaced by a Micronesian and return then to a stateside assignment. Concerning the relative success of "decentralization," he observes.

> Decentralization is just not working as an improved local [district] capability and understanding and comprehension and productivity to perform their public responsibilities, quite frankly. I don't feel I'm saying this because I'm a Headquarters type; I just think it's a question of the cultural stage of the islands, the lack of sophistication existing in the other districts [outside of the Marianas], the fact that your better people tend to have gravitated to Headquarters and work here. And your less able people, perhaps, are in the districts. You have a milieu, an environment, a climate, if you will, which is not production oriented. Decentralization simply is not working, but it's such a *shibboleth* here, it's such a watchword, that it must be carried out whether it makes sense or not, because everyone's committed to it.

Garrett, the Director of Finance in the Trust Territory, and one of the three remaining Americans to be a director at Headquarters level, believes that one of the problems for both "Micronization" and the "decentralization" efforts in the Trust Territory is the Department of Interior's *lack* of "placement program" whereby the Civil Service employees can be reassigned stateside. Garrett, who was appointed to his directorship in 1976, intends to terminate his employment by 1978. His analysis of employee problems in Finance follows:

> I'm anxious, as a taxpayer, to see some efficiency, and I'm appalled at the inefficiency that exists here [at the Headquarters]. I'm sure that . . .

it's a problem, and, of course, one of the problems is the avenue for exit. Traditionally, Civil Service people have to have some place to go, and if there's an effective return placement program, so that people can be returned to positions in the Department of Interior, in one of our other bureaus, I think that would be very effective. I could probably, well, I know of about six people right now, of those 30 [expatriates in the Department of Finance] that I could send back tomorrow, if they had a place to go. And in at least three cases they'd be management jobs taken over by Micronesians. I think that it would probably be a more effective operation. But the Interior placement program has been unsuccessful. No one ever gets placed, so they sit out here and wait. And that's a problem. We have to have support from the higher authority, and that's been a problem not only in this specific thing, but in previous attempts to implement the Financial Management System, for example. Interior has declined or neglected to support it properly.

Yoma also agrees with Jackson that "adequate staffing" is a problem at the district level in the attempt to make the "decentralization" program operate. Yoma says that "decentralization" is not a new program for Micronesia, that, back in the 1966-67 period a U.S. Congressional recommendation was made that decision-making should be concentrated more at the local levels; and he believes that Secretary Hickel attempted to spur that direction in 1969; however, not until Zeder arrived as the DOTA in early 1975 was the big push made to "decentralize." Pedrus recalls 1972 as the arrival date for "decentralization" efforts by his Department of Personnel, and defines how that process is pursued:

> Our [Personnel] department here has, probably one of the few that has, defined the process of decentralization to the districts, through memorandum to the district administrators. I believe this trend started way back in 1972, and we have periodically issued further decentralization in one system. What we hope to accomplish is full operational responsibilities by all the districts, leaving the headquarters for only established policies and standards for operations by all the districts, including headquarters, also. We do this through the training of our people here and also in the districts, because we think that the decentralization cannot succeed if our people are not well trained to do so, based on capabilities of the people in the district, and the training that they are now continually provided. We have decentralized operational responsibilities to them. . . . [We hope] to completely decentralize in the remaining areas, such as recruitment and the processing of employment for expatriate[s]. . . .

Eusebio Rechucher, Director of Research and Development in the Trust Territory Government, likes the concept of "decentralization," especially with regard to the districts making "the decision on everything that concern[s] . . . the districts," and that the "role" for his headquarters department "at this time is more an advisory capacity. We cannot tell them [the districts], or direct them, to do. So, even though we feel that . . . [a project] is best for them, we cannot tell them to do so, unless they want to. . . . We [are] willing to help them to see to it that that project is successful, or going to succeed."

Raymond Setik, a member of the House of Representatives in the Congress of Micronesia, appeared before the U.N. Trusteeship Council in 1976 and indicated that "the need to decentralize the central government merits considerable attention," and he told the U.N. members that "the [U.S.] Administration and the Congress of Micronesia are in broad, general agreement that a restructuring and reorganization of the present [Trust Territory] Government is in order."[78] Again, whether this approach to "decentralization" remains consistent after mid-1977 will depend, in part, on the new leadership brought in as a result of the change in administrations under President Carter.

How popular have the various High Commissioners been with the Micronesians and U.S. officials in the Administering Authority? Have amiable relations generally existed? So far as the islanders are concerned, Goding (1961-66) seemed to have captured their admiration the most. Perhaps being a "Kennedy man" in 1961 accounts for part of his popularity. As Salii notes, "Goding was the first person to recognize Micronesians. He got a lot of respect from us. And he tried; he was really the first man, bureaucratic-type of person, to come out here." Dwight Heine agrees, saying that "Mr. Goding was probably the most popular [of the High Commissioners] with the greatest number of Micronesians. With a few—not many, but few—never liked him." Salii also recalls that "Norwood [1966-69] was a good person. I think his basic problem was that he didn't really have enough supporters in his country [during the Vietnam War]. . . . Very little could have been done [then]."

Neas, who served under each of the High Commissioners, including the first, former U.S. Senator Elbert D. Thomas (1951-53), believes that Nucker (1956-61) was the best: "He [Nucker] took over the job from Frank [H.] Midkiff [1953-56], who decided to stay in Honolulu instead of following Headquarters to Guam in 1954. Mr. Nucker, in my opinion, was the outstanding High Commissioner of all." Craley, an American official during the terms of Norwood and Johnston (1969-76 for the latter), and who had visited the Trust Territory while a U.S. congressman during Goding's stay in Micronesia, elaborates on the "pressures" under which a High Commissioner must represent the Secretary of the Interior in far-off Washington, D.C.:

> I will state initially that both of them [Norwood and Johnston] were very nice to me in every way. . . . Neither of these two gentlemen—Bill Norwood or Ed Johnston—were, in my opinion, outstanding administrators. They were both exceptionally kind people, . . . [but] neither of them, in my opinion, were extremely strong administrators. . . . I wasn't sure that this was a failing on their part or a failing on the structure—where the High Commissioner, more or less, is a representative of the Secretary

of the Interior and, therefore, subject to guidance from Washington. But I got the feeling with both Administrations that the primary objective—the name of the game—was "Don't make any waves! Don't rock the boat! Don't create problems! If we can get by this week, or this month without any serious crises, we're doing well!"

Salii tells of the friendly relations he, in particular, and the Congress of Micronesia, generally, had with High Commissioner Johnston, recalling that the latter served longer (seven years) than any of the predecessors:

> I got along with him [Johnston] very well. He listened to the Congress of Micronesia, and he really went out of his way to follow the positions of the Congress of Micronesia. He did not lack, politically, in terms of recognizing the Congress of Micronesia, allowing the Congress to really develop into a real force. I think a lot of people say that his weakest area was in economics.

Salii's successor as senator from Palau, when Salii declined to run for reelection in 1976, was Kaleb Udui, the first Micronesian to receive a law degree and the first also to become the Legislative Counsel (from 1966-76). Udui, in response to a question about how the Congress of Micronesia feels toward the existence of an "absolute veto" over legislation by the High Commissioner, with the expectation of a sustaining of that veto by the Secretary of the Interior should the Congress of Micronesia "appeal" such action, observes:

> Yes, . . . [the congressmen were uptight] especially on issues that really had nothing to do with U.S.-Micronesian relations, but issues that are strictly local in color, import. And we think that, if there are elected representatives of the Micronesian people, then they should at least have the final say-so as to what should be their own, or what should be here. For somebody outside [i.e., the Secretary of Interior] to [sustain] . . . that veto, without really taking into consideration the general consensus of the Micronesian leadership, that appeared to be somewhat of an anomaly. Of course, we realize that, on a strictly legal basis, he's [the Secretary of Interior's] got the authority to do that, and, in the end, his concern and those of the representatives of the Micronesian people should be, and ought to be, the same.

As an example of such "vetoes" being "upheld" by the Secretary of the Interior, two bills—one to establish "a 200-mile economic zone" around the islands of the Trust Territory, and the other to require "reconfirmation hearings on executive appointments which originally called for congressional advice and consent"—were returned to the Congress of Micronesia with the High Commissioner's action sustained in May, 1977.[79] *No* vetoes to date have been overturned by the Secretary of the Interior.

Zeder, who served less than two years (1975-77) as the DOTA, brought a businessman's energetic approach toward matters involving the Trust Territory, as well as the other overseas territories for which his office is responsible (i.e., the Virgin Islands, American Samoa, and Guam), which had not been seen in recent years. Perhaps the word "sweeping" would be more apropos in describing the *changes* he enforced both in the personnel and economic areas. Zeder literally shocked the U.N. Trusteeship Council (as well as those who later read his remarks) when he personally presented a most *candid* appraisal of the weaknesses as well as the strengths found in the Administering Authority's trusteeship operation in Micronesia. That appearance at the United Nations, in June, 1976, was also the first time the Office of Territorial Affairs had prepared the material used by the DOTA.

A few excerpts from Zeder's address before the Trusteeship Council show the force with which he presented his critique. First, he said that, "over the past 12 months [from June, 1975-June, 1976], in contrast to the work schedules of my predecessors in this [DOTA] position, I have spent the greater part of my time in the Territories—about seven months." Then he proceeded to identify the "biggest single problem in the Trust Territory" in *two* words: "inadequate accountability." He stressed that "corrective action" had been taken in "eight vital areas": acounting, legal, priorities, capital improvements, maintenance, inventory, personnel, and decentralization. Perhaps the most shocking aspect in his U.N. speech of 1976 came when he described "personnel changes" which had been effected in the past year, including the first public announcement of the firing of one of the six district administrators in Micronesia, Leo A. Falcam (formerly the Executive Officer for High Commissioner Johnston):

> We have made a number of changes in key personnel both in Washington and in Saipan. More will come. High Commissioner Edward Johnston has resigned [effective June 1, 1976], and Deputy High Commissioner Coleman has assumed full responsibility for administration as Acting High Commissioner. The former chief financial officer in Saipan is now stationed here in Washington. . . . A new Public Works Officer has been appointed in Saipan and his function has been redirected. The Director of Transportation and Communications in Saipan has been replaced. . . . The Attorney General has been reassigned to another Territory in a different capacity. . . . The Director of Planning in Saipan was notified of the termination of his contract. . . . The District Administrator in Ponape has been terminated.[80]

Whereas Fred M. Zeder II may be described as a "controversial" DOTA by some, especially on Guam, it is worthwhile to note that this author, in conferring with over 200 officials, businessmen, and others, did *not* find one who denounced what might be called the "Zederization process" to make the Trust Territory Government more accountable for its policies and programs. In fact, many in the fall of 1976 who perceived that Jimmy Carter would defeat President Ford, and thus effect a "housecleaning" (appointing Democrats to replace Republicans), privately expressed the wish that President Carter would ask Zeder to remain as DOTA. From a reading of Zeder's closing report of December, 1976, in which he recommended that his successor as DOTA be someone with extensive business background, be willing to spend over half his time visiting in the territories, and be "between the early 50's to around 65" in age, it sounded as though he were writing an autobiography. In that same report, made to the Transition Committee of the Department of the Interior,[81] which was chaired by Dr. Donald F. McHenry, Zeder counseled against the appointment of either a black or a female to the position as DOTA, for various reasons. McHenry is a black; President Carter appointed Ruth G. Van Cleve as the new DOTA in April, 1977.

Zeder also counseled, in the above report, that the person appointed as High Commissioner be "a tough and demanding manager," for that position should not be conducted as though it were "a popularity contest: it's a tough and demanding management assignment." In that regard, Zeder believes that "the High Commissioner should clearly understand that he works for the DOTA," and he also suggested that the title "High Commissioner" be changed to something else, for the present term may be associated with "Colonialism." He likened the relationships which *should* exist among the High Commissioner, DOTA, Secretary of the Interior, and the Assistant Secretary-Administration and Management, to a "football team" operation:

> The owners are the Secretary of the Interior, DOTA is the coach, and the High Commissioner is the quarterback. The High Commissioner calls the plays from the field where he alone can best see and feel the action. He gets the game plan and overall strategy from the DOTA/coach. Not so incidentally, whatever you [the Transition Committee] do, don't let the Office of the Assistant Secretary-Administration and Management call the signals. They are the scorekeepers.

Finally, Zeder, in his term-ending report to the President's Transition Committee, noted what Mackenzie indicated earlier in this chapter, namely, that *alcoholism* is a problem in the islands: "Alcoholism is a major occupational hazard." For that reason, among others, Zeder recommended against selecting candidates for either the position of DOTA or High Commissioner who had lived in the islands for an extended period. On a positive note, the departing DOTA acknowledged that there are some choice American officials serving in the Micronesia:

> Locked in that fortress [the Trust Territory bureaucracy] . . . are some —not too many but some—of the most dedicated, hard-working people

imaginable. They are unusually bright, efficient, and perceptive. They are the ones who keep the whole operation from becoming a complete shambles. They possess that unique quality of patience, perseverance, and intellectual integrity that makes them invaluable. They are hard to identify. They camouflage themselves. In a society where such attributes, when spotted, are considered to represent a threat to the entrenched establishment, they lay low.[82]

President Carter, in May, 1977, saw his nominee to become the new High Commissioner, Adrian P. Winkel (former aide to U.S. Congressman Philip Burton, Democrat of California), confirmed by the U.S. Senate.[83] Winkel, in his first appearance before the U.N. Trusteeship Council, in June, 1977, said that the Trust Territory Government's "policies and programs . . . will be devoted to achieving and expediting an orderly transition to that self-government or independence of the Trust Territory . . . which is stipulated by . . . the Trust Territory Agreement between this body [the Trusteeship Council] and the United States Government"; and Winkel indicated that the Administering Authority will be "moving forward on four fronts simultaneously": administration (with emphasis on "micronization" and "decentralization"); economic development; health and education, and a capital improvements infrastructure.[84] Thus, an apparent continuation of Zeder's goals.

THE NORTHERN MARIANAS PREPARE FOR COMMONWEALTH STATUS

On December 13, 1972, Franklin Haydn Williams of San Francisco, former President of the Asia Foundation (a nonprofit institution involved in assisting Asians to solve their problems) and also the former Deputy Assistant Secretary of Defense (1958-62), spoke before the Marianas Political Status Commission on Saipan. As President Nixon's personal representative with the rank of ambassador (appointed in March, 1971), Williams acknowledged to the Marianas delegation of 15 members, headed by Chairman Edward del G. Pangelinan, that the latter's representatives, "with the knowledge of the Joint Future Status Committee [of the Congress of Micronesia], formally requested the United States to enter into *separate* talks leading to a close and permanent union with my country." (Italics mine.) Ambassador Williams reminded Pangelinan's group that the intent of the United States since 1947 had been "to develop Micronesia toward a common status upon termination of the Trusteeship Agreement"; however, since the northern Marianas, through their district legislature and appointed status commission, desired to exercise their people's "right of self-determination" with respect to their future political status, the United States, under such circumstances, would be "willing to respond affirmatively to the request that has been formally submitted to us today to enter into separate negotiations with the representatives of the Marianas in order to satisfy a desire which the Joint Committee [of the Congress of Micronesia] has already recognized."[85]

How did the United States find itself in a position to be negotiating *separately* with the Marianas District while, at the same time, attempting to reach an amicable agreement through discussions with the Congress of Micronesia's negotiating arm, the Joint Committee on Future Status, to terminate the Trusteeship Agreement of 1947 for the *whole* of those islands? This situation dates back to the first *two* "rounds of negotiations" between the American and Micronesian delegations (during October, 1969, in Washington, D.C., and May, 1970, on Saipan, respectively). Whereas the Micronesians initially opted for a "self-governing state in free association with the United States" as their first choice, and "independence" as second,[86] the U.S. position presented in May, 1970—a "commonwealth" arrangement—was not publicly announced until the report of the Political Status Delegation was presented before the Third Congress of Micronesia meeting in its Third Regular Session, on July 21, 1970. The Micronesian delegation's rationale for rejecting a "commonwealth" status is seen in the following excerpt from that report:

> The United States position [of May, 1970], which is reflected in its rejection of the Free Association and Independence [choices of the Micronesian delegation] and in its counter-proposal of what it calls Commonwealth status, is that association between Micronesia and the United States must be permanent, and that any Micronesian government must yield in certain crucial final respects to the United States. Your Delegation's position is that any Micronesian government which *permanently* ceded to the United States *ultimate* power over its laws, could not be considered an authentic self-government; and any association that foreclosed future changes in status would not be free.[87] (Italics mine.)

All of the members of the Congress of Micronesia meeting in the summer of 1970, with the *exception* of the Marianas representatives, were to reject the American offer of a "commonwealth" future status for the Trust Territory. Hence, the December, 1972, request (mentioned above) for "separate negotiations" between the Marianas District and the U.S. delegation.

The question arises, *why* would the inhabitants of the northern Marianas, through their elected representatives, favor a "commonwealth" position while all the rest of their peers in the remaining five administrative districts expressed preference for a "free association," with "independence" as an alternative? Were there some "separatist" tendencies dormant in the Marianas which suddenly came to the fore in mid-1970? What might account for a more pronounced "pro-American" future political status sentiment in the northern Marianas than apparently was found in Yap, Palau, Truk, Ponape, or the Marshall Islands at that point?

Dwight Heine believes that the *long* association of the northern Marianas with the Naval Administration was the main reason for that position. He points to the period from 1944-62—an 18-year span interrupted only by one and a half years under the Interior Department (from mid-1971 to early-1973), and says: "A whole generation was born during that [Navy] era, until 1962." Thus, Heine feels that the inhabitants of the Mariana Islands drew *closer* to the United States by virtue of the almost unbroken Naval rule than the other districts did under Interior direction.

A common belief is that the Chamorro people—predominant throughout the northern Marianas—feel a particular affinity to the Guamanians, who are of the same ethnic background. Father Arnold, at the Mt. Carmel Church on Saipan, points to the 1951-53 period as a stage when he felt that the northern Marianas wanted to "reintegrate" with Guam: "They thought that would be the easiest way to get it [i.e., a commonwealth status]. And they had a number of plebiscites [in 1961, 1963, and 1969], and every time the U.N. committee [the Visiting Missions] came out here, they [the Marianas] would ask for this [reintegration with Guam]." The last-mentioned plebiscite was conducted on November 9, 1969. Of the 4,954 registered voters in a population approaching 14,000 at the time, 65 percent voted. The choices for the political future of the Marianas District: 1,942 (or 60%) for "reintegration with Guam"; 1,116 (35%) for a "free association"; 107 (3%) for an "unincorporated territory"; and only 19 (.0006%) for "independence." The remaining 2.4 percent was scattered among "Trust Territory" (five votes), while three other choices—"commonwealth," "U.S.A." (annexation), "unincorporated territory with Japan," and "Japan" (annexation) each received one vote.[88]

However, five days earlier than the northern Marianas' third favorable "reintegration" consensus, above, there was a referendum on Guam with surprising results. The Guamanians, with only 6,408 voting (or 36% of some 18,000 registered voters), *opposed* "reintegration with the northern Marianas" by an overwhelming margin, 3,720 (58%) against to only 2,688 (42%) in favor. The surprising aspect of the Guamanians' inclination not to want to merge with the northern Marianas is that none of the political observers on the scene expected such an outcome. Joe Murphy, editor of the Guam *Daily News,* recalls that there "was no apparent opposition" on Guam to such a "reintegration" proposal. He recalls flying to Saipan with Guamanian senators on "at least three occasions before that [referendum on November 5, 1969], and everybody was quite agreeable. We couldn't find one single vocal opposition to this reunification, so it was a complete shock to all of us when we found out the next morning that it had been voted down." Murphy indicates that "there were no [political] ads in the paper [*Daily News*] either pro *or* con on the issue of 'reunification.'"

Officials at the Micronesian Area Research Center (MARC), University of Guam, who had been on Guam within eight years after World War II ended, see a certain lack in the way the Guamanian senators (of the unicameral legislature) campaigned in favor of the "reintegration" issue of 1969. Emilie G. Johnston, Curator at MARC and a resident on Guam since 1947, says that "one of the senators . . . that spoke out here at the University . . . turned off most of the people. And if he spoke elsewhere in the same manner, I can see where he didn't get the support for the northern Marianas at that time." She also feels that the lifting of the "Navy security clearance" (in 1962), which opened Guam as well as the Trust Territory to tourism, meant "that the economy was picking up and there wasn't the interest in the northern Marianas [by the Guamanians] as there has been more recently." Marjorie G. Driver, Asst. Director of MARC and on Guam since 1953, sees a "general lack of information and education as to the results that they might expect from a merger" as contributing to the "reintegration" failure. If the proposal had been "put a little more positive . . . in the plebiscite," the results might have been different. Driver feels that the negative vote was seen in "basically the way the information was conveyed to the public."

Regarding the "lack of political education," mentioned above, Murphy acknowledges that "the coverage in the press was minimal. Primarily, we didn't have the reporters or staff to do it. But there wasn't that much, there was no opposition here. Everybody thought it was a great idea." Murphy adds: "There was no political education, that's true. People just assumed that it was going to pass, and we couldn't believe that any political opposition had arisen."

How was the disappointing referendum on Guam viewed by the people in the northern Marianas? Father Arnold believes that part of the reason for Guam's rejection of the "reintegration" proposal was that the Guamanians "were afraid of their tax money. . . . They had so much tax money, and Saipan would get much more out of it than they [the Saipanese] contributed; and, therefore, they [the Guamanians] were afraid of sharing their revenues with the Saipanese." Senator Borja agrees with Father Arnold on the "financial responsibility" concern Guamanians might feel should "reintegration" have taken place in recent years: "The people of Guam apparently [were] opposed to getting the northern Marianas to their political jurisdiction because of financial responsibility, because of other problems that they have, and . . . because of that reason,

... they did not get the majority [in Guam's 1969 referendum] to really go ahead and integrate with Guam."

The question of "discrimination" has been raised by observers both in the northern Marianas and on Guam with regard to any possible "reintegration" (which, as of mid-1977, is academic due to the "commonwealth" timetable for the northern Marianas). Part of that feeling of "discrimination" dates back to the rather harsh treatment during World War II, when some of the Chamorros from the northern Marianas were employed by the Japanese military as "interpreters" on Guam in the occupation period (December, 1941-July, 1944). Murphy notes that earlier problem and why some "hard feelings" resulted therefrom: "Some of them [the Saipanese interpreters] got a little overaggressive in their duties, and there were some beatings, and so the Guamanians had sort of an adverse reaction to the Saipanese for a long period of time. I don't see it now."

From a posture of feeling "discriminated against" during the War, the more current feeling is that the Guamanians have a "superiority complex" regarding their cousins in the northern Marianas. Such a feeling is not limited just to the Mariana Islands District. Driver observes that a "poor (or country) cousin" attitude is often exhibited by Guamanians toward "other areas of the Trust Territory. In other words, at least Guam had been a center which had been more of a metropolitan situation, and there was a certain feeling that others [in Micronesia] were sort of 'country bumpkins,' as some might say."

Carl Heine wrote that "it is true that the Marianas have always wanted to rejoin their cousins in Guam, at least this is the reason advanced by the Marianas as the basis for their decision not to join with the rest of the districts of Micronesia"; and he can see, politically, that the northern Marianas have "a legitimate reason" for wanting to "reintegrate" with Guam. Where Heine differed here was in the *timing:* "I disagree with the timing and the manner in which it has been handled, particularly the way in which the United States has eagerly embraced the situation. It looks as though the trustee is colonizing the beneficiary."[89] Heine's book was completed in 1973; hence, the "reintegration" theme in the interim has shifted to one of anticipating a "commonwealth" status when the Trusteeship Agreement is expected to terminate, possibly as early as 1981.

The events in early 1971 on Saipan dramatized the desire of the people in the northern Marianas to become a "commonwealth." First, the Mariana Islands District Legislature passed a resolution (No. 30-1971) on February 19 of that year, threateningly entitled "A Resolution Relative to Advising the Security Council and Trusteeship Council of the United Nations that the Mariana Islands District of the Trust Territory of the Pacific Islands Will Secede from the Trust Territory . . . by Force of Arms If Necessary, and with or without the Approval of the United Nations." This resolution accordingly was submitted to the President of the U.N. Trusteeship Council.[90] At 4:00 A.M. the following day (February 20), an arsonist (or possibly more than one) destroyed the Congress of Micronesia's assemby chambers (both in one wooden structure), in addition to some senatorial offices in an adjacent building on Capitol Hill, Saipan, necessitating that legislative body to adjourn *sine die* with nine days remaining in the First Regular Session of the Fourth Congress.[91]

While officials on Saipan in later years commented that a single arsonist probably was responsible for the above fire, with no conspiracy involvement by the Marianas District Legislature, the question is, *why* did those Marianas legislators find it necessary to threaten "force of arms, if necessary," in their desire to secede from the Trust Territory? The eight basic reasons in Resolution No. 30-1971 (mentioned above), directed to the U.N.'s Security Council and the Trusteeship Council, include grievances against the earlier Japanese Mandate Period, as well:

> WHEREAS, contrary to the provisions of the covenants of the League of Nations, the Japanese Empire placed military fortifications throughout the islands [of Micronesia]; . . . and
>
> WHEREAS, in neither instance, [i.e., the Japanese Mandate or the later Trusteeship arrangement with the U.S.] did either the League of Nations or the United Nations consult the people [the islanders] concerned as to what their desires were regarding these arrangements; . . . and
>
> WHEREAS, in each instance, however, the people of the Mariana[s] . . . accepted and sought to make the best of their fate; and
>
> WHEREAS, . . . the people have over the years directed grievances to the Security Council and the Trusteeship Council without any favorable action; and
>
> WHEREAS, the original [U.N.] signatories in San Francisco in 1945 . . . pledged to give the people concerned self-government or independence according to the [latter's] freely expressed wishes; . . . and
>
> WHEREAS, the people of the Mariana[s] have, . . . over the last twenty years, advised both the Administering Authority and the Trusteeship Council of its political aspiration, but both have proceeded to ignore these aspirations for reasons of their own; and
>
> WHEREAS, every effort has been made to live and work with the Congress of Micronesia, but it has now become clear that all hope for the people of the Marianas of working harmoniously with the people of the Eastern and Western Caroline Islands is lost; and
>
> WHEREAS, we, the elected representatives of . . . the Mariana[s] . . . do not agree that the United Nations has any legal rights over the lives of the people of the Marianas. . . .

With the Congress of Micronesia in adjournment and the U.N. in receipt of the Marianas District Legislature's "secession" proclamation of February 19, 1971, what posture did the Administering Authority assume?

"To Foster the Development of Political Institutions..."

As sometimes appears apropos in tense, political matters, nothing immediately was done. Within a month, however, President Nixon sent his former Secretary of the Treasury, David M. Kennedy, in the latter's capacity as a special Ambassador-at-Large, to visit the Trust Territory and "familiarize himself with Micronesia's economic problems and development prospects."[92] Thus, while on Saipan in March, Ambassador Kennedy included in his itinerary a visit with Marianas leaders, including the District Legislature President, Ben Santos, and Saipan's Mayor, Vicente Sablan. Editor Murphy wrote an "open letter" to Mr. Kennedy in which the former articulated *three* "demands" Santos and the others in that district leadership felt should be met on behalf of the people of the northern Marianas as they wanted to leave the Trust Territory arrangement:

> [*First*,] a plebiscite now which will enable them to begin forming a commonwealth of the Marianas.
> [*Second*,] an end to the favored nation agreement clause so that Japanese capital can be invested on the island [of Saipan].
> [*Third*,] the removal of High Commissioner Johnston, whom they unfortunately regard as a symbol of repression.[93]

(Each of the above three "demands" was to be met by the United States within the next five years: the "favored nation agreement" was terminated in 1974, the plebiscite was held in 1975, and Johnston resigned in 1976.)

Senator Borja, from his then vantage point in the Congress of Micronesia as the senior solon from the Marianas District, indicated in a personal letter to the author (in October, 1971), that, by then, he did not think "unification with Guam" would be wise, due in part to the adverse vote on Guam (in November, 1969), which led Borja to believe that "there would probably be some measure of discrimination against the people of Saipan in union with Guam." Borja concluded by stating that he felt "the Commonwealth status offers a political future far brighter than that of [reintegration with] Guam."

The 15 members of the Marianas Status Commission were to meet with Ambassador Williams' Office of Micronesian Status Negotiations team for some 26 months, finally culminating in the signing of the "Covenant for a Commonwealth of the Northern Mariana Islands" on February 22, 1975. Less than four months later, a record 92.9 percent of the 5,000 registered voters (out of a northern Marianas population of 14,000) went to the polls to vote in a special plebiscite on whether to approve the Covenant and thus establish a Commonwealth of the Northern Marianas. The "yes" vote was 78.8 percent.[94] Thus, the Marianas islanders had exercised their "right of self-determination" option outlined in Article 6 of the Trusteeship Agreement of 1947 and promised by Ambassador Williams in December, 1972, in the initial meeting between the U.S. and Marianas teams (mentioned earlier), regarding the Marianas' future political status.

The American Congress expressed its willingness to have the northern Marianas become an unincorporated territory of the United States (a commonwealth, on the order of Puerto Rico): the U.S. House used a "voice vote" in August, 1975; the U.S. Senate, with all but one of its members participating on February 24, 1976, voted 66-23 in favor of the Covenant; a conference committee was successful in ironing out differences in the two house bills on March 12 of that year; and President Ford signed the Covenant 12 days later. Acting Secretary of the Interior Kent Frizzell, also on March 24, issued a Secretarial Order establishing a new administration for the Mariana Islands "separate from the rest of the Trust Territory."[95] Hence, the Government of the Northern Marianas was born on April 1, 1976.

President Ford appointed Erwin D. Canham, former Editor-in-Chief of the *Christian Science Monitor,* to be the Resident Commissioner of the Government of the Northern Marianas—a "caretaker government"—effective April 1, 1976. Canham was a popular choice, having previously administered the plebiscite in the northern Marianas (in mid-1975), an assignment on which he was involved for two and a half months. As his two chief staff members, Canham appointed N. Neiman Craley, Jr., as his Special Assistant, and Francisco C. Ada, to be the Executive Officer. (Craley most recently had been Special Assistant for Legislative Affairs to the High Commissioner, from 1972-76; Ada was the long-time District Administrator of the Marianas, 1969-76). The Resident Commissioner explains the "interim nature" of his Government of the Northern Marianas, and the long-range "timetable" for bringing a full-fledged commonwealth to those islands:

> The adoption of the Covenant, and its ratification by both branches of the United States Congress, created a, shall we say, "tentative" or "transitional" commonwealth status. And the [islander] people, when they voted last year, voted to become a commonwealth. The absolute, final, legal fulfillment of that commitment comes when the Trusteeship is dissolved. But long before that date, all—or nearly all—of the advantages, the elements, of commonwealth status will be achieved. And most of them will be achieved, presumably, sometime in early '78, when the first native Governor is installed. The election of the constitutional government of the Marianas will take place sometime in late '77, and I suppose very early in '78 the first Marianas indigenous Governor will take office; and a constitutional government will be in place. And it will be a commonwealth, but not final until the Trusteeship is dissolved, whenever that comes.

Canham further clarifies the relationship of the "interim government" with the Trust Territory Government, the latter expected to terminate by 1981:

> We [the Government of the Northern Marianas, or NMIG] are part of the Trust Territory, but not part of the Trust Territory Government [TTG]. We talk about the TTG and the NMIG. We are a separate government, but we are part of the Trust Territory until the Trusteeship comes to an end. And the date—1981—has been used repeatedly, but it is not a legal or binding date; it's a goal. And if, by some happy chance, negotiations with the other districts of the Trust Territory could be accomplished before that time [1981], so much better. But . . . these negotiations are difficult because of the differing aspirations of the other districts of the Trust Territory. And . . . when status negotiations are completed for all the districts, this will still have to be ratified, technically, by the Security Council of the United Nations, a body in which there are five vetoes—two of them by the two great Communist giants, who, at present, do not always agree on many issues. . . . The United States might have to say [to the U.N.], "We have done everything we can. We have reached an agreement, which is the wishes of the people, . . . and that's the best we can do!" And if one of the veto-possessing powers of the Security Council is not happy about it, we cannot prevent that. But I hope that doesn't come. I think our position will be strong, if it does, quite clearly, represent the wishes of the people [islanders] involved.

Within four days after the above interview with Resident Commissioner Canham, the Constitutional Convention opened at the Continental Hotel on Saipan (on October 18, 1976) amid "welcoming remarks" by Canham and a general feeling of expressed "unity" among the delegates from Saipan, Tinian, and Rota. However, before the convention reached its midpoint in the 50-day session, one Trust Territory Government official notes that the proceedings *almost* foundered "over issues regarding minority (Carolinian) participation in the [proposed] government and representation for the outer islands in the lower house of the bicameral legislature. Several delegates representing all factions did . . . threaten to walk out." Nevertheless, compromises were reached and the convention adjourned one day early with a proposed Constitution.

As an "updating" for events in the Marianas leading to the election of a bicameral legislature and the indigenous governor, Resident Commissioner Canham noted in a personal letter to the author (in May, 1977), the following:

> The timetable is unchanged. The Constitution reached President Carter on April 23 [1977]. He is expected to find it acceptable by mid-summer. . . . Then begin[s] a political campaign to nominate and elect the constitutional officers. Election expected in early November, inauguration of new government in early January [1978].

How has the Government of the Northern Marianas been "funded" since its start in April, 1976? From then to the end of Fiscal Year 1977 (or to September, 1977), a portion of the Trust Territory Government's annual appropriation from the U.S. Congress has been made available to the northern Marianas. After September, 1977, Canham indicates that his interim government's request for Fiscal Year 1978 (FY 78), "'as reduced by OMB [Office of Management and Budget] of $13,515,000 has been approved. The Covenant-authorized levels apply only to [the first] nine months of FY 78. In the next year it will go up to the full [12-month] amount."

Parenthetically, the residents of Guam appear to smart, somewhat, over the *careful* concern being shown in the creation of a commonwealth for the inhabitants to the north in the Marianas vis-à-vis the Organic Act of 1950, which, they feel, was more or less "forced" upon Guam without the inhabitants of that most westerly territory of the U.S. having any input. As Caldwell observes, "Financially, I think they [the northern Marianas] look better off than we [on Guam] do. They're writing their own government; they're writing their own territorial plan. We [on Guam] got handed one from the U.S. Congress called the Organic Act [of 1950]."

Professor George J. Boughton, Chairman of the History Department, University of Guam, articulates the chagrin both the "statesiders" and the Guamanians experience in being denied the right to vote on Guam for U.S. President and Vice President—a right also withheld from the islanders in the proposed Commonwealth of the Northern Marianas—believing that there is a "route" (in addition to a Constitutional amendment) to get the Presidential vote out to Guam and the northern Marianas, as well: "You can take it to the [U.S.] Supreme Court both on the bases that the President is the President of all the people—they're *all* American citizens—and that you do not deny, under the Constitution, the right to vote by any group of American citizens, in some fashion or another." Dr. Boughton adds that a visiting American political scientist told him the Ninth Circuit Court of Appeals, whose jurisdiction extends to Guam, "would love to see a court case of this nature [i.e., Guam's vote for U.S. President] brought forward." Murphy also acknowledges that the people on Guam "feel sort of rejected and [as] second-class citizens" because they do not have a franchise in federal elections. Washington, D.C., residents were given the Presidential vote opportunity through the Twenty-third Amendment in 1961. Guam and the Virgin Islands in 1972 were each given a "non-voting" delegate position in the U.S. House of Representatives (comparable to the already existing delegate for Washington, D.C., and resident commissioner from Puerto Rico); and, although such delegates are popularly elected by the people at large in the respective territories—Guam's only delegate to date being Antonio Borja Won Pat—that prerogative seems minimal compared with the U.S. citizens residing in the 50 states and Washington, D.C., exercising their franchise in Presidential elections.

Editor Murphy recalls the awkward position he experiences on visits to the states: "People that I've talked to back in the states—friends and relatives—I go back there every year or so, and they start asking me who we're going to vote for in Guam for President, and I tell them we don't have the right, and they're quite surprised. They feel, as we do [on Guam], that American citizens *should* have that right."

Thus, the "caretaker" Government of the Northern Marianas is expected to end, with a Commonwealth of the Northern Marianas joining the family of "territories of the United States" (such as Puerto Rico, the Virgin Islands, American Samoa, and Guam) in January, 1978, only awaiting termination of the Trusteeship Agreement of 1947—presumably by 1981—to make the new commonwealth a permanent political reality.

POLITICAL STATUS "OPTIONS" BY MID-1977

One of the final official acts by J. Boyd Mackenzie, Acting High Commissioner, on May 11, 1977—two weeks before the U.S. Senate confirmed Adrian P. Winkel to be Edward E. Johnston's successor as the High Commissioner—was to sign a proclamation. This was not an ordinary type of proclamation concerning a commemorative day, such as the Fourth of July or Thanksgiving; however, the results expected to accrue therefrom may give the Micronesians in the Trust Territory a measure of "independence" and certainly something for which they should be "thankful." Entitled "Calling for a Referendum in the Trust Territory of the Pacific Islands on the Proposed Constitution of the Federated States of Micronesia," Mackenzie proclaimed that, pursuant to Public Law 7-31 (passed by the Seventh Congress of Micronesia early in 1977), he designated "July 12, 1978, as the date for said Referendum to ascertain the wishes of the people of Micronesia with respect to the proposed Constitution," and Mackenzie concluded by urging "all eligible and qualified voters of Micronesia to participate fully in this historic process of self-determination through careful study, discussion and evaluation of the proposed Constitution of the Federated States of Micronesia."[96]

The above referendum, to take place in mid-1978, is an outgrowth of the Micronesian Constitutional Convention held on Saipan during a four-month period in 1975 (July 12-November 8), at which time the proposed Constitution of the Federated States of Micronesia was drafted. Public Law 7-31, also mentioned above, required the High Commissioner to designate a date for the referendum to be conducted between June 15 and August 15, 1978. (July 12 is recalled as "the day to be remembered," for the First Congress of Micronesia convened on that day in 1965, and it has been celebrated since then as a Micronesian holiday.)

There have been *two* basic problems facing Micronesians in general, and the Education for Self-Government (ESG) Program of the Trust Territory in particular. First, the "termination date" for the Trusteeship Agreement of 1947, itself. If former Director of Territorial Affairs Fred M. Zeder's public pronouncements are to be sustained by his successor, Ruth G. Van Cleve, as well as others in the decision-making process of the Carter Administration, including the most recent High Commissioner, Adrian P. Winkel, then the assumption may be made that, as Zeder said in his remarks before the Congress of Micronesia at that legislative body's special session on Ponape in mid-1976, "The Trusteeship Agreement *will* be terminated in *1981*. This fact has been known for two years and is still five years away. During the remaining time, several changes in government must be made in order to appropriately prepare Micronesia for self-government." (Italics mine.)

The second basic problem has been the *conflicting* signals coming out of the various "rounds of negotiations" (of which there have been eight as of mid-1977) vis-à-vis the product of the Micronesian Constitutional Convention in 1975. In other words, the Compact agreed upon at the Eighth Round of Negotiations (on Saipan during May 28-June 2, 1976) is in basic conflict with the Constitution drafted at the Constitutional Convention of 1975. Paul J. Bennett, State Department Liaison Officer for Micronesian Status Negotiations on Capitol Hill, Saipan, explains this conflict as follows:

> The Constitution and the Compact are inconsistent as they stand. The Constitution has been drawn up for an independent country; and the Compact envisages a status for Micronesia which is not fully independence. We've been calling it [the latter] "free association," but there's no particular magic in that term. You can call it self-government or anything else you like. The point is, the Compact envisages a Micronesia which is not fully independent, and this conflict between the two documents is going to have to be resolved in some way. Now, the easiest and the simplest way of doing this—the solution that many of the Micronesians are thinking about—is what some of them are calling a "standby clause" to be attached to the Constitution before it is submitted to a referendum by action of the Congress of Micronesia. The "standby clause" would say, essentially, that no provision of this Constitution which is in conflict with the Compact shall go into effect until or unless the Compact is terminated. . . . As I say, this is one of the remaining issues to be resolved: how we reconcile the Constitution with the Compact.

Samuel McPhetres, Program Developer and Researcher for the Education for Self-Government (ESG) Program, which is part of the Political Affairs Division in the Department of Public Affairs, Trust Territory Government, agrees with Bennett, above, with regard to the conflicting nature of the two documents, the Compact and the Constitution. McPhetres, an American official who first arrived in Micronesia in 1970 to be the Peace Corps Director for the Truk District, later being employed first by the Department of Education in the Trust Territory Government and then in his present position, believes that the conflict between the Constitution for the Federated States of Micronesia and the draft Compact of Free Association reached the point where this placed "a tremendous strain on the Micronesian people, who would like to have the Constitution but who don't want to be independent." McPhetres, an early (1962) Peace Corps volunteer to Africa, also says that a "fixed date" for the end of the Trusteeship Agreement would be helpful in the ESG's educational programming:

> We have no fixed deadlines to work against. If you take any African country, if you take any of the places under the British or French colonialism where this type of process took place, you'll find that one of the great advantages of it was that they knew, already, the date which the status they were in would terminate and the new one would begin. It would be by Administrative fiat. The colonial power would tell you, "You *will* be independent by 1977. Now, go to work!" And so they'd mount a program aiming at that particular thing, and you'd know ahead of time when the plebiscites and the referenda, and so forth, were to take place. We don't know any single date, for sure.

At least *one* date "for sure" is known in the Trust Territory since the above interview with McPhetres was held in October, 1976: the time for the referendum for a Constitution of the Federated States of Micronesia is set for July 12, 1978, as discussed earlier. Now, as to the *shape* of the proposed Constitution, such may be a *mixture* of the 1975 Constitution and the 1976 Compact. This is something for the Congress of Micronesia to determine prior to the summer of 1978.

The Political Affairs Division, which houses the ESG Program, is headed by Daiziro Nakamura, former Political Affairs Officer for the Palau District. There is one other researcher (besides McPhetres) and a secretary. The ESG Program was an outgrowth of a discussion in late 1973 among the co-Chairman of the Joint Committee on Future States of the Congress of Micronesia, Lazarus Salii, the High Commissioner Johnston, and Ambassador Franklin Haydn Williams, when those three officials met in Hawaii. The decision reached was that "political education" was an Administrative responsibility; hence, the ESG Program became operational in January, 1974. A logo was adopted, showing four elements: a seedline coconut, a Micronesian family, a ballot box, and the words "Education for Self-Government." The express purpose of the ESG Program has been "to prepare Micronesians to make their decisions concerning a new political status which will eventually replace the Trusteeship Agreement."[97]

Excerpts are here given from a Comparative Status Chart (p. 98)

COMPARATIVE STATUS CHART*

Status Option	Self-Government and Citizenship	Control of Foreign Affairs	Possibility of Status Change in Future
Free Association (According to the draft Compact as it was negotiated between the U.S. and Micronesian teams at the 8th Round of Negotiations on Saipan, June 2, 1976.)	Complete internal sovereignty with the form of government established by the Micronesian Constitution. Citizens of Micronesia would have the privileges of U.S. nationals.	The U.S. would be fully responsible for foreign affairs and diplomatic relations with other countries and protection of Micronesians traveling abroad. The U.S. would represent Micronesia at the U.N.	The Compact between the U.S. and Micronesia may be terminated or amended at any time by *mutual agreement*. After 15 years, the Compact may be terminated *unilaterally* through Micronesian plebiscite or U.S. Constitutional means.
Commonwealth (According to the "Covenant to Establish a Commonwealth of the Northern Marianas in Political Union with the United States," 1976.)	On the date of Commonwealth establishment, Marianas [or Trust Territory] citizens would choose U.S. citizen or U.S. national status. All children born later would be U.S. citizens.	The U.S. would have complete authority except as negotiated in the Commonwealth agreement. The Commonwealth Government would be permitted to establish offices abroad to promote local tourism or other economic or cultural interests.	The Commonwealth would be considered a permanent part of the U.S. and therefore could not be changed or terminated without *mutual* consent.
Independence (According to a Micronesian constitution to be drawn when the Trusteeship Agreement of 1947 is terminated and the new government has full responsibility for decision making over internal and external affairs.)	Complete internal and external sovereignty according to a Micronesian constitution. All would be Micronesian citizens according to the Constitution.	Micronesian control of all aspects of foreign relations, including military defense of the islands. As an independent nation, the Government of Micronesia could negotiate with all nations.	An independent nation may choose any direction within its capabilities. A change of status from independence to something less is rarely voluntary although it has been done.

*Adapted from material compiled by the ESG Office, Trust Territory Government. Omitted as a "status" is the category of "Trusteeship," which is the status quo; also, several other "conditions" for each "status" listed above.

"To Foster the Development of Political Institutions..." 99

prepared by the ESG Office for use in its "political education" program begun in 1974: (*Note:* McPhetres says this chart has been revised *four* times since early 1974 as the various "options" are more refined by further negotiations and public utterances. It is assumed the announced referendum for 1978 will see the ESG people making good use of the chart for comparative purposes.)

A primary reason for the Honolulu Round Table Conference, hosted by the United States during May 18-21, 1977, to which numerous Micronesian officials were invited to meet with American negotiators and others (including the newly appointed High Commissioner, Winkel, and the Director of Territorial Affairs, Van Cleve), was to reach agreement on the resumption of "formal status negotiations." Instead, the participants concurred only to "another series of informal multilateral and bilateral talks, to be held at the earliest possible date in June or July [1977]."[98]

What was the *major* stumbling block at the Eighth Round of Negotiations on Saipan (in May-June, 1976), which necessitated the above "round table" approach almost a year later? Senator Salii, in his closing remarks at the plenary session of that last "round" told the American team:

> The one area in which we have not reached full agreement is an important one to both Micronesia and the United States. We recognize Micronesia's great and legitimate interest in preserving and protecting Micronesia's ocean resources for the full economic benefit of the people of Micronesia. We share this interest and your understandable objective. Law of the Sea matters of course have global significance and the United States has world-wide interests which it must also keep fully in mind.[99]

Thus, the solution to the 200-mile "economic (or "marine") resources zone" has been the key problem. The Congress of Micronesia has advocated an "archipelago theory" for the Trust Territory, under which a straight line would be drawn between each of the outermost islands, thus giving the Micronesians a *wider* circumference than the intersecting circles of 200 miles around each island, as seen in the U.S. approach. Although the American zone was implemented on March 1, 1977, the Trust Territory and the northern Marianas were permitted to retain the 12-mile limit, which was to be extended to the 200-mile limit in late 1977. (Guam, being a territory of the United States, now has the 200-mile zone.) Resolution of the "economic resources zone" in Micronesia remains to be settled prior to the referendum on the Micronesian Constitution scheduled for July, 1978.

Militarily, many American as well as foreign observers question whether the U.S. defense interests in the western Pacific include preparing the islands of Micronesia to be a "fallback" base at the time American forces must exit the Philippines, Taiwan, and Japan, Bennett, mentioned earlier, spent most of his Foreign Service (since 1958) in Southeast Asia, and he attended the National War College, in Washington, D.C., during 1975-76. He categorizes *three* "strategic interests" for the United States in Micronesia:

> One of these—and by far the most important, I think everyone would agree—is simply the concept of denial: making sure that Micronesia is not used against us by a hostile power.
> The second interest is much more tangible and measurable, and that is continued use of the Kwajalein Missile Range [in the Marshalls]. Not because it could not be replaced somewhere else, but because we've invested a quarter of a billion [dollars], something like that, in facilities that are there; and, obviously, moving it to some other location, with the expense. That.
> And the third and, in most people's view, the least significant of the strategic interests, is the possibility of continued access to certain island land areas and harbor areas in Palau.

Bennett does *not* include the northern Marianas in the above comments, due to the "interim governmental arrangement" there since April, 1976. However, he then speaks of the possibility of using Tinian (immediately south of Saipan):

> I know there's talk of this [western portion of Micronesia] as a "fallback position" from the Philippines, but that's a fairly minor part of it. The more important interest, as far as I can make out, is in access to training areas for amphibious training, that kind of thing. There's really very little real estate left, especially in this part of the world, that can be effectively used for amphibious military training.... [Tinian] is something like the contingency possibility of using Babelthuap [in Palau]—the possibility of an air base on Tinian in what now looks like a fairly unlikely event that it would be needed in some time in the next 15 or 20 years. You see, we went through a stage before the end of Vietnam, from about '73 to '75, when the notion of a "fallback" from the western Pacific was very fashionable both in and out of Government, ... that we needed to get some contingency options in Micronesia, and that meant Tinian and Palau. This concept has very much receded in Washington.... The chances are that nothing will be done on Tinian, as things stand now, and the same is probably true in Palau. There might be some training there, but I'd be very surprised if there is military development beyond that.

United States Senator Henry M. Jackson (Democrat of Washington), Chairman of the Committee on Energy and Natural Resources (and, for a number of years before 1977, Chairman of the Interior and Insular Affairs Committee), in a personal letter to the author in May, 1977, responded to the general question of using Micronesia as a "fallback base." Senator Jackson's opinion follows:

> Your question with respect to a "fallback base" concept with regard to military options is a difficult question to answer. . . . Guam is a major component of the United States military defense interest in the Pacific. That the islands of Micronesia are strategic is evident from their status as the only strategic trusteeship under the U.N. However, with the exception of the ballistic missile testing program at Kwajalein and the nuclear testing of the 1950's [in the Marshalls], the U.S. defense interest in the area has been one of denial of the area rather than one of fortification as happened under the Japanese mandate. That policy of denial rather than actual use has not altered to my knowledge.

Salii, after nine years as the chief Micronesian negotiator (1967-76), views U.S. "defense aims" in the islands as follows: "I don't see anything extensive here in the foreseeable future. I think they've got what they require now. . . . I don't see the need for the United States to build a big base in Palau for conventional type of warfare. . . . The Palauans will give the options that the United States insists on. I am sure of that." Senator Borja, who was involved in negotiating with the United States over the future use of Tinian for military purposes, recalls the two years he spent on that: "The status [of Tinian] is very much in limbo. . . . [We] really came up with a six years' plan in developing first stage and second. But those have really dropped down [in priority] because of [U.S.] Congressional actions and budgetary problems." However, Borja believes that, eventually, Tinian will see some military development by the Americans: "In the interest for national defense, they [the U.S.] will further develop Tinian and not because of the close-down of other places [such as Japan or Taiwan], . . . because maybe there's another place that it's much, much better than Tinian."

A discussion of "political development" in Micronesia would not be complete without acknowledging that there has *not* been the emergence of territory-wide political parties. As Craley, a former Democratic U.S. Congressman and, for several years, the Trust Territory Government's Director of Public Affairs, notes:

> We have two districts that have had political party structures: the Marianas, which is going through an interesting development now. The last reelection here, in the Marianas, has seen a gradual changeover from the old Popular [Party] dominance to the Territorial dominance. When I first came here in '67 to work in the Trust Territory, Palau had two parties: the Progressives and the Liberals. And at that time the Progressives were in power, but very shortly thereafter they went out and the Liberals came in, and the Liberals remained in power until recently, and now, this election [in November, 1976] for the Congress [of Micronesia], they're running on one ticket. Both parties [in Palau] have gotten together, for some reason. . . . I don't feel that political parties [in Micronesia] were, or are, that important. They're a facet that we've certainly brought along with us, and two districts have picked them up in varying forms.

Possibly one of the most helpful developments to bring "self-government" to the Trust Territory was the passage of Public Law 7-54 in April, 1977. This law established "the process by which District governments can be chartered by the Trust Territory. Chartering, if approved, means that a district could possibly have its own government, including an *elected* chief executive, whether he is called a governor or a district administrator." (Italics mine.) As of mid-1977, three districts —Truk, Ponape, and Kosrae—were in "varying stages" of completing their charters; additionally, Yap and Palau were expected to commence work on their charters.[100] Until such chartering is completed, or the political status of the Trust Territory is changed by virtue of the 1978 referendum and following constitutional procedures agreed upon between the United States and Micronesia, the chief executive officers (headed by the district administrator) will continue to be appointed by the High Commissioner.

As a final observation on how well the Administering Authority has fulfilled the first of four "goals" of Article 6 of the Trusteeship Agreement of 1947, the author wishes that the following *negative* item could have been avoided from the outset. In late-December, 1976, some weeks after his 10-week field trip to Japan and Micronesia, he received a telephone call from a staff member of the U.S. Senate Select Committee on Intelligence, who indicated that the committee was planning to convene on January 10, 1977, in closed session, to consider "CIA spying charges" publicized in mid-December, 1976, by Bob Woodward (of "Watergate" reportorial fame) in the *Washington Post*. Thus, this author was asked for background material relating to the political development in Micronesia over the last few years, and, among other things, his own opinion as to *why* certain key officials in the Ford Administration (and the earlier Nixon Administration) would want individuals or groups in the Trust Territory "bugged."

That the above Senate Select Committee was to make its findings known, in part, in the spring of 1977, and confirmed that the CIA indeed had engaged in such spying, is not as significant here as the *effects* of the clandestine acts on both American and Micronesian officials in the Trust Territory Government, not to mention censure from developing nations and the Communist world. As one American official told this writer in a personal letter after the press releases of December 13, 1976: "While few of us were surprised by the Woodward revelations, it was a serious setback, both moral and political, to hear that they [the charges] were real. When I say 'not surprised,' I mean that to think that the CIA was actually carrying out operations in the T.T. has been expected and assumed for many years." Resident Commissioner Canham, on Saipan, responded to a query by this author as to whether the "spying" had involved the separate negotiations for the northern Marianas since 1973.

Canham wrote in May, 1977: "The CIA spying did not touch the Marianas negotiations at all." The Resident Commissioner then articulated the chagrin felt by many officials both in Washington and Micronesia when he concluded: "What tragic stupidity!"

The reaction of the Congress of Micronesia leadership to the "spying" episode was swift. In a letter to the U.N. Trusteeship Council in January, 1977, Senate President Tosiwo Nakayama, of Truk, and House Speaker Bethwel Henry, of Ponape, asked that council "to take a stand on the ... [CIA's] reported bugging and wiretapping of Micronesians engaged in talks with the United States on their islands' future."[101] The "round table" gathering in Honolulu (in May, 1977) saw the "CIA issue" resurface, with the officials from the Congress of Micronesia present continuing to insist on "further information from the United States Government" regarding the nature and names of individuals who may have conducted such spying within the Trust Territory, and indicating that this information must be forthcoming before they (the Micronesians) would agree to resumption of any "formal negotiations." Only the Palauan and the Marshallese delegations—both of which have requested "separate negotiations" with regard to their respective future status—viewed the "CIA incident" as "a thing of the past."[102]

Finally, the U.N. Trusteeship Council, at its June, 1977, annual meeting, was told by Senator Ambilos Iehsi, of Ponape, that, while the Congress of Micronesia membership was confident that the United States had halted any "CIA spying" activities, and accepted the American assurances concerning the future, there were still some "unanswered" questions which the Ponapean legislator "hoped to have resolved in the near future."[103]

The following chapter focuses on the second "goal" in Article 6: namely, the "economic advancement and self-sufficiency" of Micronesians since 1947.

Notes for Chapter 1

1. See Dorothy E. Richard, Cdr., USNR, *United States Naval Administration of the Trust Territory of the Pacific Islands,* II (Washington, D.C.: Government Printing Office, 1957), 72.
2. For a chronology of these Wartime encounters, see Robert R. Robbins, "United States Trusteeship for the Territory of the Pacific Islands" (*State Department Bulletin* of May 4, 1947), pp. 785-86.
3. "The Navy set the Indians to work cleaning their village; the ship's surgeon established a dispensary ashore and started a health and sanitation program; naval personnel put a compulsory educational system in effect and helped the missionaries of the New York Board

of Home Missions to establish a manual training school for boys; members of the ship's crew [the U.S.S. *Jamestown*] repaired a building for use as a school. As a result of information gained while investigating the habits and customs of the people, Commander [Henry] Glass ordered the abolition of an existing system of slavery, forbade witch doctors to practice, and broke up a long standing tribal feud." Richard, *op. cit.,* I, 2 and 3.
4. *Ibid.*
5. Guam was placed under the Navy following the Treaty of Paris in 1898 and remained so, except for the two-and-a-half-year occupation by the Japanese (December, 1941-July, 1944), until 1950. American Samoa, originally referred to as "the islands of eastern Samoa," came under the jurisdiction of the Navy from 1900 until transferred to the Department of the Interior in 1951. Both Guam and American Samoa are unincorporated territories of the United States. See Ruth G. Van Cleve, *The Office of Territorial Affairs* (New York: Praeger Publishers, 1974), pp. 81 and 74.
6. Richard, *op. cit.,* I, 7 and 8.
7. *Ibid.,* pp. 46 and 47.
8. *Ibid.,* pp. 47, 48, 52, and 53. Neas says that "specialized" courses—for individuals who would serve, say, as "claims officers"—were held at various points across the nation. For instance, he recalls a "claims officer training school" at a small college near Nashville, Tennessee, where the military literally took over that college for this purpose. The University of Michigan, at Ann Arbor, made space available for a school to train those reserve officers who would become Judge Advocate General personnel.
9. Statement of Fred M. Zeder II, Director, Office of Territorial Affairs, U.S. Department of the Interior, before the United Nations Trusteeship Council, New York City, June 29, 1976, Exhibit A, p. 2.
10. Ironically, President Truman later designated Dublon to become the "permanent site" for the Territorial government headquarters; however, no move to Dublon was possible. Why? The 1953 *Annual Report* of Interior blamed a lack of funds "with which to construct housing, office, and other facilities." See U.S., Department of Interior, *Annual Report to the Secretary of the Interior, for the Fiscal Year ended June 30, 1953* (Washington, D.C.: Government Printing Office, 1953), p. 367.
11. Richard, *op. cit.,* I, 243.
12. *Ibid.,* pp. 246-47, and 249-50.
13. See Norman Meller, *The Congress of Micronesia* (Honolulu: University of Hawaii Press, 1969), pp. 291-305 and 291 footnote.
14. *The Forrestal Diaries,* p. 21, as quoted in Richard, *op. cit.,* II, 60-61.

"To Foster the Development of Political Institutions..." 105

15. Chief of Staff, U.S. Army memorandum, dated 6 December 1945, as quoted in Richard, *op. cit.*, III, 4-6.
16. Harold L. Ickes, of Illinois, initially was appointed Secretary of the Interior by President Franklin D. Roosevelt in March, 1933, and remained in that position until March, 1946 (which was 11 months into President Harry S. Truman's first term). Prior to Secretary Ickes' service in five different administrations (four of Roosevelt's and the first of Truman's), the next longest term by an Interior Secretary was Franklin Knight Lane (1913-20), under President Woodrow Wilson; since Ickes' day, only one such secretary has come close to his tenure: Stewart L. Udall, who, under Presidents Kennedy and Johnson, served eight years (from 1961-69). The Department of the Interior was established in 1849. See *The Official Associated Press Almanac, 1973* (New York: Almanac Publishing Company, Inc., 1972), pp. 197-207; also see Office of the Federal Register, *United States Government Organization Manual, 1976/77* (Washington, D.C.: Government Printing Office, 1976), p. 294.
17. See Richard, *op. cit.*, III, 18-19.
18. *Ibid.*, p. 29. *Collier's* Magazine ceased publication on January 4, 1957.
19. See U.S., Congress, Senate, Senator Mansfield speaking for H. J. Res. 233, 80th Cong., 1st sess., July 10, 1947, *Congressional Record*, XCIII, 8732-33.
20. See U.S., Congress, House, Representative Engle speaking in favor of the Trusteeship Agreement but not under administration of military, S.J. Res. 143, 80th Cong., 1st sess., July 17, 1947, *Appendix to Congressional Record*, p. A3591.
21. *Ibid.*, p. A3592.
22. See U.S., Department of Interior, *Annual Report of the Secretary of the Interior, for the Fiscal Year ended June 30, 1948* (Washington, D.C.: Government Printing Office, 1948), p. 411.
23. *Ibid.* The term "Pacific islands," as used within the context of the late 1940s by the Truman Administration, referred not only to the Trust Territory of the Pacific Islands but to Guam and American Samoa as well.
24. Unpublished manuscript, Rear Admiral C. H. Wright, Chief of Naval Operations Files, as quoted in Richard, *op. cit.*, III, 51.
25. Richard, *op. cit.*, III, 169.
26. *Ibid.*, p. 157.
27. *Ibid.*, II, 298.
28. Daniel T. Hughes and Sherwood G. Lingenfelter, eds., *Political Development in Micronesia* (Columbus, Ohio: Ohio State University Press, 1974), p. 21.

29. For an overview of the development of district legislatures in the Trust Territory, see chap. 3 in Meller, *op. cit.*, pp. 43-90.
30. Richard, *op. cit.*, III, 288.
31. Van Cleve, *op. cit.*, pp. 9 and 10.
32. *Ibid.*, p. 9.
33. See Martin Shapiro, ed., *The Pentagon Papers and the Courts* (San Francisco: Chandler Publishing Company, 1972), p. 10. Murray, a former Peace Corps volunteer in Micronesia, referred to Saipan under the Naval Administration (from 1953-62) as "a super-secret training base for Chinese Nationalists who planned assaults on mainland China." (See Steve Murray, "The Americanization of Micronesia: Paradise Lost," *Ramparts* [February, 1971], p. 37).
34. U.S., Department of Interior, *Annual Report of the Secretary of the Interior, for the Fiscal Year ended June 30, 1953* (Washington, D.C.: Government Printing Office, 1953), p. 368.
35. From the verbatim transcript of the remarks of Robert R. Robbins at the symposium "Political Development in Micronesia," American Anthropological Association annual meeting, New York City, November 18, 1971.
36. See U.S., Department of Interior, *Annual Report of the Secretary of the Interior, for the Fiscal Year ended June 30, 1954* (Washington, D.C.: Government Printing Office, 1954), pp. 367 and 375-77.
37. See U.S., Department of Interior, *Annual Report of the Secretary of the Interior, for the Fiscal Year ended June 30, 1955* (Washington, D.C.: Government Printing Office, 1955), pp. 365 and 372.
38. U.S., Department of Interior, *Annual Report of the Secretary of the Interior, for the Fiscal Year ended June 30, 1956* (Washington, D.C.: Government Printing Office, 1956), p. 337.
39. See Robert R. Robbins, "United States Territories in Mid-Century" (paper prepared for the Conference on the History of the Territories, National Archives and Research Service, Washington, D.C., November 3-4, 1969), pp. 60-61.
40. See U.S., Department of Interior, *Annual Report . . . for 1955*, p. 374.
41. See U.S., Department of Interior, *Annual Report . . . for 1956*, pp. 337, 344, and 346.
42. See U.S., Department of Interior, *Annual Report of the Secretary of the Interior, for the Fiscal Year ended June 30, 1957* (Washington, D.C.: Government Printing Office, 1957), pp. 361-62.
43. U.S., Department of Interior, *Annual Report of the Secretary of the Interior, for the Fiscal Year ended June 30, 1959* (Washington, D.C.: Government Printing Office, 1959), p. 366. This report also stated that, with the chartering of Yap and those numerous

muncipalities, "plus the conversion of a bicameral congress [in the Marshal Islands] to a unicameral body, progress in political development was well ahead of the target dates set." (*Ibid.*, p. 374.) Thus, by the end of Fiscal Year 1959, each of the district congresses (or legislatures) was unicameral in structure. Only in the Marshalls and Ponape had the respective congresses begun originally with bicameral bodies. (See Meller, *The Congress of Micronesia*, pp. 76-77.)

44. See U.S., Department of Interior, *Annual Report of the Secretary of the Interior, for the Fiscal Year ended June 30, 1960* (Washington, D.C.: Government Printing Office, 1960), pp. 310-11. Meller wrote that it was at the 1958 meeting that the delegates voted to call their committee the "Inter-District Advisory Committee to the High Commissioner," a title which was to change to the "Council of Micronesia" in 1961. (See Meller, *The Congress of Micronesia*, pp. 184-85.)

45. See United Nations, Trusteeship Council *Provisional Verbatim Record of the Fourteen Hundred and Fifty-first Meeting*, T/PV.1451 (2 July 1976), p. 28.

46. See U.S. Department of Interior, *Annual Report . . . for 1953*, p. 367.

47. Van Cleve, *op. cit.*, p. 130.

48. See Footnote 52 in the Introduction, herein, for a listing of the other trusteeships in the post-World War II era.

49. The names of Salii's fellow islanders attending the University of Hawaii during the late 1950s and early 1960s read like a "Who's Who" in the Micronesian leadership which was to come forth by the *mid*-1960s throughout the six administrative districts. For example, Heine became the first islander to be a district administrator and then the first Speaker of the House of Representatives in the Congress of Micronesia; Oiterong was one of the first Micronesians to receive a master's degree and is a long-time director of education in the Palau District; Nakayama, from Truk, was to become the President of the Senate in the Congress of Micronesia; DeBrum, a District Administrator in the Marshalls; Falcam, an Executive Officer to the High Commissioner, then a District Administrator in Ponape, and presently, Liaison Officer for the Micronesian Washington Office; and both Olter and Henry, Ponapeans, were to become members of the Congress of Micronesia—Olter in the Senate, and Henry as Speaker of the House.

50. Other members of the Solomon Mission in 1963 were: Richard Cooper, Council of Economic Advisers; Paul Dale, Peace Corps; Donald Lindholm and Howard Schnoor, then Bureau of the Budget; Dr. Pedro Sanchez, Commissioner of Education, Virgin

Islands; and Cleo Shook, Consultant. Richard Taitano, Director of the then Office of Territories, and Naval Commander Charles Chamberlain, Pacific Command, also were members.

51. See Janos Gereben, "Cleveland Bares His Role in Micronesian Policy," *Honolulu Star-Bulletin,* July 30, 1971, p. A-1.
52. See "The Solomon Report from the Young Micronesian," *Micronitor,* July 10, 1971, p. 3.
53. Statement of Zeder, . . . Exhibit A, p. 3.
54. Gereben, "Cleveland Bares His Role in Micronesian Policy," p. A-1.
55. Excerpts from a tape recording of Kurt Ludwig, former Assistant Political Affairs Officer, Trust Territory Government, Saipan. Recorded in Salem, Ohio, in the summer of 1969. Ludwig later became the Secretary of the American Assembly of Columbia University, in New York City.
56. Van Cleve, *op. cit.,* p. 138.
57. *Ibid.*
58. See Meller, *The Congress of Micronesia,* p. 291.
59. See *Remarks of Professor Robert R. Robbins of Tufts University, First Legislative Counsel of the Congress of Micronesia, before the House of Representatives,* Capitol Hill, Saipan, January 18, 1971, p. 1. (Mimeographed.) July 12 is an official holiday—"Micronesia Day"—in the Trust Territory, and succeeding sessions of the Congress of Micronesia ceremoniously have begun on that day unless such falls on a Sunday. (In 1970, for example, the holiday was observed on Monday, July 13.)
60. From the remarks of Robbins, "Political Development in Micronesia."
61. See U.S., Congress, House, *A House Joint Resolution to Establish the Commission on the Future Political Status of the Trust Territory of the Pacific Islands (Micronesia),* H.J. Res. 594, 90th Cong., 1st sess., 1967. The nine members would be composed of five persons appointed by the U.S. President; two U.S. senators; and two members from the U.S. House.
62. See U.S. Representative Patsy T. Mink, "Micronesia: Our Bungled Trust," *Texas International Law Forum,* VI, 2 (January, 1971), 199. Doubtless, if we had available the memoirs or a biography of former U.S. Congressman Wayne N. Aspinall, erstwhile chairman of the House Committee on Interior and Insular Affairs, we would have a better appreciation of the accusation that "piqueness" on his part, above all else, was responsible for failure of the U.S. Government to establish a Micronesian status commission. One source close to the scene at that time later commented that there were possibly three reasons for Aspinall's "inaction" as committee

chairman to *move* the commission proposal: first, Aspinall did not like to do anything in a hurry, and almost no major territorial legislation over the years was ever passed unless it had been introduced in at least one previous Congress, which Johnson's proposal had not; second, that chairman was "healthily skeptical" about commissions in general, viewing them as most often an excuse for not making "hard decisions"; and finally, he did not have a high regard for the Senate in "territorial matters," feeling that the senators were generally "sloppy" in that area, being too hasty, ill-informed, and inclined to do the wrong thing. On the surface, Congressman Aspinall might say that, if the commission resolution were passed and appointments made, the new Administration (Nixon's, in 1969) would want its own appointees; thus, the passage of the resolution prior to 1969 would be "a great waste."

63. See United Nations, Trusteeship Council, 34th Session, 1967, *Report of the United Nations Visiting Mission to the Trust Territory of the Pacific Islands, May 29-June 30, 1967,* T/1668, Supplement No. 2, p. 3.
64. *Ibid.,* pp. 41-42.
65. *Ibid.,* p. 48.
66. See *Highlights,* May 1, 1969, p. 9.
67. See Office of the High Commissioner, *Opening Statement by High Commissioner W. R. Norwood to the 35th Session of the Trusteeship Council, May 28, 1968,* released by the Department of Public Affairs, Saipan: [1968,] p. 2. (Mimeographed.)
68. See Mink, "Micronesia: Our Bungled Trust," p. 199.
69. See U.S., Congress, Senate, *A Senate Concurrent Resolution To Express the Sense of Congress on Including Trust Territory of the Pacific Islands in the State of Hawaii,* S. Con. Res. 50, 89th Cong., 1st sess., 1965, *Congressional Record,* CXI, 20841-45. This resolution was referred to the Senate Committee on Interior and Insular Affairs, where it died.
70. *Statement of Representative Jacob Sawachi, of the Congress of Micronesia, to the 35th Session of the Trusteeship Council, May 27, 1968,* released by the Department of Public Affairs, Saipan: [1968,] p. 1. (Mimeographed.)
71. See Trust Territory of the Pacific Islands, Congress, *Report of the Future Political Status Commission,* 3d Cong., 2d sess., July, 1969, p. 7.
72. See Trust Territory of the Pacific Islands, Congress, House, *A House Joint Resolution Extending the Life of the Future Political Status Commission of the Congress of Micronesia and Requiring a Final Report To Be Submitted during the Fifth Regular Session of the Congress in July, 1969,* H.J. Res. 10, 2d Cong., 4th reg. sess.,

1968. (*Note:* The "Fifth Regular Session" was to become the "Second Regular Session" of the Third Congress in July, 1969; hence, the "First Regular Session" of the Seventh Congress, which convened during January-March, 1977, was the most current as of mid-1977.)

73. From "Unification in Micronesia," A position paper prepared for use of the Joint Committee on Future Status during meetings with a U.S. delegation at Hana, Maui, Hawaii, October 4-12, 1971. (Mimeographed.)
74. See "Secretary Hickel Calls for Micronesian-American Partnership," *Highlights,* May 15, 1969, p. 1.
75. *Ibid.,* p. 6. Ironically, Hickel, himself, was to lose his own Executive position when President Nixon fired him in December, 1970.
76. See "Interview: Edward E. Johnston," *Micronesian Reporter,* XVIII (2d Quarter, 1970), p. 4.
77. Statement of Zeder, . . . p. 7.
78. Statement of Raymond Setik, Congressman, House of Representatives, Congress of Micronesia, Before the United Nations Trusteeship Council, New York City, June 29, 1976, p. 62.
79. See "Vetoes Upheld," *ESG Notes, LXVI* (May 20, 1977), p. 6.
80. See Statement of Zeder, . . . pp. 3-6. Falcam apparently was "forewarned" by Zeder of the pending termination, according to a number of sources, several weeks before Zeder's public firing of him. Ironically, the special session of the Congress of Micronesia, meeting in July-August, 1976, appointed Falcam to be their Washington, D.C., Representative at a salary of $25,000, slightly more than he was receiving as a District Administrator. In this latter capacity, Falcam was to find himself conferring on occasion with the DOTA as well as the Secretary of the Interior—the two men responsible for his firing.
81. See Office of Territorial Affairs, *Report to the Transition Committee, Department of the Interior, from Fred M. Zeder II, Director of Territorial Affairs,* December 9, 1976, 10 pp. (Administratively Restricted.)
82. *Ibid.,* pp. 5-7. The author feels that those officials who so graciously shared their candid opinions with him over the past 11 years are counted among "the most dedicated [and] hard-working" type Zeder found in Micronesia.
83. See "New HiCom Nominated," *ESG Notes,* LXV (May 6, 1977), 8; also see "Late Bulletin," *ESG Notes,* LXVI (May 20, 1977), p. 6.
84. See "Statement by Adrian P. Winkel, Special Representative to the Trusteeship Council on the Trust Territory of the Pacific Islands, June 6, 1977," United States Mission to the United Nations, Press Release USUN-34 (77), June 7, 1977. (23 pp.)

"To Foster the Development of Political Institutions . . ." 111

85. See "Special Edition: The Marianas Status Talks," *Highlights*, December 20, 1972, p. 2. Background on the "rounds of negotiations" (as of 1973) between the U.S. and Micronesia, including the Marianas status talks, are compiled in a 36-page handout, entitled "Fourteen Questions," prepared by the Education for Self-Government (ESG) Program in the Political Affairs Division, Department of Public Affairs, Trust Territory Government, Saipan, 1973.
86. See Trust Territory of the Pacific Islands, Congress, *Report of the Future Political Status Commission*, 3d Cong., 2d sess., July, 1969, p. 8.
87. Trust Territory of the Pacific Islands, Congress, *Report of the Political Status Delegation of the Congress of Micronesia*, 3d Cong., 3d reg. sess., July, 1970, pp. 7-8. This report also told of "executive meetings" held between the U.S. (headed by then Asst. Secretary of Interior Harrison Loesch) and the Micronesian delegation, in Washington, D.C., during January, 1970, when the American position was to present the islanders with a "draft bill" under which Micronesia would become an "unincorporated territory" of the United States, similar to Guam or the Virgin Islands. The report in July, 1970, referred to this earlier American offer as being "almost totally objectionable." (*Ibid.*, p. 4.)
88. United Nations, Trusteeship Council, 37th Session, 1970, *Report of the United Nations Visiting Mission to the Trust Territory of the Pacific Islands*, T/1713, Supplement No. 2, p. 172.
89. See Carl Heine, *Micronesia at the Crossroads: A Reappraisal of the Micronesian Political Dilemma* (Honolulu: The University Press of Hawaii, 1974), p. 172.
90. United Nations, Trusteeship Council, 38th March 1971, *Communication Received from the Third Mariana Islands District Legislature Concerning the Trust Territory of the Pacific Islands*, T/COM.10/L.70. The date of the "cover letter" from the Marianas Legislature was 4 March 1971.
91. See "Congress of Micronesia Buildings Burn; Members Adjourn First Session," *Highlights*, February 22, 1971, pp. 1-4. This was the first of two fires to occur on Capitol Hill, Saipan, in less than a year. In late November, 1971, an arsonist (or more than one) caused an estimated $50,000 in damage to the High Commissioner's residence while he and his wife were on a visit to Guam. (See "Reward Offered," *Highlights*, December 15, 1971, p. 5.) Concerning the Congressional buildings' fire, Professor Robert R. Robbins, the former Legislative Counsel (in 1965), had addressed the House of Representatives on Capitol Hill in mid-January, 1971—only 33 days before the fire—and commented on the rather plain, yet prac-

tical, approach to the design and construction of those buildings (the frames of which, Robbins said, "were scrounged from the boondocks" on Saipan) : "We are told by some late arrivals [after 1965] that these provisional buildings are rather awful and unbecoming the dignity of the Congress. . . . I would like to express the personal view that these simple and modest buildings are genuine, sincere, and prideful products of provisional times and circumstances." The former Legislative Counsel also remarked: "While in Saipan five years ago, I did not pose as an architect, but I am willing to have it said that I was a scrounger. Nonetheless, I drew up the original projection for this complex." See *Remarks of Professor . . . Robbins,* p. 1.

92. See "Kennedy to Visit T.T., *Highlights,* March 1, 1971,p. 3. A *faux pas* was committed by Ambassador Kennedy when he canceled a visit to Yap, although his plane flew over Yap on the trip to Palau. Other than Yap, all the districts were visited by him.

93. See Joseph Murphy, Editor, *Pacific Daily News,* "Saipan Awaits Amb. Kennedy," Guam *Pacific Daily News,* March 18, 1971, p. 1.

94. For islander reactions to the Covenant signing, see Mike Malone, "Marianas Special News Analysis: Marianas Leaders Approve Commonwealth," *Micronesian Independent,* V, 7 (February 28, 1975), cover, and 1 and 2; for the plebiscite results, see "Marianas Voters Approve Commonwealth," *Highlights,* June 15, 1975, pp. 1 and 2.

95. See "President Signs the Covenant," *Highlights,* April 1, 1976, p. 2. Interestingly, the final flurry of Congressional and Presidential approval during March, 1976, was occurring at a time when the U.N. Visiting Mission was making its periodic tour (every three years) of the Trust Territory. A negative critique of the American approval of the Covenant came from José A. Cabranes, former special counsel to the Governor of the Commonwealth of Puerto Rico and more recently, legal adviser of Yale University. Cabranes challenges the "value" of such an annexation in his article, entitled "Annexation of the Marianas, a 'Dismal Story,'" *New York Times,* April 17, 1976, p. 21.

96. See "Proclamation," *ESG Notes,* LXVI (May 20, 1977), 1 and 4.

97. See "ESG Supplement," in *Highlights,* February 1, 1974, unnumbered.

98. "[Joint] Press Release on Behalf of Micronesian-U.S. Conference, May 18-21, 1977, Honolulu, Hawaii," as an attachment to personal letter from Ruth G. Van Cleve, Director, Office of Territorial Affairs, Washington, D.C., June 24, 1977.

99. See Office for Micronesian Status Negotiations, *Micronesian Status Negotiations, Eighth Round, May 28-June 2, 1976, at Saipan, Northern Mariana Islands,* Washington, D.C., 1976, pp. 2 and 3.
100. See "District Chartering Progressing," *ESG Notes,* LXIV (April 22, 1977), pp. 1 and 3.
101. See "Congress of Micronesia Seeks U.N. Stand on Bugs," *ESG Notes,* LXI (January 28, 1977), 3. Reaction in the American press to the U.S. Senate Select Committee on Intelligence releasing its report on the "CIA bugging"—which release on May 3, 1977, was a brief, four-page effort omitting the names and sources of the CIA "operatives"—was typified in a *Los Angeles Times* editorial. "The Central Intelligence Agency managed to forget those basic commitments [of the U.N. Charter, chapter 12] in its snooping actions in Micronesia in 1975 and 1976," the editorial noted, "and [the then Secretary of State] Henry Kissinger forgot them, too, when he approved, in advance, the CIA's covert operations in the scattering of Pacific Islands [Micronesia]." (See "Snoopery Without Manners," *Los Angeles Times,* May 5, 1977, Part II, p. 6.)
102. See "Multilateral US-Micro Talks to Continue," *ESG Notes,* LXVI (May 20, 1977), 4.
103. See "Micro Reps Address UN Council," *ESG Notes,* LXVII (June 10, 1977), 4.

Chapter 2

"To Promote Economic Advancement and Self-Sufficiency..."

When the degree of "economic advancement" or "self-sufficiency" of the Micronesians under American Administration since 1947 is discussed, the usual reaction of scholars, journalists, or other observers of events in the Trust Territory over the past decade has been to dismiss earlier periods as "nonproductive." An example of such a view is that of Reverend John F. X. Condon, S.J. Father Condon, presently a pastor on Guam, was assigned to the Yap District (from 1947-73). In a personal letter to the author in 1971, this longtime missionary characterized development—or the lack of such—in Micronesia quite succinctly: "Don't look for 'positive results of the Interior Department' before 1963; there was complete stagnation in all branches of the T.T. [Trust Territory] Government before then."

Coupled with the above stereotype of "stagnation" under Interior prior to the early 1960s is that of "the good old Navy days," when "everything was free!" This chapter probes into those earlier eras and concludes with the thrust found in the economic sphere as the islanders approach the late 1970s.

HOW GOOD WERE "THE OLD NAVY DAYS"?

The political efforts under the Navy were examined in the preceding chapter. Some of the same problems which the Naval Administration faced in structuring a workable operation were present in the economic area as well, especially while World War II was still being fought in parts of Micronesia (as late as mid-1945). Thus, Dwight Heine, a Marshallese, reflects on the "mystery" which was the annual budget: "During Navy Time [1944-51], we really don't know what our budget was, because there are many ways Navy can draw things here and there. Medicine, for instance. We did not know where it comes from. Or, if you need

"*To Promote Economic Advancement and Self-Sufficiency* . . ."

papers [i.e., office materials], you will get it. Who, what account they charge, we don't know, but we never run out of those things." Heine also remembers the high quality of Naval personnel, some of whom were assigned as supervisors over those Micronesians employed by the Navy throughout the six districts:

> The Navy who came—they had them, like the doctors, they won't come now. . . . The only reason they came out here [before 1951] was because they were in uniform. Medical doctors. Or take some of the fellows [during the Navy Period] I worked with. One was from Columbia—a professor of international law. (Laugh.) This kind of professor—Dr. so-and-so. . . . Very top-notch people in their field. And that is why we felt so much [sadness] when they left. They left, they take number of manpower—men who can handle a job. You see, when they hire this Micronesian, not because they needed us, because we were slow, we were not as good worker as the Americans, but to give us some learning—give us a chance to learn something.

The salaries paid Micronesians under the Naval Administration included a number of "fringe benefits" not normally considered in the payment of an indigenous work corps. Senator Olympio Borja, in the northern Marianas, recalls the stated salaries as being relatively low, but the additional allowances attractive:

> I was getting 25¢ a day. I used to work for . . . [the military] hospital, helping the nurses, the corpsmen, and so forth. At that time they [the Navy] giving us the houses and the clothing free from the [military] supplies. And that 25¢ it practically goes by for your own necessities and for expenses. . . . And then the salary go on for $1 a day. . . . During the military time, most of the surplus they have they giving it to the people, whenever they have an emergency—typhoon or something—again, they were giving it.

JoeTen (José Tenorio), a leading entrepreneur on Saipan, reflects on the Navy Period after World War II and also says that "everything is free, and we thought that, we had the impression that the United States is really a rich country, that, you know, they have many things that they can even throw away—just like clothes." The type of clothes JoeTen remembers being made readily available to the Micronesians were the khaki uniform items: "Those military shirts and pants, eh? You can wear it, khaki, eh? You can wear it even if you just go to the [Navy] warehouse and change it for the new one. You don't have to wash [the clothes]. Shoes, as well. And they give us the impression that I think we happy to have new work [under the Navy]."

Maynard Neas, whose first assignment in the Trust Territory was to be the Acting District Administrator in the Marshall Islands when the Interior Department replaced the Navy in mid-1951, attributes *two* factors for Navy's relative success in the islands compared with the difficulties which Interior was to face: "The Navy Administration had better communication with the islands, more frequent field trips, and more things to give away—surplus goods." Neas also comments on the *real* "Navy budget," which he feels was possibly five or six times as much as that listed as available through U.S. Congressional appropriations or Naval funds, and concludes that the availability of goods and services at little or no cost to the Micronesians enhanced the Navy's image:

> Their [Naval] budget didn't show exactly what they had. But they were spending, those guys, some of us could figure out, if you count the shipping and air service, and one thing and another that they had for free, they were operating at a level somewhere around $25 [million] to $30 million budget in the 1940s and '50 through [mid-] '51. Here, all at once, we [the Interior Department] were there with practically nothing. And there was complaint, not any violent complaint, but certainly the Marshallese that I worked with didn't hesitate to tell us, "We wish the Navy would come back!" Now, under the Navy, the field ships didn't charge a fare for passengers; the airplanes didn't charge fares. . . . They [the Micronesians] went as Government guests, or, you know, on Government business, but if they needed to go somewhere, why, there was no such thing as buying a ticket.

Commander Richard, in her comprehensive retelling of the Navy Period, wrote that "the Navy at no time considered that the free distribution of supplies to the natives in the Central Pacific islands was to continue indefinitely," and she observed that, in addition to the "relief" measures taken to ensure the immediate needs of the Micronesians, "there were also 'rehabilitation' supplies of agricultural tools and fishing gear to assist them in establishing a self-sustaining economy as soon as possible. When money became available, food and clothing and minor luxuries were to become incentive goods to be sold in stores under military government supervision."[1]

The U.S. Navy realized before its occupation of Micronesia in the latter part of the War (1944-45) that the islanders' economy would be completely disrupted as a result of the American campaign against Japanese shipping and the combined bombardment/amphibious landings required throughout Micronesia. Thus, the Navy's stated objective— "to restore the islands to their normal degree of self-sufficiency"—was attempted as soon as the "assault period" was completed in the respective island areas. Richard said that the Navy "went into business on a scale never before attempted by a United States military organization" in its effort to fulfill the stated instructions issued by the Naval Commander in the Pacific: namely, to reestablish "public utilities, industry, fishing, agriculture, storage facilities, coastal shipping, and port facilities for ocean-going vessels."[2]

The wages paid initially by the Naval Administration to the indigenes was commensurate to what the islanders received in the pre-War days from the Japanese; thus, the daily salary ranged from 70 sen (17½¢) and graduated to two yen (or about 50¢),[3] in addition to the "fringe benefits" referred to previously by Heine, et al.

As for the industries involved in the Navy's rehabilitation efforts, the sugar growing in the northern Marianas, principally Saipan, was not attempted; rather, the fields were to be converted to rice and vegetable crops; interest was expressed to rehabilitate the copra industry, and fishing also received a high priority. A difficulty to be confronted in restoring fishing as a potential source of food throughout Micronesia during the whole of the Navy Period (1944-51) was that the islanders had *lost* the art of "deep sea" fishing: in other words, during the long Japanese Period (1914-45), the Micronesians had confined their fishing to lagoon and off-the-reef fishing. The Japanese fishermen, meanwhile, had conducted the deep sea fishing operations.[4]

William H. Stewart, Deputy Director of the Department of Resources and Development in the Trust Territory Government, feels that the Navy "goofed" when it fostered what his department refers to as the "10% companies":

> The Navy established island trading companies, and when they organized these companies and drew up the charter and bylaws, they had a provision in those documents that no one owner could own more than 10% of the stock. We call these companies "10% companies." In the case of KITCO [Kwajalein Importing and Trading Company], in the Marshall Islands, I think it's a 20% company. At any rate, these companies eventually changed their names. In the Marshalls, it became the Western Carolines Trading Company [WCTC]; in Yap, YCO—the Yap Cooperative Association; in Truk, it's the Truk Trading Company [TTC].

Stewart points out that the Navy's desire to keep the stockholder shares low (usually no more than 10%) was to have *a harmful* effect in the ensuing three decades:

> They're [the island trading companies are] in serious difficulty now. ... WCTC was one of these 10% companies, and the net result was, that, over the years—since no one owned a majority of the ownership—they did not exercise, the stockholders did not exercise, the interest that might have been exercised should one of them have owned a majority of the interest. Now, I don't know why the Navy put that restriction in the bylaws, and the charter, but that restriction has caused us a great deal of trouble, because every one of those companies have experienced financial difficulties 30 years after the fact. They could have all done very well under the proper management.

The Truk Trading Company (TTC), discussed above by Stewart, is an example of Micronesians being placed in executive positions during the Navy Period when such had not been done previously under the Japanese Mandate years. The TTC became the first islander-owned trading company in the Trust Territory with the opening of a small store in the Michitou Village, on Moen Island, in 1948. While the initial manager of the TTC was an American (Henry Chatroop, from Australia), appointed by the Naval Administration, the first TTC President was Artie Moses, a Micronesian. The best-known successor as President was Petrus Mailo, the late Chief of Moen, who served in that executive position for TTC (technically, in his later years, at least, as *both* President and Chairman of the all-Micronesian, 15-member Board of Directors) from 1954 until his death in 1971.[5] Thus, although the TTC, along with other island trading companies mentioned by Stewart, above, were to suffer over the years through the absence of interested majority-share stockholders, at least the Micronesians did occupy some executive offices in business ventures for the first time.

A number of successful indigenous entrepreneurs started their business careers with humble beginnings during the Navy Period. Senator Borja recalls that he and his wife had "a very small store known as [a] 'mom and pop store.' And that was originally an idea from my wife." Similarly, JoeTen and his wife started their own small retail store in Chalan Kanoa, Saipan, in 1949.

Two areas of potential "self-sufficiency" in the economic development of Micronesia under the Naval Administration were *discouraged* in the first few years by the Navy: taxation and foreign investment (both of which were to *plague* the Administering Authority down to the late 1970s, as well). Concerning the former revenue method, although staff officers from time to time encouraged taxation as a means of helping to defray the costs of the Administration and, at the same time, making the Micronesians more responsible in the support of their own local governments, as well as erasing from the minds of the islanders that the United States, or its Naval Administration in Micronesia, "operated on a philanthropic basis," the military commanders disagreed. Hence, the Island Commander Majuro (in the Marshalls) disapproved all suggestions for such taxation, with the Commanding Officer (Commander-in-Chief of Pacific Operations, or CinCPOA) concurring, as follows:

> With respect to taxes, I personally am in complete accord with your views. I believe the imposition of a head tax or anything similar thereto under any kind of disguise would be most unwise as such taxes have always been regarded in the Pacific Areas as a symbol of oppression. Moreover I can see no need of any direct tax for raising the little revenue that should be required for governing the Islands. I believe that the "off-island" profits from the handicraft and other similar sources of revenue should be ample.[6]

The only difficulty with the "handicraft profits" during the Navy Period was that the customers—in the absence of any tourism in those early years—were the Naval personnel, themselves; thus, with the eventual withdrawal of these military customers, the handicraft industry was in a state of decline by the time the Interior Department arrived on the scene in mid-1951.

The second lost opportunity in the economic sphere by the Navy was foreign investment. The Peter Paul Candy Company, makers of the coconut candy bar Mounds, expressed interest in putting a dessicating plant in Micronesia. Captain William F. Jennings, the CinCPOA military government officer for the islands, opposed such proposed civilian commercial interests from outside the islands. Richard wrote that Captain Jennings "fought all such attempts at [foreign] exploitation lest they encroach upon the meager resources of the islands and reduce the people to cheap labor."[7]

When a form of taxation was permitted in Micronesia, it was first limited to local (or municipal) taxes only. The categories involved as of May, 1947, included five types: head taxes from residents (applicable only to males between the ages of 18 and 60, set at $2 per year); license fees for businesses conducted entirely within the confines of the municipality (not to exceed $10 annually); sales taxes on retail luxury items in the municipality; property taxes on possessions within the municipality; and fees for private use of municipal properties and services. Should the islander be unable to pay in cash "without undue hardship," he could "work off his taxes" on designated municipal projects. Income taxes were not levied. Customs taxes on imported goods also were prohibited by the Navy.[8]

Critics of American rule in Micronesia in the post-World War II era often point to the tremendous economic development experienced during the three decades of Japanese Administration and ask, "Why did the United States *fail* in restoring that earlier economic climate?" Richard attributed the inability of the Naval Period to "restore the artificial, capitalistic type of prewar economy" to a decision of the Joint Chiefs of Staff in December, 1945. That decision? To repatriate all aliens. Thus, when the repatriation was completed by the end of 1946, this "took both the artisans and the majority of unskilled labor from the islands, and left only a small, untrained native labor supply. This was a death blow for the Marianas, the Western Carolines and Ponape, which had had thriving communities under the Japanese." Richard added that the Marshalls and Truk did not suffer as much from the repatriation, for those two areas were less developed, economically, during the Japanese Mandate Period.[9] It is recalled from the introductory chapter that, by mid-1945, there were three times as many Japanese, Koreans, Okinawans, and Formosans in Micronesia as there were indigenes.[10]

Another problem confronting the Naval Administration was the difficulty in convincing the islanders that "cash crops" should replace the traditional "subsistence economy." The latter preference of the Micronesians saw a large incidence of "accidental deaths" among poultry and hogs provided by the Navy for restocking purposes; and fishing in the northern Marianas waned after the repatriation, in part due to the "disinterest of the natives" in that vocation.[11] Again, these were difficulties to be a continuing concern throughout the succeeding years of Interior's Administration after 1951.

The Naval Administration had its own internal problems to resolve in addition to striving to bring the Micronesians to a point of "self-sufficiency" in the economic sphere. First, the "demobilization" which began with the end of World War II saw large numbers of trained military personnel leaving the Navy to return to civilian life, especially the hundreds who had been trained at Columbia and Princeton during the War. Richard characterized the situation by mid-1946 as also affecting the number of vessels available to Micronesia: "Usually it was the lack of men and ships that complicated all phases of operation. . . . The personnel problem worsened steadily . . . until by the summer of '46 there was no military government staff deserving of that appellation at any command" in Micronesia. Such drastic cutbacks in manpower and vessels adversely affected support of the outer islands throughout Micronesia: "Supply of the outlying areas, especially of the Carolines, failed miserably during '46. Demobilization of key personnel and their replacement by insufficient and inexperienced personnel at the supply centers created much of the confusion, [and] no commercial shipping to the islands was allowed. . . . All transportation was by naval ships and planes."[12]

What was the situation in Micronesia as the Naval Period drew to a close in mid-1951? Just prior to Interior's assumption of the responsibility to be the Administering Authority, arrangements were made for a commercial shipping line to replace the Naval vessels; the island trading companies (mentioned earlier) were functioning; the Bank of America had begun operating in Micronesia; fishing remained almost entirely at the "subsistence" level; and, beginning in mid-1947, the Japanese Government had contracted to mine phosphate on Angaur, in the Palau District. Small indigenous businesses were encouraged and fostered. However, the improvement of the "economic condition" in Micronesia during the Navy Period "continued to be one of the most difficult and trying administrative problems." As Richard concluded with regard to the second "goal" of Article 6 under the Navy (1944-51):

"To Promote Economic Advancement and Self-Sufficiency . . ."   121

Fortunately, the wording of the Trusteeship Agreement did not demand self-sufficiency but only promotion toward that goal. People who knew the area had little hope that the goal would ever be reached. The islands were as geographically isolated as ever, the natural resources were as poor and the people continued to lack the training and capability to develop spontaneously additional sources of revenue and diversification of economy.[13]

In summary, perhaps the *best* description of Naval efforts throughout Micronesia in the post-War era leading to the advent of the Interior Department in mid-1951 comes from the Naval officer coordinating the infrastructure program for the Trust Territory in 1977: Lieutenant Commander James Wood, on Guam.[14] Commander Wood sees wisdom in the traditional "Navy way" of doing things, and adds an appreciation for the former Japanese Mandate Period:

> I think the old bullheaded approach, like when the Navy was down there [in the Trust Territory], is best. . . . They [the Navy] went in there, built these things [the infrastructure], and everybody was happy, people were working. And they're [the Micronesians are] not that mad at the Japanese. You know, a few of the old ones have gotten a little pinorochi beat over their head, but the Japanese did a hell of a lot down there. Of course, they [the Japanese] didn't have to go by the rules, . . . and they were doing it for the Japanese, but, there were a lot of spin-off benefits.

HOW BAD WAS THE "RUST TERRITORY PERIOD" UNDER INTERIOR?

Numerous observers would say "Amen!" to Professor Robbins' characterization of the pre-1963 period of the Interior Department's efforts in Micronesia as being "retrogressive," for which a nickname—referring to the *physical* appearance in the Trust Territory—was later to become quite commonplace and, apparently, descriptive, as seen in the following commentary:

> In retrospect, . . . [Interior's pre-1963 Micronesian policy] has been shown to be *retrogressive* in economic and social matters, as additional funds to cover rising costs were not provided, to say nothing of additional funds for development programs. The general corrosion in the islands which occurred in this period caused observers to refer to them as *"The Rust Territory,"* and the tempo of life as such that, by comparison, the prior regime of Japanese rule could be considered the age of "The Great Society" in Micronesia.[15]

No one with whom this writer has conferred in the past decade will extol the achievements of the Department of the Interior's first dozen years (1951-63) in Micronesia. There were many problems encountered as Interior attempted to build upon the Navy's efforts in the islands but with only a fraction of the funding or logistical support previously available to the Naval Administration there. Representative of the sentiment expressed by those long-time civilian officials whose employment in the Trust Territory by Interior dates back to the 1950s is that of J. Boyd Mackenzie, whose first assignment (in 1954) was to be the Island Development Officer in the Marshalls District. In response to a question on how "keenly felt" the *absence* of sufficient funding was in Micronesia during that decade of the "Rust Territory," Mackenzie says:

> I don't think it [the insufficient funding] was "keenly felt" in that particular example. I think they were still going through sort of a transitional period, having been under the military [Navy] in which it was a completely different form of life, really, where the military [Navy] had a lot of money, and they were able to do a lot more personal things for the people than the Trust Territory [Interior Department], after [Interior] . . . got it in 1951. I think this is where the difference was. Granted, at that time the War had been over just a little while. Evidences of the War were still very, very strong in all of the islands [in 1951], wherever there had been a major battle, wherever there had been military stationed, there was this evidence of the presence of U.S. war machinery.

Mackenzie debunks the comparison sometimes made that the U.S. Navy was able to perform *better* than the Interior Department on similarly *low* expenditures, and justifies his position on the basis that the Navy listed most of its expenditures under the category of "training," and thus received U.S. military funding for such, as was discussed earlier (see chapter 1).

An example of the spartan budgetary allocations from the U.S. Congress for Interior's operations in the Trust Territory during the mid-1950s (excluding the northern Marianas, which was separately administered by the Navy from 1953-62) is found in two *Annual Reports* which highlighted "significant events" as follows in the economic development of Micronesia: an appropriation of $700,000 for "new construction" in 1955;[16] and the announcement that the budget appropriation for Fiscal Year 1957—expected to cover *all* expenditures by Interior in Micronesia —would be $6,250,000.[17]

Dwight Heine recalls that the annual budget "ceiling" for the Interior Department in the Trust Territory that first decade following 1951 was $7 million, and that the Administering Authority, through the High Commissioner, lived within that small yearly amount. Heine says that, many years later, he had lunch with one of the former High Commissioners, Frank H. Midkiff (who had served during 1953-56): "He [Midkiff] told me—I forgot the name of the person [in Washington, D.C.] who told him—'Never ask over $7 million, or else!' I don't know why."

MEANWHILE, THE U.S. NAVY DEPARTS THE MARIANAS

What economic impact did the Navy's 10-year administration in the northern Marianas have on those islanders' economic growth? JoeTen, who, in the opinion of James M. Bower (Manager of the Saipan Branch, Bank of Hawaii, since 1975), "is the most successful man in the western Pacific, bar none," remembers that decade as one in which most of the Saipanese were employed, but *not* by the Navy: "I think the majority of the people [in the northern Marianas during 1953-62] were so happy to have the CIA [see chapter 1] so that they can keep employment; otherwise, we just, with the Navy, we kind of so scared—afraid that we don't have no job." Was JoeTen thus happy to see the Interior Department replace the U.S. Naval Administration in 1962? "We [in the Marianas] find out that [we're] kind of a little bit behind because the administration between the civilian government and the military is two different things, and we feel that we're kind of behind in terms of administration." Probably, JoeTen's reflections here are based on hindsight in the late 1970s, with the full awareness of what was to transpire *after* 1962. It is recalled that, prior to 1962, the Interior's total rule in the northern Marianas had only consumed 18 months (from mid-1951 to early 1953). JoeTen also had the knowledge of Interior's efforts in other districts during the decade of Naval Administration in the Marianas from 1953.

Eusebio Rechucher, a Palauan who became Director of Resources and Development in early 1976 for the Trust Territory Government, first arrived on Saipan in 1962 at the time when that headquarters had been transferred from Guam shortly after the departure of the Naval Administration. His opinion of the northern Marianas in 1962? "There was no development in this island [Saipan]. The Navy just move out, and nothing really going on. Even this main road to the airport, it's all tangantangan trees,[18] covered in the road, so that you have to go through —under the trees. At that time there were very few vehicles running in Saipan. Maybe mostly Jeeps." Rechucher's view is that economic development generally throughout Micronesia began with the Kennedy Administration's interest in the islands, and he cites 1962 as that *pivotal* year for the islanders' economy.

Francisco C. Ada, Executive Officer to the Resident Commissioner of the Northern Marianas (see chapter 1), recalls that, prior to the end of the "security restriction" imposed in the Marianas (from 1953-62), economic growth under the U.S. Navy was almost nonexistent:

> Really, there wasn't much of, shall I say, planning. The situation of these [years under Navy] . . . was merely to keep things running as it is. At that time, we were also confronted with the so-called "security restriction." . . . Not until the late President Kennedy took administration—that

was during the Kennedy Administration which lifted the so-called "security restriction." Prior to that, of course, everybody coming into Guam, even, had to undergo a certain kind of security pass, so, therefore, there was practically no economic development of any significance.

Not mentioned in the above interview with Ada was the fact of employment by the CIA of large numbers of islanders in the Marianas during that Navy Period.

"STUDIES AREN'T WORTH A DAMN!" . . .

With the above "words of wisdom," Fred M. Zeder II, then Director of Territorial Affairs (DOTA) in the Department of the Interior, told an assembly of Congress of Micronesia members, representatives of district legislatures, and the United Nations Development Plan (UNDP) task force, all gathered for a UNDP meeting on Truk in May, 1976, that "it isn't what we know that counts, it's what we do about what we know." He then counseled those present: "It is going to be up to you as individuals to do something about it."[19] The "it" to which the former DOTA referred was the collection of recommendations in studies—mostly economically oriented—which had been performed on behalf of the United States Government with regard to Micronesia, dating back to 1946. Those studies were to be enumerated as an addendum to Zeder's remarks before the U.N. Trusteeship Council the following month.[20] That listing included surveys, projects, and reports compiled by groups both from within the federal government and through foundations, associations, and commercial enterprises. The estimated cost to American taxpayers for these endeavors, covering the period from 1946-72, is $5 million. (Excluded from that amount, Zeder said, are the sums expended by the U.S. Naval Administration for "logistical support" of studies conducted in the Trust Territory up to 1951.)

Zeder's "shock treatment" at the 1976 UNDP meeting on Truk, above, as well as his later appearance before the U.N. Trusteeship Council, verbalized in admittedly frank language a feeling expressed by numerous American, Micronesian, and foreign officials, businessmen, and others to this author during his field trip to the Pacific (in the fall of 1976) and through follow-up correspondence. Perhaps the word *catalyst* may be a fair appraisal for the worth of the manifold bound volumes compiled by well-intentioned groups who usually visited in Micronesia to glean firsthand impressions of the economic problems. By "catalyst," one may only hope that some of the recommendations have influenced later actions. Still, Zeder's concern for an estimated $5 million tax expenditure over the years is well taken. Following are but two such studies which were researched by teams of businessmen and scholars in the four

"To Promote Economic Advancement and Self-Sufficiency . . ." 125

years following the Kennedy Administration's interest in the Trust Territory: the "Solomon Report" of 1963 and the "Nathan Report" of 1966.

The salient features of the "Solomon Mission" commissioned by President Kennedy were discussed earlier (see chapter 1). Focusing on the economic findings contained in that report, one was particularly pointed: "The economy [in Micronesia] has remained relatively dormant and in many ways, retrogressed."[21] The recommendations by the Solomon Mission to correct weak economic endeavors in the Trust Territory included a proposal that $42.1 million for an "optimal capital investment program" be instituted for a four-year period (Fiscal Years 1965-68), as follows:[22]

Area of Endeavor	Cost (in Millions)
Education	$ 9.9
Health	2.4
Public Safety and Judiciary	.9
Economic Development Fund	5.0
Transportation	1.5
Communication and Radio	2.7
Public Works	13.0
Equipment Replacement	2.5
Housing Assistance	1.2
TOTAL PROPOSED EXPENDITURES, 1965-68	$42.1

Who would provide the money for the above expenditures recommended by the Solomon Mission in 1963? That 10-man team envisioned a favorable response from "private Micronesian and US capital" during that four-year period (1965-68); however, the report further indicated that "the limited prospects for the growth of the private economy [in Micronesia] dictate that, for the foreseeable future, this will continue to be a deficit area notwithstanding the development that will result from the proposed program." The Solomon team also felt that "prospects would be brighter, and the post-1968 need for subsidization reduced," *if* the U.S. Government would only *cancel* its "import duties on processed fish" and "eliminate . . . entry restrictions (except in the Kwajalein area) on Japanese businessmen, technicians, and fishing vessels." An optimistic, long-range result of the above "investments" and "accommodations" was expressed in the Solomon Report as follows: "In the still more distant future [beyond Fiscal Year 1968], although not now foreseeable, what looks like a 'Micronesian folly'—justifiable only for its strategic value— may well develop into a viable economy based on American residents and tourists."[23]

The other "mission" to visit Micronesia was a three-man group from the Robert R. Nathan Associates, Inc., of Washington, D.C., which toured the Trust Territory during 1965-66, devoting "more than nine man-months traveling in the districts, ... [involving] all district center islands and at least ten other islands in the Trust Territory were visited one or more times by one or more members of the team."[24] The team's report, running some 735 pages, was published on Saipan in three volumes in December, 1966, as the *Economic Development Plan for the Trust Territory of the Pacific Islands* (or, simply, the "Nathan Report"), a proposed long-range plan for developing Micronesia.

Two proposals in the Nathan Report are apropos to the problems of economic development in Micronesia during the latter 1960s and into the 1970s. The first dealt with the need to bring in "outside investment" to *counter* "monopolies" which might arise among a few islander businessmen:

> The explicit or implicit policies tending to restrict Micronesian development to Micronesians are giving a few Micronesian businessmen a monopolistic status and allowing them to operate without high regard for efficiency to charge high prices, and to slow the pace of development. . . . The introduction of outside resources will create competition among suppliers and producers, stimulate efficiency, provide a greater variety of goods and services, and protect consumers from unreasonable monopoly prices. . . . The introduction of new businesses, financed and managed and manned in large part by outsiders will, over time, greatly benefit Micronesian businessmen and workers.[25]

The second proposal in the Nathan Report involves the suggestion in 1966 that the U.S. Congress, which was then supplying almost 90 percent of the "total monies" received in the Trust Territory that year—through appropriations and grants—would be able to "raise the standard of living for the people of Micronesia to any level chosen and [to] maintain such a level for the foreseeable future without a viable and internally strong economy" in those islands; and the report gave, as an example of the appropriation which the American legislators *might* approve to "raise the standard of living" for those islanders, an amount "equal to $1,500 per man, woman, and child in Micronesia."[26]

THE ANNUAL BUDGETS SKYROCKET AFTER 1963

Earlier references in this chapter to the annual appropriations by the U.S. Congress (in the post-Naval Period from 1951) have depicted low amounts which contributed to a lag in economic growth under the Interior Department. Van Cleve pictures that decade as a period in which the yearly budgets for Micronesia "were calculated to permit what was essentially a holding operation," and she said that such federal funds, ranging between $4.2 million and $5.2 million during most of the 1950s, "were sufficient to keep the vessels and planes moving, to pay the salaries of about 100 Americans and 500 to 1,000 Micronesians [employed] in the TT Government, to supply hospitals, . . . and to conduct limited government programs, as in copra production and fisheries research."[27]

The more than *doubling* of the annual budget for Micronesia by the American Congress in Fiscal Year 1963—to $15 million—would seem to be a "turning point" in the overall development of the Trust Territory. Dwight Heine's response as to whether President Kennedy's support of increased annual appropriations made a *big* change all of a sudden in Micronesia is: "Oh, and how! Really, it was so sudden, it's not one of those things they talk about at times. But certainly, something ought to be done [i.e., the thinking by Kennedy's Administration]. That is what is popular. . . . We found out that he [Kennedy] was able to blaze through all this jungle and try to meet the desire and need of this area. And not only this area, [but American] Samoa as well."

That $15 million appropriation approved in 1963 was to increase several fold in succeeding years: to $25 million in Fiscal Year (FY) 1967, to $50 million by FY 71, and to $72 million by FY 1975. The yearly amount requested for FY 1978 was $83 million. None of the above amounts include the "supplemental" appropriations, usually obtained from the U.S. Congress in the spring. Thus, the "supplemental" for FY 77 was $21 million, boosting the total amount from Congress that year ($85 million regular appropriation and the $21 million supplemental) to $106 million.[28] These annual budgets, listed above, do *not* include the various federal grants-in-aid monies made available to Micronesia, as will be discussed later in this chapter.

What overall effect did the sharply increased annual budget have on the economic development *and* self-sufficiency of the Micronesians after 1963? Father Hezel, S.J., in Truk, wrote an article in 1971 in which he reviewed development throughout the Trust Territory since the early 1960s. After quoting another Jesuit priest as noting that "the real poverty in Micronesia is its wealth," Father Hezel pointed to the vastly increased number of automobiles and air-conditioned supermarkets in the Trust Territory (e.g., some 140 cars on Ebeye, an island in the Marshalls barely one-tenth of a square mile). Father Hezel attributed this modernized life style for the islanders, or "new-found affluence," to the Administering Authority's change in policy during the early 1960s: "The period of 'benign neglect' that had characterized its [Interior's] relationship with these islands since the end of World War II was halted. The flow of dollars began as the U.S. stepped up its yearly subsidy from $7 million in 1962 to $70 million last year [1970]," and, while indicating that most of the budget increase had been placed in educational and health services, with some new construction of the infrastructure and improved utilities, he pointed to a questionable increase in the number of governmental jobs: "One of the most notable effects of expansion of the infrastructure was the multiplicity of government jobs within a burgeoning bureaucracy. From $2.5 million in 1961 the total wages paid to government-employed Micronesians has swelled to more than $20 million today [1971]. Meanwhile little was done to stimulate local productivity."[29]

A consensus is readily found in Micronesia to substantiate the two key points Father Hezel made in his article, above, concerning effects of a tenfold (and *more,* by mid-1977) increase in the annual budgets since the early 1960s: namely, the large number of islanders employed by the Trust Territory Government and the lack of development in the local private sector of Micronesia. Reverend Mack Williams, a General Baptist missionary to Micronesia (specifically assigned as Pastor of the Saipan Community Church from 1972 until he and his family returned to the United States in the summer of 1977), feels that "office work" has destroyed interest in the more traditional vocations, especially that of agriculture and cattle raising in the northern Marianas:

> They [the islanders] all work in the office! Here, again, it comes—I don't know if you should say "work ethic" or what—we [the Administering Authority] have built, the thinking is, that the job is to work in an office, behind a desk. And if you go out and farm, or work with the cattle, or truck patching, that this is demeaning, second class. And I do not know, we have failed here. But, in saying that we have failed, . . . I think we have been more generous, kind. I think the failing has not been intentional, but in some way we have failed, and I do not think I would have had the wisdom to have seen it ahead of time or directed it differently. . . . But, we have failed them in that we have made them think that "office work" is superior to out on the farm. I'm persuaded that most of them could make a whole lot more money if they would farm than what they do in the office.

Reverend Williams' critique of the emphasis on desk jobs, above, is shared by Micronesian officials in the Trust Territory Government as well. Ramon Rechecebei, a Palauan, and Coordinator of the Marine Resources Division in the Department of Resources and Development, sees "the main problem" as one of getting the Micronesians involved again in another traditional livelihood—*fishing*—and indicates a hopeful solution: "I would say Government is employing 7,000 Micronesians. That's a lot of people being involved. . . . So, once we reduce the Government work force, maybe it would get some good people who may be able to get into fishing business."

Stewart, mentioned earlier, was in charge of conducting the most recent census for the Trust Territory (in 1973). That census showed, among other things, that the growth in Micronesia is 3.6 percent annually. Stewart updated the 1973 census information for an article he wrote in 1976, entitled "Micronesia by the Year 2000—New Ideas." Under a heading of "Micronesia's New Government," he discussed the "large government payroll" involving both Micronesians and Americans, and concluded in his article that a solution to the population growth vis-à-vis employment opportunities must be found in the *private* sector:

> One thing seems certain, the Trust Territory Government as we have known it in the past is going to change. It is doubtful that the large government payroll, recruitment cost and fringe benefits for about 7,500 Micronesians and 725 non-Micronesians [mostly Americans] can be maintained at $31.1 million and $8.8 million, respectively, from a total grant budget of $61 million (1975) simply to manage the affairs of some 115,000 Micronesians, about half of whom live on outer islands and see little direct benefit from this payroll. Of the half [55,400] that remains in the district center where most government activity is concentrated, almost 50% of this population [or 27,700] is under the age of 17 and not now in the labor force. These young people, about 55,000 in all [in district centers and outer islands], will need jobs. It is impossible to conceive that the government will absorb them. Employment opportunities must be created in the private sector, and quickly. Investment concepts must be identified, . . . their feasibility must be documented, and attempts made to locate the financing to bring the endeavor about.[30]

Before turning to the subject of more recent efforts to provide Micronesians with employment opportunities through the private sector, including foreign investment possibilities, the attention here is focused on the development of a *majority* Micronesian stockholder endeavor which began in 1968: Air Micronesia, Inc.

THE ADVENT OF "AIR MIKE"

Transportation in Micronesia was the gravest immediate problem after the Naval Administration departed in 1951. The question of what could be done to *replace* the Navy's vessels and aircraft to meet the needs of the incoming Interior Department's Administering Authority, as well as those of the islanders spread over some three million square miles of the central and western Pacific, demanded a workable program. Interior's resolution of that problem was to recommend to President Truman (in 1951) that "seven naval vessels . . . and four Navy amphibious planes (PBY-5A's) [be] under contract with private firms." This plan was approved, with contracts awarded to two airlines: Pacific Micronesian Line (a subsidiary of Pacific Far East Line) and Transocean Air Lines.[31]

By 1954, the Trust Territory Government was still referring to transportation in general as "a difficult problem," and sought an Air Force "loan" of three SA-16 Albatross aircraft (also amphibious) to replace the above four Navy planes, which, by that time, "could not be continued in use without major and expensive repairs." After modifications on the SA-16 (adapting these planes for civilian use), the Civil Aeronautics Board (CAB) issued a certification for the use of those Air Force planes in Micronesia.[32]

Some of the longtime U.S. officials in the Trust Territory Government recall the "old days" in which some "close calls" were made in the PBY-5A and SA-16 landings. Possibly the *most* air miles logged in Micronesia to date are attributable to J. Boyd Mackenzie, whose air travel in those islands began in 1954. Mackenzie's experiences include a flight in 1959 with his bride of two days aboard an SA-16, when that plane lost *both* engines and the pilot dropped the aircraft from 5,000 feet to 150 feet. He recalls that flight originated in Guam and was headed for Truk:

> The pilot was able to get one engine restarted, and we turned back for Guam. . . . We began throwing things overboard to lighten the plane. At that time also on board the plane was the High Commissioner, Delmas Nucker, and . . . John Spivey, the Executive Officer. . . . Everything we owned went overboard, including the empty seats. . . . But we still could not get high enough to land at the airstrip at Guam, so we tried to make a water landing in Apra Harbor. . . . Upon our landing, just as we touched water, we lost the good engine, and a tugboat had to tow the plane into the harbor itself.

Other rather unnerving experiences for MacKenzie in amphibious planes include an engine catching on fire on a takeoff from Kwajalein; a number of takeoffs from lagoons in complete darkness ("not knowing where we were or if we were going to end up on the reef"); losing the cowling off an engine while in flight; "and taking off from Ponape once . . . [when they] made four tries before finally getting off the water." However, Mackenzie also was severely injured in one crash (in 1961): "While landing in Palau, the plane [a SA-16 with 15 passengers aboard] . . . crashed, and . . . I was badly injured with a fractured back. I was flown from Palau to the Naval Hospital [on Guam] in a cast, [where] . . . I spent three months."[33]

By 1964, air transportation in the Trust Territory consisted of the following: "Service three times a week to Saipan by a 57-passenger DC-4 aircraft; once a week by SA-16 aircraft from Guam to Yap, Palau, Truk, Ponape, and Majuro; and an average of two DC-4 flights per month from Guam to Yap-Angaur in Palau and from Guam to Truk-Majuro." Additionally, "as in the past, emergency flights for medical and other reasons are made between outlying islands and district centers."[34] Others who recall "the old days" of amphibious air travel include Michael F. Caldwell, now an official at the University of Guam: "When I first traveled in Micronesia [in the early 1960s], it was by [a] 16-passenger sea plane which sometimes flew and sometimes didn't, depending on the occasion."³⁵ David S. Robbins, then an American high school student from Massachusetts (and the son of the first Legislative Counsel in Micronesia), first toured the islands in 1965. His appreciation for the later (1968) advent of Air Micronesia and jet travel is summed up in one sentence: "Well, all I can say is, 'Thank God that the SA-16 is gone!' "³⁶

The Congress of Micronesia's first Legislative Counsel, Professor Robbins, told an audience in 1967 that the matter of "bumping" on air flights in the islands was a rather *commonplace* problem for the Trust Territory Government personnel in the years immediately preceding Air Micronesia's appearance:

> Important events such as the travels of U.S. congressional parties and Trusteeship Council visiting missions strain the plane schedules [in 1967 and earlier] and require that they be revamped. [For instance,] a male nurse from the Marshall Islands who had taken a child to the Naval hospital in Guam for surgery and whose patient died en route might be "bumped" repeatedly in attempting to return home on the weekly flight. Or moving from the Marshalls or Ponape, an officer of junior grade employed at the High Commissioner's Headquarters, on Saipan, might be away from his job an inordinate amount of time because he was either "bumped" before he started or "bumped" at the crowded and water-short administrative center of Truk.³⁷

Reverend Henry Dykema, Pastor of the Faith Presbyterian Reformed Church, in East Agana, Guam, who first came to the western Pacific in 1965, has traveled extensively throughout the islands of Micronesia. When asked to comment on the "basic difference" between air transportation as provided by Pan American Airways (Pan Am) during 1965-68 vis-à-vis the later Air Micronesia service (from 1968), Reverend Dykema says: "I think [the basic difference was] the quality of the service and the frequency of service. . . . I just feel that Pan Am was not as deeply interested in the needs of the people as Air Mike [Micronesia] is. I think they [Pan Am] were in there more for the economics of it." Reverend Dykema qualifies the above view on Pan Am by adding: "It must be recognized that the airports have been significantly improved since Pan Am serviced them [the islands] and Air Mike today is able to use a better plane, providing a better service than what Pan Am could in those days using the SA-16's, for example, in Ponape, having to land in the water."

The Congress of Micronesia's Senate Interim Committee, which, along with a counterpart committee from the House of Representatives, toured the Trust Territory in early 1967 to check, among other factors, on the "economic needs" of the islanders, stressed that "air transportation," as an "essential facility" or service in the encouragement of "tourism," was *inadequate*—especially as that committee considered tourism's potentiality as "a major source of income" for those islands. The report which those Micronesian legislators prepared also critiqued the Trust Territory's air service—stating that "the present aircraft and attendant equipment are old, slow, outmoded and insufficient for tourists needs—and made *four* recommendations for the Congress of Micronesia to ponder:

> [First,] explore possibilities of greater frequency of air service to each of the districts;
> [Second,] accelerate airfield construction in Ponape;
> [Third,] replace present air fleet with more modern aircraft; [and
> Fourth,] extend and resurface existing runways and install lights and other necessary accessories.[38]

The 1967 U.N. Visiting Mission, which toured Micronesia almost on the heels of the Senate and House Interim Committees, mentioned above, was quite *negative* in its appraisal of "air services" for the Trust Territory, including the requirement for *all* tourists to enter Micronesia *only* through Guam:

> The Trust Territory air service which is operated under contract by Pan American Airways using aircraft provided by the Trust Territory Government, comprises two DC-4s on its main routes and two SA-16 amphibians to serve Ponape and certain smaller islands. The services provided are neither sufficient nor sufficiently regular and there is a requirement for improved air services.
> At present [in 1967], any traveller to the Trust Territory has to enter through Guam. The Nathan Report [in 1966] notes that an air traveller from the United States visiting the Marshall Islands would be flying 7,200 miles more than would be necessary if direct services to the Marshall Islands from Hawaii were available. Tourists do not like to travel the same route twice if it is as long as this, and this would be avoided if Majuro airport could be used for flights into and out of the Trust Territory.[39]

High Commissioner Norwood, in his annual appearance before the U.N. Trusteeship Council in May, 1968, reminded that body that the previous year, following his earlier meetings in New York, he had flown back to Guam mostly "by jet aircraft; but when I arrived on the island of Guam, the then threshold of Micronesia, I transferred to a DC-4 propeller driven aircraft to re-enter the slower tempo of Micronesian life and progress." Norwood continued:

> This year [1968], when these [U.N.] meetings are completed, I expect to return by jet aircraft all the way. I shall be flying from Honolulu, Hawaii, to Majuro, in the Eastern Carolines, by way of Johnston Island. And if I choose to do so, I could continue on through Micronesia to Okinawa, and proceed from there to major cities of the Far East.[40]

"To Promote Economic Advancement and Self-Sufficiency . . ."

Norwood then outlined for the U.N. Trusteeship Council the arrangements for "new commercial jet air services" in the Trust Territory that year, to be provided by Continental Airlines. A key feature in Continental replacing Pan Am was "Micronesian involvement in the ownership and operation of Air Micronesia, Inc. The airline is owned 31 percent by Continental Airlines, 20 percent by Aloha Airlines from Hawaii, and 49 percent by the United Micronesia Development Association [UMDA]." Two other aspects in this contract with Continental Airlines were a "training program for Micronesian personnel" to work in Air Mike's operation and the "construction of six hotels by Continental, one in each district."[41]

In retrospect, *modifications* were necessary in the above contractual arrangements between the Trust Territory Government and Air Micronesia, Inc., which was begun as a subsidiary of Continental Airlines. First, the ownership shares have shifted in *favor* of Micronesian involvement so that, by mid-1977, UMDA held "60 percent, and Continental and Aloha Airlines [owned] . . . 30 and 10 percent of the shares, respectively. Continental, in turn, owns 32 percent of the stock in UMDA." Second, the initial requirement to build *six* Continental luxury hotels in the Trust Territory was reduced to *three* when the districts of Yap, Ponape, and the Marshalls each, separately, refused to approve Continental's plans for such structures. (The three hotels built during the period from 1968-77 by Continental are: on Truk and Palau [56 rooms each], and on Saipan [185 rooms], each being fully air-conditioned. The author heard that the Palau hotel was offered for sale by Continental in 1976 due to declining tourism in that district.)[42]

Without exception, everyone with whom this writer spoke in the fall of 1976 was in agreement that the advent of "Air Mike," as Air Micronesia is nicknamed, has been a "plus" in the Administering Authority's efforts to bring the islanders along the path to self-sufficiency. William D. Jackson, Program Development Officer in the Community Development Division of the Trust Territory Government, who arrived in Micronesia in 1968, articulates the unanimous view apparently held by officials in the islands: "I think that [Air Micronesia's] operation has done wonders. It may not be first class all the way, but they've taken the local people and put them in [the operation] at the very beginning."

Alex P. Luzama, a Ponapean, and the highest ranking islander in the Air Mike operation to date (as Regional Service Supervisor, one of two such positions directly under the American General Manager, Gene D. Hassing), is the best example of a Micronesian beginning at the bottom (handling baggage on the ramp at the old Saipan airport) and rising to an executive management position. Luzama, whose first job after finishing junior high school in Ponape was to work for an American official at the agricultural station on the island of Ponape, was *nonpaying*—almost. For eight weeks during 1962-63, when no other work could be found, he was a general cleanup boy at that former Japanese facility. His duties might include cutting the grass with his machete, sweeping the office, or painting. "Little things," as Luzama recalls. "Every 4:30 [P.M.], when everybody's going, my boss would call me in and say, 'Well,' (he'll give me a little box [of C-rations], and say:) 'this is the pay what you do.' And I went home, and I was very happy because I've done something, you know, I get paid for." After that initial apprenticeship, Luzama was paid 17¢ an hour. His second job—in the Ponape District Finance Office —paid him 33¢ an hour. When his mother moved to Saipan in order to continue her job as domestic help to an American family, Alex followed her. He applied for a job at the Trust Territory Government headquarters on Capitol Hill, passed the general education test and, although he could not type, was assigned to the Communications Headquarters Radio Room. Luzama truthfully told his U.S. supervisor of the typing inability, with the latter replying: "Well, try!" His salary at first was between 42-47¢ per hour, considerably higher than the salary he left in Ponape. Within four years (by 1968), he was earning 92¢ an hour (or, about $157 per month).

At that latter point, in May, 1968, Air Mike made its inaugural flight to Saipan. Interested in "new challenges," Luzama accepted a position to be Chief of Communications for that new airlines on Saipan, handling the teletype and radio operation. When Luzama informed his American supervisor (John Welch) on Capitol Hill of his intended job switching, he recalls Welch advising him to remain with the Government: "Well, I don't think it's good for you to work with the private industries," Luzama recalls him saying. "I think you should stay with the Government, because you have been working with us here. . . . Your work is very good, and I want you to stay." Ironically, when Luzama reported to Air Mike 30 days later to begin his new job, his boss, Jerry Harrington (now Reservations Supervisor for Continental Airlines in Honolulu), sadly told him that the "teletype equipment" had been taken away because it was not functioning properly, and offered Luzama an alternative job: "Maybe we can start you on the ramp, loading cargo and baggage." Luzama replied: "I don't mind." Thus, he took a cut in pay ($135 a month to start with Air Mike) to spend three months on the ramp, followed by office duties, training conducted by Trans World Airlines (TWA) on Okinawa, and assignment as Assistant Station Manager (1970-75) and his present responsibilities as Regional Service Supervisor in the Western District (which includes the northern Marianas, Palau, and Yap areas). His most recent duties are to "train the employees in ticketing, reservations, cargo handling, other related, like handling of restricted articles and customer service, and also work[ing] with the managers—train the managers in managing their employees." (The other Regional Service Manager—for the Eastern District—is an American.)

Hassing, the General Manager of Air Mike, says that, "of the total of 225 employees assigned to the Air Micronesia operation, approximately 75 of those are actually Continental Airlines employes, on loan to Air Micronesia." That means 67 percent of the employees in Air Mike are islanders. Hassing believes that, by 1978, the total number of "expatriates" (mainly Americans—although some Japanese are employed in Guam and Saipan as ticket counter clerks to service tourists coming from Japan) may be as low as 55-60: "We're constantly evaluating jobs that are presently filled by Continental employees to determine if there are any Micronesians that are qualified to handle those.... Just three years ago, we had well over 100 Continental people out here, and now we're down to 75, and I perceive within the next two years, we'll probably reduce it another 15 or 20 people."

Has Air Mike been active in preparing islanders through more formal schooling than on-the-job training? Hassing recounts that his company has sponsored Micronesians from throughout the Trust Territory in two-year courses at the University of Guam, with about a third of them still with Air Mike:

> We have several employees who are on scholarship program at the University of Guam for two years. The company went out to the districts and selected candidates and put them on scholarships through school, and upon graduation we didn't guarantee them jobs, but we offered them the first priority of jobs that were available. And I think we had, initially, 12 students, and seven of them finished the two years. And I believe five of them are still working for us. Three of them are now station managers. As far as going beyond that into training, maybe helping a Micronesian to college for obtaining a business degree, it's a possibility. We really haven't focused in on that.

Luzama recalls another Air Mike-sponsored training program in 1974 that was unsuccessful. He blames the districts for a "poor screening" of those candidates who were nominated to become mechanics for the airlines: "When they went to school [in Guam], they just didn't make it —except one Palauan that I know. One Palauan that made it."

How efficient have Air Mike's Boeing 727 jet flights and the older DC-6AB aircraft (until phased out in 1974) been over the years since 1968? Dennis L. Duncan, of the Asia Division of the Bank of America, whose travel in Micronesia dates back to 1969, feels that Air Mike "has done an excellent job," and he indicates why he holds that view:

> I can only praise Air Mike as an employer who also operates in Micronesia. I think Air Mike has done an excellent job. That may not be shared by everyone, but their service is as regular as can be expected with

the facilities that they have and the distances that are involved. The pilots are outstanding, I think. They're really super people. The mechanics can repair the aircraft with baling wire, it seems like, and get it back up in the air. While I can't comment intelligently on their safety record, I'm pleased as pink to fly on Air Mike. It's always a white knuckle landing because of the crushed coral runways . . . in Truk and Ponape. The new airports in Majuro and Saipan are outstanding. But, outside of those [latter] two, it's barnstorming, I'm sure.

Air Micronesia's five-year contract with the Trust Territory Government expired in 1973. In the three years prior to that, politics became prominent in the Civil Aeronautics Board (CAB) over *which* airline—Air Mike or Pan Am—should be the "principal air carrier" in the Trust Territory after May, 1973. Robert L. Park, the "hearing examiner" (and presently the Chief Administrative Law Judge for the CAB), felt strongly that Continental/Air Micronesia ought to "be awarded the authority to conduct air services to, from and within the Trust Territory." The CAB, however, by a three-to-two vote, *declined* to heed Park's advice: accordingly, President Nixon was asked by the CAB to grant the air routes to Pan Am, which, as mentioned earlier, had operated in Micronesia prior to 1968. Fortunately for Air Mike, President Nixon requested the CAB to study the matter further. One year later, in 1971, the CAB changed its mind and favored Air Mike, stating that, by comparison, the proposed plans by both Pan Am and Northwest Airlines "could not or would not provide adequate air service to the Trust Territory," and concluded that the plan by Continental/Air Micronesia "is clearly superior, . . . [and] holds out the best promise for the rapid and effective development of a self-sufficient, locally oriented, and viable pattern of inter-island air service." The CAB also acknowledged that testimony was received from the Departments of State, Justice, and Interior (the Department of Transportation abstaining), each favoring Air Mike's continuance in the Trust Territory. Thus, the CAB recognized, in its opinion of May 4, 1971, that "no agency or department of government urges selection of any other carrier" than Air Mike to continue the franchise due to expire in 1973.[43]

How were the Micronesians reacting during the same time that Air Mike and Pan Am were facing a showdown in Washington, D.C., over the contract for the Trust Territory's air service after 1973? One of the legislators, Senator Tosiwo Nakayama, of Truk, stated in an interview with Micronesian News Service (an organ of the Trust Territory Government) that he had written to President Nixon in May, 1970, imploring the American Chief Executive to "support" Air Mike's bid. After citing the number of stockholders from the Truk District who had joined the UMDA (i.e., 514 invested $56,210), with the understanding that they

"*To Promote Economic Advancement and Self-Sufficiency . . .*"

were participating in an airline which would "become the internal airline for the Trust Territory," Senator Nakayama concluded:

> To people who earned their small investments [in UMDA] under difficulty—for many, their only money income from copra production which barely earns 10 cents per hour—the dissolution of Air Micronesia will mean a great financial loss. Great as this financial loss would be, the loss of the opportunity, in partnership with Americans, to develop their own air industry is, in my opinion, an even greater ultimate loss.[44]

The support of the Congress of Micronesia was quite strong in favor of Air Mike, although one representative from the Marshalls, Ataji L. Balos, told this writer in the summer of 1970 that he personally would like to see *two* U.S. airlines in Micronesia, that the "competition" between, say, Continental and Pan American, might be *desirable* from the islanders' standpoint. Thus, the Third Congress of Micronesia in its regular session of 1970 passed a resolution (H.J. Res. 76) in which it was "resolved by the House, . . . the Senate concurring, that the [CAB], with the approval of the [U.S.] President, . . . [be] requested to issue a certificate of public convenience and necessity to Continental/Air Micronesia."

Air Mike does *not* have an "exclusive franchise" in the Trust Territory. Elizabeth Udui, Chief of the Foreign Investment Branch in the Department of Resources and Development of the Trust Territory Government, says that Air Mike did have such an arrangement until 1974; however, since then, air service "has been under [the CAB], so they [the CAB] give out the permits" to airlines. Air Mike now has a "permanent permit" to operate in the Trust Territory.

TOURISM'S SUCCESS STILL DEPENDENT ON AIR MIKE

Tourism in the Trust Territory surpassed copra as the largest "export income earner" by 1971 and is referred to as Micronesia's "invisible export" (the earnings therefrom totaling close to $2 million and employing more than 500 islanders in 1976, excluding the figures for the northern Marianas[45]), and relies heavily on the operation of Air Mike's three weekly jet flights from and to Honolulu, in addition to daily flights among the districts by Air Mike's three Boeing 727s. An event in mid-1976 was to give momentary encouragement to the tourist industry in Micronesia; another, in the fall of that year, was to test the mettle of Air Mike's pilot corps at a time when the parent Continental Airlines experienced its first pilot strike in that company's 42-year history.

Regarding the "momentary encouragement," such came on June 24,

1976, when President Ford approved the CAB's award to Continental/Air Micronesia of "authority to provide the first direct U.S.-flag service between Saipan . . . and points in Japan."[46] The President of Air Micronesia, Donald L. Beck, and the then Vice President and General Manager, Barrie G. Duggan, in a "To the Stockholders" letter dated July 1, 1976 (in the *Annual Report* of 1975 for Air Mike, which was not released until mid-1976), referred to Ford's "route approval" between Saipan and Japan as "the most important day for your air service since operations were begun more than eight years ago. . . . The award is effective August 28, 1976, and Continental/Air Micronesia will begin service as soon as possible."[47] Unfortunately, the "as soon as possible" flight service between those two areas was still in limbo by mid-1977 and may not be inaugurated until 1978, if then. A number of sources in the Tokyo area told this writer in the fall of 1976 that the Japanese Diet (the national congress) would not approve *another* American airline to have landing rights at Haneda, Tokyo's international airport barely 20 minutes by rapid transit to the downtown area. The Japanese Government's refusal to permit Continental/Air Micronesia to land at Haneda Airport is mainly due to the already congested nature at that facility; also, two U.S. flag ships already land there (Pan Am and Northwest Orient).

The Diet is expected to grant approval to Continental/Air Micronesia to land at Narita Airport, in the neighboring prefecture (county) of Chiba, when this airport is completed; however, Narita is a commuting distance of at least *two* hours by train, possibly three to three and a half by car, to Tokyo. Robert S. Webb, an American official in the Hitachi Zosen CBI Ltd., in Tokyo, says that the Narita Airport facility has been "sitting completed for three years except for utilities and fuel, and they'll have to resurface the runways" before it is ready for service. In a follow-up comment through a personal letter to the author in the spring of 1977, Webb reiterates the expected delay for Narita's opening, and comments on demonstrations by environmental groups opposed to another airport being used due to the pollution problems: "The demonstrations continue . . . [but] it appears that the auxiliary work for the facility also continues. Prime Minister Fukuda indicated, when he took office [in December, 1976], that the Narita Airport would open in the third quarter of [1977]. . . . He later modified that statement to the first quarter of 1978. The airline people feel that it will be at least the end of 1978 before Narita is operable." Hassing, in a personal letter to this writer in June, 1977, is more optimistic as to when Continental/Air Micronesia flights will be approved to land in Japan:

> In regard to the service between Saipan/Tokyo, there still has not been a satisfactory agreement reached between Japan and United States. The Japanese Government has agreed to allow Air Micronesia to start service

"*To Promote Economic Advancement and Self-Sufficiency* . . ." 139

on a temporary authority which will expire on December 31, 1977. The U.S. and Continental/Air Micronesia find this totally unacceptable since it would not be practical to gear up an operation for a temporary service. The Japanese Government will not give any assurance that a temporary authority would be converted to permanent authority at the end of [1977]. . . . Consequently, the negotiation is still going on. We're very optimistic that an agreement will be reached within the very near future that would allow us to commence a full schedule of flights on a permanent basis in the late summer or early fall of 1977.

(Not mentioned by Hassing in the above observation is that the question of "air routes" is part of a *larger* problem between the U.S. and Japan, including Japanese demands for landing rights in such cities as Chicago. This problem will be discussed in chapter 5.)

The "testing of the mettle" of Air Mike's pilots occurred during October 23-December 11, 1976, when, as mentioned earlier, Continental Airlines was struck by its pilots' union for the first time. The points of contention by that union are not as important here as the response of those pilots assigned to fly Air Mike's three jets. Hassing outlines the "strike demands" as follows. "Higher wages, reduced working hours, and [an attempt] . . . to tell management how the airline should be staffed as far as pilot staffing is concerned." He recalls that the company had met, prior to the strike, the first demand: the "wage increases"; but Continental felt that the questions of "reduced working hours" and "working conditions" were financially unfeasible. How did the Air Mike pilots respond? Hassing indicated their cooperative attitude—even as 99 percent of the other Continental pilots voted to strike—in the following letter of June, 1977:

> The pilot strike did have a significant financial impact on Air Micronesia. The final agreement reached was a compromise on both the part of the company and the pilot's union. We [Air Mike] did suffer some loss of revenue during the strike, even though Air Micronesia continued to operate, due to a 33% reduction in service [while Continental was *totally* shut down]. However, due to the fact that *the [Air Mike] pilots volunteered to keep the airline operating* prevented a major setback in development and growth of the young airline. The most significant impact of this new contract is the requirement to add three additional pilots to fly the same number of hours that were being flown prior to the strike at an annual added cost of approximately $300,000. (Italics mine.)

Financially speaking, while Air Mike's flights have helped make tourism the leading "export" of the Trust Territory, the airline, itself, experienced a $10.5 million loss in its first eight years of operation (1968-76), which was somewhat more than anticipated. Hassing recalls that, "in 1975, . . . we did break even for the first [time]. . . . And [1976] appears as though it could have been a break-even year, if not a small profit year, except for . . . [the] strike situation." Other reasons for earlier deficit operations by Air Mike? The main one was the energy crisis of 1973, which, in turn, affected fuel costs and necessitated numerous fare increases. Thus, it costs *more* to fly Air Mike one way from Guam to Koror, Palau (714 miles) than to travel from Guam to Tokyo (a distance of 1,300 miles) via Pan Am, Japan Airline (JAL), or some other foreign carrier.

In summary, the role of Air Micronesia, Inc., is to furnish the Trust Territory, under a permanent permit from the CAB, adequate air transportation. In addition, Hassing observes that Air Mike's plans are to "help develop the Micronesians," which is seen in part by the formation of UMDA as the *major* stockholder, and to turn over, eventually, the management of the airline to the islanders:

> Continental Airlines has made a commitment to the people of Micronesia and the Board of Directors of Air Micronesia [which includes six islanders among its 13 members], that we intend to turn the airline over to the people of Micronesia some day, to be operated by themselves, on their own, . . . without being on a subsidy from Continental Airlines. . . . Air Micronesia will probably need technical support [from Continental] for many, many years to come in the area of engineering, pilots, pilot training, airplane financing, and so on. But, as far as the management of the company, our goal is to turn it over to the [Micronesian] people that have been hired by Air Micronesia and trained by Continental Airlines to run the airline.

AFTER TOURISM, WHAT?

As discussed earlier in this chapter, tourists to the Trust Territory principally have visited the northern Marianas, with only some 25 percent venturing on to other districts. Since the interim Government of the Northern Marianas was established in April, 1976, the statistics on tourists in Micronesia for 1976 omit the northern Marianas. Thus, High Commissioner Winkel told the U.N. Trusteeship Council in June, 1977, that, without the Marianas, "there were 17,713 visitors to five of the six districts (excluding Kosrae) of Micronesia in 1976. The [tourism] industry is starting out bright for this year [1977] with an estimated 27 percent increase . . . [in] the first quarter of 1977 as compared to the same period last year." Winkel went on to report that "there are 29 hotels in five of the six districts [the new district of Kosrae having none] with some 450 rooms. . . . Twenty-six of these 29 hotels are Micronesian owned and 23 have Micronesian managers. Unlike . . . many other parts of the Pacific, tourism development in the Trust Territory largely is in the hands of local entrepreneurs."[48]

Under the "decentralization" efforts of the Trust Territory Govern-

"*To Promote Economic Advancement and Self-Sufficiency . . .*" 141

ment, by which the six administrative districts are given wide latitude to make their own decisions in matters respecting their home islands, the Office of Tourism in the Department of Resources and Development, headed by Mike Ashman, has attempted to encourage and assist in the setting up of "tourist commissions" throughout Micronesia. Have Ashman and his assistant, Ihlen Joseph, a Ponapean, been successful in this endeavor? Ihlen recalls "mixed results," with a negative response from the Marshalls and Yap regarding tourism in general:

> When the [Trust Territory] Government created this Office [of Tourism] about six years ago, Mike Ashman was selected and one of his main objectives was to establish a tourist commission in each of the districts. We finally got every district to have a tourist commission which, in their hands, rests the development of tourism at their own pace. This commission [in each district] will be responsible for laws and regulations—everything concerning tourism development. We got every district to have a tourist commission. But, the weakest district that we can see now is Marshalls. They have a tourist commission which has been inactive for three years now. . . . And second to that is Yap.

Surprisingly, the Office of Tourism on Capitol Hill does *not* become involved in developing "tour packages" with either Air Mike, Pan Am (which has direct flights from Honolulu and Tokyo to Guam), or JAL. Again, Ihlen repeats the "decentralization" theme in that regard: "The development of tourism . . . rests within the district. We [in the Office of Tourism] print, independently, our travel guides, certain issues within our limited budget. We actually don't put together any kind of [tour] package. . . . We left that to the private sectors, especially the airline[s]."

The "limited budget" for Ashman's two-man headquarters office is about $60,000 annually. Ashman and Ihlen spend about 35 percent of their time traveling to the districts, or other areas (such as Tonga or the west coast of the U.S.) to glean or exchange ideas. Ashman did invite one of the chapters of the Pacific Area Travel Association (PATA) to hold an "out-of-the-country seminar" in Micronesia during late 1976 at that chapter's own expense, to acquaint those travel agents from Vancouver, San Francisco, and Los Angeles with the districts of Yap, Palau, an Truk (in addition to a visit to Saipan). Continental's hotels in Micronesia also cooperated with the PATA chapter in that visit to the Trust Territory.

The primary market for tourists to Micronesia is Japan. Ihlen estimates that, for 1976, about 53 percent of the vacationers were Japanese. In earlier years, the Americans were predominant. Other than Saipan, in the northern Marianas, the second choice of Japanese tourists is the Truk Lagoon, with its treasure of sunken war vessels from World War II attracting deep sea divers. Palau also has an attraction, having been the headquarters under the Japanese Mandate Period. Ponape and the Marshalls are minimal in attracting tourists, and Kosrae (the newest of the six districts) has yet to build its first hotel. Yap remains indifferent to the tourist trade, although a pleasant place to visit. (See chapter 5 for a further discussion of Japanese interests in the islands.)

What endeavors have been put forth by the Administering Authority to *augment* the "invisible export" of tourism since the late 1960s? In the view of two American anthropologists, very little at all. They believe that "the greatest single deficiency" in the United States' plans for a Micronesian nation-state is "the lack of economic development, particularly development utilizing local markets and establishing functional interdependency between the various island districts." Hughes and Lingenfelter thus concluded: "The tons of fish, rice, and sugar imported each year from Japan, Australia, and the United States might just as easily be produced and marketed within the Territory itself. The sad fact is that almost nothing is produced within the Territory for marketing in the other districts."[49]

If the above criticism by the two anthropologists, who, individually, spent a number of years researching in the districts of Micronesia, is correct, then the disturbing query must be made: *Where* has all the money gone which the U.S. Congress has appropriated since 1947, augmented to a considerable extent by federal grants-in-aid and other sources of funding? Zeder answered *part* of that spending question when he referred to the over $5 million worth of "studies" made in Micronesia between 1946-73. Still, the Fiscal Year 1977 funding for the Trust Territory probably *exceeded* $110 million (i.e., $85 million appropriated initially by the U.S. Congress *plus* the $21 million "supplemental" payment approved in April, 1977, mentioned earlier, *plus* the various grants-in-aid programs, such as the Federal Aviation Administration [FAA] in the construction of airports throughout Micronesia). Not calculated in the estimated $110 million budget for 1977 is the assistance given by *other* American groups involved in the Trust Territory's development: the U.S. Navy (for logistical planning and coordination for the Capital Improvement Program [C.I.P.], the Peace Corps Volunteers (over 200 on an average in the islands in recent years), and the military civic actions teams (MCATs), all of which are discussed in chapter 3, following.

That the above money is pouring into Micronesia is not denied. The criticisms center on *how* such funds are spent. Roger Gale, who lived on Guam in the early 1970s, pinpoints the problem on the large annual budgets and number of Trust Territory Government jobs available to the islanders: "There's no justification for spending that kind of money. . . . That's the problem. And there's very little self-reliant growth. Fifty-eight percent of the working population worked for the Trust

"*To Promote Economic Advancement and Self-Sufficiency* . . ." 143

Territory Government until a couple of years ago, and there's very little private employment." Former DOTA Zeder agrees with Gale. In his remarks before the U.N. Trusteeship Council (in 1976), Zeder said that, to counter the approximately $100 million funding from various U.S. grants, mentioned previously, "it is estimated that [in 1976] Micronesia will generate from taxes,, tourism and exports around $17.5 million. This is an optimistic figure, and it has been somewhat misrepresented in the past." Zeder then explained to that U.N. council that the Trust Territory has actually been operating at a *deficit* in recent years:

> The fact is, that, of previously reported and hoped for revenue in the future, 33% must be immediately returned to the districts and cannot be used to support the ever-increasing [Trust Territory] government obligations. In addition, more than three million is required to fund the Congress of Micronesia and its activities ($1.7 million for congressional salaries and expenses and $1.4 million for social security and other peripheral operations). This leaves an operating deficit for one year alone of around $87 million. Over the past five years [1971-76], the operating deficit is half a billion dollars.[50]

(Zeder's replacement as DOTA, Van Cleve, did not address the 1977 U.N. session; Winkel, the new High Commissioner, did not comment on present revenue amounts specifically, concentrating instead on "future possibilities.")

Lazarus Salii acknowledges that programming in the economic sphere for Micronesia has two basic problems: "There is no work force here. The labor situation [in the islands] is bad. Small population. Not as skilled as a labor force, so they have to import [workers] from the Philippines, [and] they have to import the car[s] to Micronesia." Thomas E. Tavares, in the Department of Transportation and Communications for the Trust Territory Government, believes that the "labor shortage" in Micronesia was realized in the early 1960s, but he feels the Administering Authority approached a solution to that problem in the *wrong* manner:

> We [the Government] couldn't bring anybody in from the states except for the supervisory-type of positions, and I will say, if we did bring in people from the states—carpenters, plumbers, what have you—I think we would have accomplished a hell of a lot more than we have done in the past, whereby we would have [had] skilled people working with the local people, side by side, and they [the local islanders] would have [had] a chance to learn, or have a precedent, than we could as supervisors trying to build a project and train at the same time.

Tavares remembers that it was in 1968 when Interior informed the American officials they were responsible to *train* the Micronesians: "[This] became a reality about 1968, when we were told we would have to really train [them] . . . to take over an expatriate's-type position. . . . Previous to that, we just trained them because we needed the people to work and learn the skills so that we can accomplish our mission." Father Arnold, on Saipan, agrees with Tavares and says that "blue collar"-type Americans should have been sent to Micronesia as "examples" of what the islander youths might want to emulate:

> Many years ago, I think we [the Americans] did the wrong thing. We should have sent out blue-collared men. Because, what does a young boy [islander] have to look up to today, eh? What American has prestige on this island [of Saipan]? It's not a plumber or a carpenter or a bricklayer. They're all in the office someplace. And this is his image of America, until he goes to America, himself. But as he's growing up, that's the image that everybody has of an American. Therefore, their [the Micronesians'] whole thrust is to get a desk [white-collared] job.

(This author recalls an American in the Trust Territory telling him that a Micronesian family was "shocked" to visit in the United States and see adult males cutting lawns or adult females working as waitresses. Those activities simply did not jibe with that islander family's "stereotypes" of typical Americans, based on what is found in the Trust Territory, where hundreds of Americans hold "white collar" positions as officials.)

Another observation by Tavares centers on the "transferring" of appropriated funds from a designated project to some other, or others, which was/were *unfunded* at that time. As an example, he cites appropriations earmarked for the "road systems" in Micronesia: "Many times, [funding] was put into the [roads] project, and before the project has started, money was taken out of the road system and put into a hospital project or it worked like a 'pork barrel' type of [action]. . . ." Wally Kluver, Manager of the Bank of Hawaii's Ponape Branch, and a longtime observer in Micronesia (since 1970), gives a more specific example of the "siphoning off" of funds from one approved project and the use— or misuse—of such funds in other areas. Recalling his surprise upon returning to Ponape after nearly seven years (in late 1976), Kluver says: "What's really been appalling to me out here is the amount of money that we've pumped into various programs and how it's been siphoned off, misused, stolen, completely misappropriated, and nothing accomplished. On the streets of Ponape [Island], the roads still haven't been paved. No sidewalks. I expected . . . [to see] some progress. I don't see any progress at all in seven years. I see regression." (Inasmuch as Ponape Island has been designated as the future capital of Micronesia, to be occupied by the headquarters in 1981 at the earliest, some improvements in the roads should be forthcoming. The Congress of Micronesia in 1977

"*To Promote Economic Advancement and Self-Sufficiency...*"   145

made its move to Ponape, occupying the former Kasalelia Inn Hotel facility.)

A second American banker, George Burns, at the Bank of America on Saipan, whose experiences in the Pacific date back 20 years, feels that the islanders are "waiting for the Government to do everything for them." He blames part of that dependency on the "Government payroll" emphasis at the sacrifice of growth in the "private sector":

> I think they've [the islanders have] been kind of lulled into a few things here, expecting the Government to do too much, I think, rather than doing some on their own. Particularly, the private sector in the economy here [on Saipan]: there's very limited—other than the T.T. Government here—employment, gainful employment outside of the Government. And, basically, the whole economy is based on the Government payroll here, that's been created on Capitol Hill. And you're going to have to look in the private sector to create something to replace this over the next period of years, and not to be so dependent on a Government payroll.

Former Senator Amaraich, a Trukese, feels that there was *never* "any systematic plan" for the economic development of Micronesia by the Administering Authority. He notes that "experts would be sent out" to the islands, possibly in the agricultural or fisheries areas, "but they had no plans to follow." Thus, Amaraich says, "when their contracts would be finished, Micronesia would find itself with, say, a project in chicken raising or banana growing, which would be dropped when the experts left." Father Hugh F. Costigan, S.J., at the Ponape Agriculture and Trade School (PATS), and a missionary in Micronesia for 30 years, sees the same lack of planning as noted by Amaraich in the above, and adds: "We [the Trust Territory] are always importing too much. The main thrust of our agricultural industry is to produce the commodities we need in our daily life for which we have the natural resources but through underdevelopment we are still forced to import from foreign countries."

Maynard Neas expresses disappointment that the "Nathan Report" of 1966 did not grasp a number of points he feels crucial to the economic growth in Micronesia. Asked to "make an analysis" of that report at the request of the then Director of the Department of Resources and Development in the Trust Territory Government, Paul Windsor, Neas' response was: "My best recommendation right now [in 1966] is to give it [the Nation Report] back to them and tell them to do it right!" Neas adds that he believed that report "was a bunch of words, but it didn't say anything. . . . It was, I guess, the best that they could do, but it simply didn't meet what I had in mind." Neas accordingly outlines the *four* recommendations he would have made if writing that 1966 economic study of the Nathan team:

[*First,*] I was looking . . . for [a recommendation] that would establish . . . some kind of group that would explore the world for people . . . that have got some kind of scholarly work going and that this [the Trust Territory] is the best place to do it. . . . I've always advocated that. Let's find these people that are interested in the islands of the Pacific, and make known to them what kind of places of study and subjects that are available [in Micronesia]. In other words, here we'll treat you, we'll give you visas, and we'll give you everything except money. We want you to come up and spend some money, . . . to help our economy and also to help us study this thing [the economic needs]. . . . Our scholars need the area for their study.

[*Second,*] to give [Micronesia] . . . something like Hong Kong had, a free port type of thing.

[*Third,*] tax incentives. Companies want to locate their corporate offices here and get a tax shelter, and occasionally make a lot of jobs—and they're 20th century jobs, not going back 100 years ago.

[*Finally,*] find a way to put a whole atoll to work just like the United States did with Eniwetok and Bikini [in the Marshalls], . . . for peaceful uses.

EDLF: THE "IDEAL" FAILS THE TEST

The history behind the now defunct Economic Development Loan Fund (EDLF) dates to 1956, when a "revolving fund" was established through annual appropriations acts of the U.S. Congress, to be used "for loans to locally-owned trading companies for expansion and other development purposes." In 1964, some $368,000 was available for such loans in that fund. During the Eighty-seventh and Eighty-eighth Congresses (1962-63), "legislation was introduced . . . for its [the revolving fund's] transfer to the Territory's General Economic Development Fund." Thus, the *Annual Report* for 1964 reviewed the establishment of the Trust Territory's Economic Development Fund (in FY 1963), which had an initial deposit of $100,000 and included two Micronesians on its loan committee. The kinds of loans made initially were of the "small scale type," for such business as the Micronesian Products Center "to set up a revolving fund for purchases of handicraft, [and] to the Palau Handicraft and Woodworkers Guild to expand operations." The EDLF in 1964 "guaranteed loans worth some $104,000 with commercial banks."[51]

Four years later (in 1968), three U.S. senators introduced a bill "to extend the provisions of the Small Business Act to the Trust Territory," and that action was followed closely by the Micronesian Senate on Saipan passing a joint resolution (S.J. Res. 6) in favor of the above American legislation. The Micronesian resolution indicated that the islanders were "in complete support" of the Congress of Micronesia's action in this regard, and that the people of the Trust Territory "consider the development of small business the single most important factor in the progress of a free economy" in Micronesia.⁵² The U.S. Congress did pass the above act. Of particular interest here is the participation of that Small Business Act *with* the EDLF, the effect being that it would thereafter be possible, through the Small Business Administration (SBA) loan program, for the SBA "in participation with the [EDLF] . . . and/or commercial banks . . . [to] lend $150,000. The SBA may guarantee a maximum of $350,000 or not more than 90% of a bank loan, whichever is less."⁵³

In August, 1976, a report entitled "The Administrative, Cultural, and Geographic Environment Influencing the Management of the Economic Development Fund in the Trust Territory of the Pacific Islands," was submitted as an addendum to the "Annual Report of the Fiscal Condition of the Economic Development Fund for the Year Ended June 30, 1975," prepared by the Chairman of the EDLF, William H. Stewart, to the then Acting High Commissioner, Peter T. Coleman. An entry on p. 19 of this addendum report indicated the following: "In May, 1969, the EDLF Board of Directors was encouraged to speed up their lending activity, and relax standards and sound lending procedures so as to reduce the rather high level funds available for loans, so that when a request to the U.S. Congress was made for additional funds, the balance available would be reduced so as to better enhance the chance of additional appropriations." That entry continued with acknowledgments that the above advice was received: "Nothing is on record to substantiate this particular activity except the loan records for that period. If such is true, it occurred many years ago [in 1969]; but the matter was recalled in the August 20th [1976] meeting by the Acting High Commissioner [Coleman] and many people in the Government who remember that period of the fund's history also testify to this fact." The entry concluded with the overall effect of granting "looser" loans: "Loans made under such pressured circumstances have certainly contributed to the high delinquency level." This writer was informed by a source in Micronesia that the above instructions of May, 1969, came from "a high official in the Department of Interior," who visited the Trust Territory Government headquarters on Capitol Hill, Saipan, that month and reportedly said to those U.S. and Micronesians assembled as the EDLF Board of Directors: "All right, now you people have a lot of money in the Economic Development Loan Fund. I want you to lend it!" When someone present replied, "Well, one of the reasons we haven't loaned the money in the past is because the loan applicants can't meet the criteria and justify a loan under prudent and reasonable qualifications," the above Interior visitor gave those assembled what was described as "a terrible tongue-lashing." The visiting official admonished them: "Forget that [i.e., the prudent and reasonable qualifications]!" In other words, the EDLF Board of Directors was *strongly* advised by Interior, in essence, to "give the money away," as the high amount of "loan delinquencies" which followed would seem to indicate.

The EDLF program was frozen in mid-1975 due to the *high* "delinquency rate" accrued. With a total of $5 million in the EDLF account (mainly from appropriations of the U.S. Congress), a total of $1.8 million in loans had been made. Of that $1.8 million, about $1,250,000 became delinquent. That is a "delinquency rate" of about *69* percent. J. Knox McConnell, President and Chief Executive Officer of the Micronesia Development Bank, who inherited the EDLF program in late 1976, refers to that lending process as "a disaster," and gives examples of the types of loans (mostly in the $6,000-$10,000 range) that "did nothing, really, for the economy" in Micronesia:

> A man would come in [to the EDLF office] and say, "I need $3,000 to start a piggery." Well, to support himself, and to get the pigs and to get the ground, and lease the ground for $3,000, there was no way that he could do something like this. So he gave up, abandoned the farm, and, as a result, the loan went bad. Same thing with the fishing vessel. An individual would come in and say, "I need $10,000 to buy a boat and an engine, and I want to fish." Economically, this just was not the way to go. As a result of it, a lot of the loans went bad.

McConnell, an experienced banker from Pennsylvania whose commission as President of the Micronesia Development Bank (MDB) in 1976 was to release the EDLF money for the use of that bank and to run the bank in "a prudent, honest, and forthright manner," does not expect that the Attorney General's Office in the Trust Territory Government, headed by Daniel J. High, will be able to recover much more than $150,000 of the $1,250,000 in delinquent accounts (or, just over 10%). Many of those delinquencies (as of late 1976) were 21, 30, or 40 months in arrears. Would the MDB make *new* loans to parties who have *delinquent* ones? McConnell's response follows:

> We're going to keep a file, and I think if they want to try to restructure that [first] loan again, I'd try to help them. . . . I'd look at them just like any other credit risk because, after all, I still think people are people, and I think they know the moral responsibility that they have. For instance, we have a project in Ponape, and it was a small hotel. It shut down. I got all the people together and talked to them, [and said:] "Here, we have a good chance of opening it [the hotel] up again, under the same people." They need a few more thousand dollars. I don't think they were completely wrong on their project. They asked for help [the first time], and never got the help. And I think it's a good, honest mistake. I'm willing to help this people. God forbid if they make the second mistake on me, because I'm just not going to tolerate [that]. But I think I sort of live by the rules that my father laid down to me—that everybody should enjoy one mistake in their life, and, you know, if it's an honest mistake.

"*To Promote Economic Advancement and Self-Sufficiency . . .*" 149

The MDB President recalls making the following statement to one of the Micronesian officials in the Trust Territory Government: "It would have been better for us to give $300 to every Micronesian as a direct grant, and forget about the loan program." He explains the *rationale* behind such a proposed grant: "This is an unusual thing. You sit down with your [loan] group, and you make a loan [of $15,000] in an hour. You decide you're going to do it. But, remember this: you make that loan in an hour, but you have to live with it, then, for 12 or 14 years."

POTENTIAL PROJECTS THROUGH THE MICRONESIA DEVELOPMENT BANK

Originally conceived as a *commercial* banking endeavor in 1972, through the Congress of Micronesia's "Bank of Micronesia Act" (which became Public Law 4C-31), such a commercial operation failed to materialize by the target date of April, 1973. J. Knox McConnell recalls that an accounting firm, Haskins and Sells, visited Micronesia and recommended that a *development* bank would have a greater impact on the economy and the islanders. The first President of the Micronesia Development Bank in 1975 was Joe Perez, of Guam. He was followed shortly thereafter (in early 1976) by McConnell, a commercial banker with 22 years' experience, and who had started two banks and several finance companies in Pennsylvania. McConnell originally was recruited by the former DOTA, Zeder, to work in the Department of Resources and Development in an effort to "promote projects" for the Trust Territory; then, as a replacement for Perez when the latter's contract was terminated.

During a series of three interviews in the fall of 1976, McConnell outlined for this writer *five* "potential projects" which the MDB would consider supporting (with the stipulation that at least *51* percent of such loans would be Micronesian involvement):

> FIRST, a *feeder airline*. Inter-island transportation, especially involving the outer islands, is needed in Micronesia. This proposal would involve a tri-lander airplane converted to carry 12 passengers and 1,000 lbs. of cargo. This could service the newest district, Kosrae (formerly Kusaie), which lacks a jet runway for Air Mike's 727's. Hopefully, Micronesians would be trained to pilot this one-person crew aircraft. Gene D. Hassing, General Manager of Air Mike, would like to see such a "feeder operation" to augment his carrier's jet service.
>
> SECOND, a *motorbike assembly plant*. Disassembled motorbikes shipped from the Benton Harbor, Michigan, area, via Chicago and Honolulu on Continental Airlines and then by Air Mike to Ponape all within a four-day period. A one-passenger motorbike might be assembled on Ponape for

$700; a two-passenger, three-wheeler, for $1,100—both prices cheaper than importing Japanese models already assembled. A $15,000 investment might be sufficient for the marketing and advertising. From this concept might spring other projects, such as the assembling of tractors or tillers, and involve general distributors throughout the Trust Territory districts.

THIRD, a *Ponape pepper industry*. A supply of the pepper grown in Ponape was shipped to Richard Bonnet, President of the American Culinary Federation in Pennsylvania and the head chef at the Oak Mont Country Club in that state. Bonnet's response: "We're presently using [Ponapean] pepper at the Oak Mont Country Club. In my professional opinion, it's truly a gourmet product, and I can assure you of my utmost cooperation in the endeavor to market Ponape pepper in the United States."

FOURTH, a *diagnostic clinic*. This might involve American doctors who would treat Japanese tourists visiting on Saipan during the summer season. Possibly housed in one of the luxury hotels on that island, a proposed name for the clinic might be the "Pacific Medical Pavilion."

FIFTH, *"The Battle of Saipan."* With current interest focused on World War II films involving events or personalities (i.e., *The Battle of Midway* and *MacArthur*) from that earlier war in the Pacific, there might be a possibility of filming this most famous battle in Micronesia. This would involve an American producer and some actors from Japan, the latter having a relatively short jet flight (some 1,300 miles) for this location. The Northern Marianas might receive 5-8% of the box office receipts and the intangible publicity as a spur to tourism.

Again, the above projects were simply those being considered as revenue-producing *possibilities* in Micronesia more recently. High Commissioner Winkel, in his June, 1977, appearance before the U.N. Trusteeship Council, referred to the Ponape pepper possibility, and others not listed above, as being researched during the 1976-77 period in attempts to attract foreign investors to Micronesia: "Prospectuses were completed for a pepper industry in Ponape, for a forty acre vegetable farm and a commercial piggery. Other projects under discussion include a soap factory to utilize oil from the coconut oil mill and a containerized transshipment facility to ship frozen fish."[54]

The Micronesia Development Bank was able to begin limited operations in late 1976 when the then DOTA, Zeder, released $500,000 of the remaining EDLF balance of $3.2 million. After the failure of the ELDF program in the past decade (with the $1,250,000 in delinquent accounts by mid-1975), the MDB President, McConnell, would not be faulted for scrutinizing development loans very carefully. "The first year, I'm going to close every loan myself," he observes. Additionally, he recruited Mike Cocchilla, an experienced American accountant in the banking community (and the holder of a master's degree), whose main duties in the Trust Territory are "to work with [islander] people who have a problem in their business. He'll be traveling in the Territory. . . . We're setting up two [field] offices: one in Truk and one in Palau. By the end of [1977], ... we will have a field office in every district."

TAXATION IN MICRONESIA: THE DECLINE AND RISE?

High Commissioner Winkel informed the U.N. Trusteeship Council in June, 1977, that plans had been laid "for assuring an effective implementation and administration of the new progressive income tax law enacted during the first regular session of the 7th Congress of Micronesia at the recommendation of the UNDP [United Nations Development Program, to be discussed shortly]."[55] Prior to the passage of a progressive income tax law by the Congress of Micronesia (Public Law 7-32), in the spring of 1977, the mentality in the Trust Territory Government, as well as among the islanders during the past three decades, had appeared to *mirror* the early views by U.S. Naval commanders discussed earlier in this chapter, that, "with respect to taxes, ... [there is] no need of any direct tax for raising the little revenue that should be required for governing the Islands."[56]

William H. Stewart, Deputy Director of the Department of Resources and Development in the Trust Territory Government, while assigned to the Economic Development Office in Honolulu during 1976-77, drafted a "listing of investment incentives" for distribution to prospective foreign investors in Micronesia. Under the heading of "Low Taxes," Stewart indicated the following attractive "tax breaks:"

—1% on gross revenue over $10,000
—3% on salaries and wages
—1.5% social security tax on covered wages matched by employer
—Low import duties on raw material
—No corporation tax
—No real estate tax
—No inventory or processing tax
—No discrimination tax on outside investment
—Rebate on import duties on business equipment
—Rebate on imported raw material when processed export

Under "Trade," Stewart listed the following inducements:

—No U.S. quotas on manufactured items
—Preferential U.S. tariff treatment
—Located within major Pacific sea lanes
—Direct shipping service to Japan, Far East, and U.S. West Coast ports

The new graduated income tax is to become effective January 1, 1978. In the meantime, there has been considerable opposition to the new tax, which is not surprising in consideration of the unbelievably *low* tax profile in the Trust Territory over the past several years. A special session of the Congress of Micronesia was to consider "proposed amendments" to the new tax law at that legislature's late-summer, 1977, gathering. If the law, as passed, remains intact, the actual "graduated income tax" would increase from the present 3-4 percent to 6-8 percent of an individual's adjusted gross income; also, the "gross receipts" tax of 1 percent would give way to 25 percent tax on "net profits."[57]

If the Micronesians continue to express their displeasure with having to pay a higher personal income tax, part of their unhappiness may be their inability to fathom the uses to which *taxes* are put, as well as the prohibitions placed on tax money. With the $100 million-plus amounts yearly pouring into the Trust Territory from the U.S. Government in recent times, the temptation must be to think there is a "bottomless well" from which Micronesia can always turn to draw more funds. One U.S. official told this writer of a member of the Congress of Micronesia in recent years who was hesitant to see that islander legislature appropriate funds for a particular project, plaintively inquiring, "Can't we [the Trust Territory Government] get the money from some American *grant* rather than spend *our* [the Congress of Micronesia's] funds?" (Italics mine.)

Another American official recalls chatting with a U.S. college-educated Micronesian department head in the Trust Territory Government at a social gathering. That Micronesian, who had lived in the United States for several years while a student, broached the topic of a recently appropriated $3 million from the U.S. Congress for "economic development." He inquired of the American, "What are we going to do with it [the $3 million], as far as development is concerned?" The American's reply, below, is instructive from a number of standpoints, the main one being that even some *key* Micronesian officials appear unaware of the use and prohibitions on U.S. tax dollars:

> Do you want R. and D. [Research and Development in the Trust Territory Government] to build a tuna fish canning plant with the $3 million the [U.S.] Government has appropriated? We can sure do it. Who's going to manage it? Are you going to manage it? Are you going to hire a high-powered fish processing manager to do it? That's fine. Who gets the revenues? The Government? Does the U.S. Government want us to use [U.S.] Congressionally appropriated money to build productive endeavors? Because we sure as hell can do it. The Congress [of Micronesia] would be very happy to have that done.

Another use of American tax revenue which has been flowing to the islands of Micronesia since the mid-1960s is from the U.S. Department of Agriculture (USDA) in the form of food stuffs. Inasmuch as most

"*To Promote Economic Advancement and Self-Sufficiency ...*"   153

Micronesians, especially in the private sector, earn less than the "poverty level" in the United States (which, in mid-1977, was a maximum "net adjusted income" of $6,804 for an American family of four),[58] such food items are distributed to them. Father Arnold, on Saipan, expects that the USDA food distribution program eventually will be reduced as the northern Marianas become a commonwealth in the next few years. Meanwhile, he feels that some of these programs are *poorly* managed in the islands, and he places part of the blame on the officials in Washington, D.C.:

> They're [the officials are] sitting back in Washington, they appoint local boys [islanders] here [on Saipan] to run them, and they really do not understand the whole situation. I see people getting USDA [foods], and I know their kids are taking care of these old people. I know that they won't starve. But, if they can get this free from the Government, more power to them! I mean, they do it, see, and I don't know what local, what level they cut off income that you're eligible to it. Before you know it, it's so low that 50 percent of the Saipanese will qualify because the wage scale is way down. Now, they can use the help, there's no doubt about it. I suppose it helps them, and you hate to see the people lose something [like that]. But whether it's really necessary or not is another problem.

Senator Borja recollects that the USDA program began in Micronesia around 1965, when farmers could not depend on their crops and needed assistance. From that start, the USDA food program spread to the schoolchildren, then others:

> [The USDA experimented or gave] it to the schools, students, and so forth, finally extend the benefits to some of the low income. And from that time, of course, the people got so used to it, with 10 years and so forth, and I do know that USDA is one of the most, let's say, people relying upon, for some of their income—either to supplement or to provide for these needy people—and I think that program has been really looking upon from the people, and any effects . . . that may effect reductions in getting some, . . . I believe the impact [of such reductions] will be pretty great on account that they're so used to it, . . . and the people has been enjoying very much, I think, as a result of this. They like very much the United States. (Laugh.)

A longtime American official, in surveying the operation of the USDA program in Micronesia, believes that, by providing canned chicken and butter to the villagers in the outer islands throughout Micronesia, "we [the Administering Authority] are making cripples out of people who have been self-sufficient since the beginning of their inhabitation of the islands. And if you give a man canned chicken and he doesn't have to fish, he will say: 'Give me a canned chicken. I don't have to go fish!

The hell with that!'" In addition to USDA foodstuffs imported at no cost to the islanders, they, in turn, use their discretionary income to spend more than $1 million on canned fish (not including frozen fish) and another $1 million on alcoholic beverages, all of which is imported for a population smaller than the size of Western Samoa (which has about 150,000).

Tokuichi Kuribayashi, a former official during the Japanese Mandate Period (see the introductory chapter), recalled in a letter to the then DOTA, Zeder, in July, 1976, that he (Kuribayashi) had been astonished to see, during a visit to Palau in 1974, that, at a party there, he looked forward "with anticipation to partake and fill myself with the tasty meat of genuine local chicken. However, what I found was meat of chicken commonly known as broiler that has been reared by integrating system. I actually did not eat any of it but partook myself of fish." Kuribayashi later asked the Palauan District Administrator, Thomas O. Remengesau, "Why is it that they [the Micronesians] do not raise chicken under more natural conditions like they did during the days of the Japanese mandate? [That is,] let the poultry roam about amongst the coconut plantations." Kuribayashi referred to his 1974 question to the Palauan District Administrator, mentioning to Zeder in the above letter: "If the poultry were raised under natural conditions [in Micronesia], I explained [to Remengesau], there will be no expenses to be incurred in construction of a fowl yard, in imported feeds, and above all, it will be possible to obtain tastier eggs, and meat." Kuribayashi also conversed and exchanged correspondence with Rev. Hugh F. Costigan, S.J., at the Ponape Agriculture and Trade School (mentioned earlier). Father Costigan told this writer, in a letter dated March, 1977, that he (Costigan) is "totally in agreement with him under certain conditions. These conditions are not always easy to meet: fairly large tracts of land, a certain amount of fencing, protection from hungry villagers, and some sort of feed and watering program." Thus, Father Costigan says that PATS has "gone more for the broiler raising under controlled conditions. Our primary objective in farm development today is to raise enough corn and other crops to supply a small feed mill and thus provide adequate protein at a reasonable price, for people to raise chickens in their backyards as a subsistence project."

Unfortunately, the role of "subsistence farming" has remained in Micronesia. The United States, meanwhile, has a virtual monopoly for importation of poultry into not only the Trust Territory but also in Eastern Samoa and Guam. In 1975, the U.S. supplied "virtually all of the 907 tons of poultry valued at $1 million imported in 1975 [into Micronesia]."[59] Imports are costly for the islanders, but locally grown items are even more so. As one Trust Territory Government official notes, "We financed poultry farms and sawmills only to have our lumber and our fresh eggs compete with imported lumber and cold-storage eggs.

Our eggs here [in the islands] run maybe $1.35 a dozen because the feed costs are so high. But they're fresh eggs. The price of cold-storage eggs from Australia was $1.00 a dozen." That same official points to the *dilemma* faced by the Trust Territory Government over imports vs. the limited local products: "Are you going to raise the tariff on imported eggs to protect your infant industry and, in effect, sort of penalize the people [the importers] for an inefficient operation [by the islanders]?" Another official indicates that he feels badly that agriculture has not been developed in the Trust Territory the way it should. Referring specifically to the situation on Saipan, he says: "They need markets in Japan. It's a shame when they have to buy fruit that comes from Ecuador when they could be growing things right here!" As an example, he refers to the new $10 million airport on Saipan and the visibility of Japanese tourists who come primarily to Guam and the northern Marianas: "Even if they [the Saipanese] had a vegetable stand at the airport, when the Japanese are leaving, they could buy our melons from Saipan for 50¢ instead of $17 [the cost of cantaloupe in Tokyo], or whatever it is, in Japan, and these could be 'certified' as free of disease."

THERE ARE SOME SUCCESSFUL ISLANDER BUSINESSMEN

Earlier in this chapter, reference was made to High Commissioner Winkel's comment that 26 of the 29 hotels in the Trust Territory are Micronesian-owned, with 23 of those managed by islanders. There are a number of other Micronesians who have been successful entrepreneurs, including those of particular note on Saipan—JoeTen, M. S. Villagomez, and Senator and Mrs. Borja. For instance, Joseph Tamag (a former senator in the Congress of Micronesia), in Yap, has done well as a store owner and contractor; F. Kazuo Asao, a wholesaler in Koror, Palau, who, for several years, also ran a popular nightclub (called "The Factory," after a better-known establishment in Los Angeles); Bob Reimers, on Majuro, in the Marshalls, whose interests involve a large wholesale and retail business; and Ponape Automotive and Marine Inc. (PAMI), a Ford Agency which is Micronesian with an American head, Gary De Broff.

The growth of credit unions in Micronesia has been quite striking since the mid-1960s. The *Annual Report* for FY 1964, for example, showed a total of 26 credit unions in the Trust Territory that year; however, only 18 of those were "chartered" (that is, operating with the official sanction of the Trust Territory Government). By 1972, there were forty-four such groups in Micronesia, having a total membership of about 10,000, or just under 10 percent of the islands' total population. Most of those credit unions were relatively small. Charles Sicard, a longtime Small Business official in the Department of Resources and Development for the Trust Territory Government, wrote in 1972 that "the future of the small credit union [in Micronesia] greatly depends on the quantity of technical assistance and leadership provided in each district; but credit unions are now very definitely a part of Micronesian life."[60] High Commissioner Winkel, in his 1977 U.N. speech, stressed the tremendous growth in the number of such credit unions, as well as the significance of cooperatives (such as the Yap Cooperative Association, discussed earlier), and the flow of money involved in small loans:

> Seventy-two cooperatives and 43 credit unions continue to serve as the backbone of many island communities. Cooperative gross sales and revenues as of March 31, 1977, are approaching 12 million dollars worth of business, a 13 per cent increase over the previous year. During the past eleven years [1966-77], over $30 million dollars have been loaned and repaid by Micronesians to their credit unions.[61]

Although agriculture has been disappointing as a revenue-producing source, an example of one cooperative attempting to encourage the local farmers to participate in a "cash crop" economy (instead of the traditional "subsistence farming" approach noted earlier by Father Costigan at PATS) is the Saipan Farmer's Market Cooperative Association (FMCA), managed since its start in 1973 by Gregorio C. Cabrera. Supported in part by an EDLF loan of $5,000 (which was reduced through *regular* repayments to only $3,400 by the fall of 1976), the FMCA showed a profit of $584 for August, 1976, with the inventory that month valued at $3,000. Cabrera's accounting continued to be handled by the Trust Territory Government's Department of Finance even after the formation of the interim Government of the Northern Marianas, in April, 1976. Cabrera points to a "logistical problem" experienced by the FMCA even with Guam only 70 air miles to the south of Saipan: "We import this feed from Hawaii and some from Australia, and some from Guam. I got the feed from Hawaii more cheap than Guam's. I don't know why. Guam is very close to Saipan, but it's very high price. And not good quality feed from Guam. I tried many times from Guam feed, but not good quality feed to the animals, chickens, like that."

WILL THE UNDP BE A "BREAKTHROUGH"?

As noted earlier, former Trukese Senator Andon Amaraich believes that there was *never* any "systematic plan" for the economic development of Micronesia by the Administration: "Experts would be sent out, but they had no plans to follow." The most recent "group of experts" sent out to the Trust Territory was a team from the United Nations in 1975. Those indi-

"To Promote Economic Advancement and Self-Sufficiency..." 157

viduals completed their surveys and submitted such as the "United Nations Development Program" (UNDP) to the Congress of Micronesia in 1976, which, in turn, incorporated the UNDP's recommendations as its own in the "Five Year Indicative Development Plan (1976-1981)," a 177-page effort. One official in the Trust Territory Government says that the Congress of Micronesia, through its various committees, "made adaptations and revisions and encroachments" on the UNDP. High Commissioner Winkel expressed the use of the UNDP by that Congress quite clearly: "The United Nations Development Programme designed [the Congress of Micronesia's] Five Year Indicative Development Plan."[62]

Jean-Pierre Dumas, whose responsibilities as a member of the above U.N. team in Micronesia during 1975-76 included doing an economic "case study" of Kusaie (which became the district of Kosrae in January, 1977), says that there are *four* "priorities" which should be pursued if Micronesia is to become "self-sufficient" in the economic sphere: first, marine resources; second, agriculture; third, tourism; and fourth, foreign investment. Dumas *deplores* the almost total dependency on "imports" by the Trust Territory, and points to the almost nonexistent tax structure in Micronesia (until the new system is to begin, effective January 1, 1978, as discussed previously in this chapter), and how absurd it seems when Japan fishes in Micronesian waters and then sells the product back to the islanders:

> When you [the Trust Territory] import tuna food from Japan, the Japanese has to pay only one percent [to Micronesia]; and often they fish, this fish came in [from] the T.T.P.I. water, economic water. They [the Japanese] send it back [to Japan], they can it in Japan, and they send it back out here, in the T.T.P.I., and [they] . . . pay one percent. If you want to export [canned] tuna to Japan, you have to pay 20 percent [to Japan]. The Japanese are not, don't bluff. They're serious in business.

Dumas also agrees with some of the American officials quoted earlier with regard to the ability of the Micronesians to survive without heavy dependence on imported foods: "Even if Americans tomorrow leave this country like that [snapping his fingers together], nobody will starve to death. They [the islanders] can go back to the reef to fish; they can go to get their coconut and to have taro and breadfruit. And this is natural food; you don't need foreign [imports]." How well the Congress of Micronesia's Five Year Indicative Plan (1976-81) will do in implementing the UNDP's recommendations remains to be seen.

"MICRONESIANS DON'T WANT FOREIGN INVESTMENT!"

Although the above quotation comes from an American official in the Trust Territory Government, it is reiterated by others, including the

Director of Resources and Development at the headquarters, Eusebio Rechucher, a Palauan. Rechucher qualifies his response by indicating that the "anti-foreign investment" feeling is one in *some* of the *districts,* rather than at the Trust Territory Government headquarters level:

> Our [the Trust Territory's] biggest problem will be, as far as [foreign] investment concerned, will be the districts, because some of the districts don't believe in outside investment. So that's the deal that it's going to be a real problem. . . . Let's say, investment from Japan or United States or any country that want to come and invest a big amount of money, let's say, to maybe build a hotel or a fisheries complex, and so forth. If he say, "We're going to do it ourselves, without outside investment," it can be done, but it's going to take much longer period of time, because when you have a big company, then they have manpower and know-how, and also a means to get their products to the market, and without depending on anyone. But if you're going to rely on our transportation system, our present system, . . . then it's going to be very hard for anyone to market our products outside, especially when you deal with a small quantity, then you have a real problem.

Rechucher elaborates on the *dichotomy* which exists between the Micronesians' desire to keep "foreign investment" *out* of the islands, and their desire, at the same time, to *import* the products which, with some effort, could be produced within Micronesia: "A lot of people question . . . why they [the Micronesians] don't have fresh fish, why they go to the store to buy, say, a can of sardines. . . . I think it's [the canned fish is] something that they don't have, and they know the taste of it. . . . [Also,] corned beef. So, I think it's natural." The Director of Resources and Development sees a "solution" for the above dilemma: "The only way I believe we will be able to prevent on this is to impose a high tax on the canned food. Maybe we will prevent these people from [eating canned goods]. (Laugh.)"

Not all districts in the Trust Territory are opposed to "foreign investors" coming to the islands, however. Possibly Palau, since the northern Marianas formed their own interim government in 1976, is the most developed of the areas (excluding the Kwajalein missile test range in the Marshalls). Elizabeth Udui says that Palau at present has three large American business involvements in that district's area: "They have Van Camp, they have a Continental Hotel, and they have a coconut oil mill. And these are all million-dollar investments. They do not have any smaller investments; they have only those three large [ones]."

(The growth of "joint-ventures," a development principally confined to Saipan as of mid-1977, as well as the possibility of a "supertanker facility" in Palau by the early 1980s, are discussed in chapter 5, for both topics involve Japanese present and future interests in Micronesia.)

In conclusion, "foreign investment" in Micronesia is a fairly recent

"*To Promote Economic Advancement and Self-Sufficiency...*"

event, for, in Udui's view, "there really wasn't any interest, or any permissible, . . . until about 1969, '70, until the Foreign Investment Act was passed by the Congress of Micronesia." That act in 1970 was highly restrictive. So, although the then Secretary of the Interior, Rogers C. B. Morton, ordered the lifting of restrictions on *foreign* investment in the Trust Territory, effective April 1, 1974, thus allowing individuals and commercial investors "from any of the world's community of nations . . . to apply for business permits in Micronesia," subject to review by the High Commissioner with regard to matters of security and the general welfare of the Micronesian peoples,[63] there has been no big rush of foreign investors applying to come into Micronesia in recent years. Part of that hesitancy, of course, is attributable to the uncertain political status of the Trust Territory in the next number of years as the Trusteeship approaches its termination.

Chapter 3 addresses the third goal of Article 6 in the Trusteeship Agreement of 1947: the social advancement of the Micronesians under American rule.

NOTES FOR CHAPTER 2

1. Dorothy E. Richard, Cdr., USNR, *United States Naval Administration of the Trust Territory of the Pacific Islands,* I (Washington, D.C.: Government Printing Office, 1957), 255.
2. *Ibid.,* pp. 252 and 259.
3. *Ibid.,* p. 264.
4. *Ibid.,* pp. 302, 306, and 307.
5. For accounts of this indigenous leader's career, see "Micronesians Mourn Chief Petrus' Death," *Highlights,* September 15, 1971, pp. 1, 4, and 5; also, *Micronesian Reporter,* XIX (4th Quarter, 1971), 25-29.
6. Richard, *op. cit.,* I, 219.
7. *Ibid.,* p. 314. As will be mentioned later in this chapter, a similar proposal for a "dessicating plant" was being studied in mid-1977.
8. See Dorothy E. Richard, Cdr., USNR, *United States Naval Administration of the Trust Territory of the Pacific Islands,* II (Washington, D.C.: Government Printing Office, 1957), 331-32.
9. *Ibid.,* p. 406.
10. That figure for the total number of aliens in Micronesia by the end of World War II was 147,000. The islanders at that time numbered some 45,000.
11. Richard, *op. cit.,* II, 453 and 462.
12. *Ibid.,* pp. 229, 230, and 244

13. Dorothy E. Richard, Cdr., USNR, *United States Naval Administration of the Trust Territory of the Pacific Islands*, III (Washington, D.C.: Government Printing Office, 1957), 619.
14. Commander Wood's official title is twofold: "Resident Officer-in-Charge of Construction (ROICC) for the Trust Territory of the Pacific Islands (TTPI), and the Program Coordinator for the Capital Improvement Program (CIP) of the TTPI." His office is on Guam. He began performing these duties in early 1976 and will probably remain in this capacity for a minimum of two years.
15. See Robert R. Robbins, "United States Territories in Mid-Century" (paper prepared for the Conference on the History of the Territories, National Archives and Research Service, Washington, D.C., November 3-4, 1969), p. 61. The relatively *wide* use of corrugated sheet metal in the construction of homes, especially in Palau—which seems the warmest and most humid of the six districts (probably due to its closeness to the Equator)—is still seen in the late 1970s. One would be hard-pressed to find a *more* heat-generating material than iron to use as the roof of a house in the islands. (Chapter 3 will discuss a new process developed in Denmark and tested in Africa to replace sheet metal in homes.)
16. See U.S., Department of Interior, *Annual Report of the Secretary of the Interior, for the Fiscal Year ended June 30, 1955* (Washington, D.C.: Government Printing Office, 1955), p. 373. Even considering the *greater* "buying power" of the dollar in the mid-1950s, the sum of $700,000 to spend for construction in such a vast area as Micronesia seems almost ludicrous in hindsight.
17. See U.S., Department of Interior, *Annual Report of the Secretary of the Interior, for the Fiscal Year ended June 30, 1956* (Washington, D.C.: Government Printing Office, 1956), p. 346.
18. The tremendous overgrowth of the tangantangan (a castor-oil plant), which appears as a nondescript shrub-tree on Saipan, infested that island as a result of a seeding project involving U.S. military planes immediately following World War II, when so much of the vegetation was destroyed by the fierce bombardment and amphibious landing. The tangantangan remain very much in view to the visitor in the late 1970s.
19. Speech by Fred M. Zeder II, Director of Territorial Affairs, before the United Nations Development Plan Meeting, Moen, Truk, May 6, 1976, p. 8. (Mimeographed.)
20. See Statement of Fred M. Zeder II, Director, Office of Territorial Affairs, U.S. Department of the Interior, before the United Nations Trusteeship Council, New York City, June 29, 1976, Exhibit A (3 pp.).

"To Promote Economic Advancement and Self-Sufficiency . . ."   161

21. See "The Solomon Report from the Young Micronesian," *Micronitor* (now *Micronesian Independent*), July 10, 1971, p. 3.
22. *Ibid.*, p. 12.
23. *Ibid.*, pp. 13 and 14.
24. See *Economic Development Plan for the Trust Territory of the Pacific Islands,* Vol. I, Elbert V. Bowden, Chief of Mission (Saipan: Robert R. Nathan Associates, Inc., December 1, 1966), preface, p. 1.
25. *Ibid.*, pp. 101-102.
26. *Ibid.*, p. 83. Considering that the Nathan Mission based its figures on a Micronesian population of about 90,000 in 1966, the total cost of the proposed $1,500 per inhabitant appropriation by the U.S. Congress would amount to some $135 million.
27. See Ruth G. Van Cleve, *The Office of Territorial Affairs* (New York: Praeger Publishers, 1974), p. 129.
28. See U.S., Department of State, *28th Annual Report to the United Nations on the Administration of the Trust Territory of the Pacific Islands, for the Fiscal Year ended June 30, 1975* (Washington, D.C.: Government Printing Office, 1976), p. 28; also see "Supplemental Budget for T.T. Approved," *Highlights,* May 1, 1977, p. 1.
29. See Francis X. Hezel, S.J., "Micronesia Ten Years After" (article by Father Hezel at Xavier High School, Moen, Truk [ca. 1971]), 3 pp. (Mimeographed.)
30. See William H. Stewart, "Micronesia by the Year 2000—New Ideas" (article drafted while Stewart was assigned as Deputy Director, Economic Development Office, Trust Territory Government, Honolulu, November, 1976), 7 pp. (Mimeographed.)
31. See U.S., Department of Interior, *Annual Report of the Secretary of the Interior, for the Fiscal Year ended 1951* (Washington, D.C.: Government Printing Office, 1951), p. 415. Assisting Interior in this program planning were the Navy Department, the Civil Aeronautics Administration (CAA—which was transferred to the Federal Aviation Agency [FAA] in 1958), and several private shipping firms and airlines.
32. See U.S., Department of Interior, *Annual Report of the Secretary of the Interior, for the Fiscal Year ended 1954* (Washington, D.C.: Government Printing Office, 1954), p. 376.
33. See "Interview: James Boyd Mackenzie," *Micronesian Reporter,* XIX (4th Quarter, 1971), 4.
34. See U.S., Department of State, *17th Annual Report to the United Nations on the Administration of the Trust Territory of the Pacific Islands, for the Fiscal Year ended June 30, 1964* (Washington, D.C.: Government Printing Office, 1965), p. 81.

35. From the verbatim transcript of "The Department of Social Sciences Presents 'Current Topics,' " a tape of a live broadcast interview, Radio Station WGGL-FM, Houghton, Michigan, April 13, 1971.
36. From a taped interview with Thomas A. Elliott and David S. Robbins, Medford, Massachusetts, March 25, 1971.
37. See Robert R. Robbins, "Trust Territory of the Pacific Islands: The Development of a Polity" (paper presented at the panel, "Liquidation of the American Dependent Empire," New England Political Science Association annual meeting, Amherst, April 29, 1967), p. 7.
38. See Trust Territory of the Pacific Islands, Congress, Senate, Interim Committee, *Report to the Senate, Congress of Micronesia*, unnumbered report, 2d Cong., 3d reg. sess., 1967.
39. See United Nations, Trusteeship Council, 34th Session, 1967, *Report of the United Nations Visiting Mission to the Trust Territory of the Pacific Islands, May 29-June 30, 1967*, T/1668, Supplement No. 2, pp. 25-26.
40. See Office of the High Commissioner, *Opening Statement by High Commissioner W. R. Norwood to the 35th Session of the Trusteeship Council, May 28, 1968*, released by the Department of Public Affairs, Saipan [1968], p. 1.
41. *Ibid.*, pp. 4 and 5.
42. The most recent report available from Air Micronesia, Inc., as of mid-1977 was *Air Micronesia Annual Report: 1975*, A President's report, Los Angeles: July 1, 1976. (Unnumbered pages.)
43. See Appendix to Civil Aeronautics Board, *Docket 17353: Pacific Islands Local Service Investigation*, Order 71-7-170, Washington, D.C.: Decided on May 4, 1971, p. 1. This writer queried an official in the Trust Territory Government on Saipan in the summer of 1970 to see why the CAB was initially opposed to Air Mike's continuance after 1973. The response was that Secor D. Browne, then Chairman of the CAB, was "a close personal friend" of Pan Am's President.
44. See "Congress of Micronesia Still Wants Air Mike," *Pacific Daily News*, August 28, 1970, p. 29.
45. See *Statement by Adrian P. Winkel, Special Representative to the Trusteeship Council on the Trust Territory of the Pacific Islands, June 6, 1977*, United States Mission to the United Nations, Press Release USUN-34 (77), June 7, 1977, p. 11. If the former Mariana Islands District were included in High Commissioner Winkel's figure for 1976, the "earnings" would have been appreciably higher. In 1975, when the Marianas District was included, the total was $4.9 million (the Marianas accounting for 74% of the tourist visitors). See U.S., Department of State, *28th Annual Report to the United Nations . . . [for] 1975*, p. 32.

"*To Promote Economic Advancement and Self-Sufficiency* . . ." 163

46. See Civil Aeronautics Board, "CAB News Summary," July 8, 1976, p. 3. The CAB's decision, approved by Ford, affirmed an earlier opinion of the CAB issued in August, 1975, and had the effect of "denying" the applications of Northwest and Pan Am for such service between Saipan and Japan.
47. See *Air Micronesia Annual Report: 1975,* p. 1.
48. See *Statement by* . . . *Winkel,* p. 11.
49. See Daniel T. Hughes and Sherwood G. Lingenfelter, eds., *Political Development in Micronesia* (Columbus, Ohio: Ohio State University Press, 1974), p. 200.
50. See Statement of . . . Zeder, pp. 10 and 11.
51. See U.S., Department of State, *17th Annual Report to the United Nations* . . . [*for 1964*], pp. 49-50.
52. See Trust Territory of the Pacific Islands, Congress, Senate, *A Senate Joint Resolution Endorsing United States Senate Bill 3070 Extending Provisions of the Small Business Act to the Trust Territory of the Pacific Islands,* S.J. Res. 6, 2d Cong., 4th reg. sess., 1968.
53. See U.S., Department of State, *22d Annual Report to the United Nations on the Administration of the Trust Territory of the Pacific Islands, for the Fiscal Year ended June 30, 1969* (Washington, D.C.: Government Printing Office, 1970), p. 40.
54. See *Statement by* . . . *Winkel,* p. 12.
55. *Ibid.,* p. 7.
56. See Richard, *op. cit.,* I, 219.
57. See *ESG Notes,* LXI (April 1, 1977), pp. 1 and 3; also see "Tax Law Examined," *ESG Notes,* LXV (May 6, 1977), p. 4.
58. The U.S. Department of Agriculture uses a maximum "net adjusted income" of $567 per month for a family of four, and $245 (or $2,940 yearly) for a single individual in computing the "poverty level" for eligibility to receive food stamps in the United States. (Foodstuffs are not made available within the states.)
59. See Steven D. Yoder, "A Look at Poultry Markets in the Pacific Islands," *Foreign Agriculture,* XV, 22 (May 30, 1977), 5 and 6.
60. See Charles Sicard, "Truk Credit Union Marks Tenth Anniversary," *Highlights,* March 15, 1972, p. 4.
61. See *Statement by* . . . *Winkel,* p. 12.
62. *Ibid.,* p. 3.
63. See "Interior Secretary Morton Issues Major Policy Statement, Orders Lifting of Restrictions on Foreign Investment," *Highlights,* January 25, 1974, pp. 1-3.

Chapter 3

"To Promote the Social Advancement of the Inhabitants..."

This chapter is intended to be a potpourri of several topics, briefly sketched, which, to some readers, might better be placed in the preceding chapter (on the "economic development and self-sufficiency" of the Micronesians). However, this writer feels that the following subjects are germane to the "social advancement" of the islanders and thus are treated here. It is to be hoped that the patient reader will see the wisdom of this topical approach in an evaluation of how well the American Administrations over the years since World War II have "protected the rights and fundamental freedoms" of the islanders while, at the same time, attempting to "improve the standard of living" throughout the Trust Territory.

HEALTH CARE: A CONTINUING HIGH PRIORITY

Commander Richard, in her third volume on the "Naval Administration in the Trust Territory," acknowledged that "improvement in the health of the Micronesians continued to be one of the principal aims of the [Naval] administration during the trusteeship period [1947-51]," and she wrote that "the Naval Medical Department had performed an outstanding and spectacular job during the military government era [1944-47]." She concluded: "The islanders had, for the most part, accepted the health program willingly and gratefully." An exception Richard noted in the Micronesians' full acceptance of the Naval approach to health programming was some lingering dependency by islanders on "witchcraft" practices: "There were still some people who sought dispensary care only after native medicine and witchcraft had failed."[1]

Dr. Ngas Kansou, Deputy Director of Health Services for the Trust Territory Government, recalls the U.S. Navy's emphasis on providing medical services to the Micronesians: "I would say that that was the first thing that the Navy did. I think they realized that . . . the area was not a healthy place and Japanese and natives were sick, . . . so the area was not that healthy." Dr. Kansou points to a *difference* in the approach to medical care by the Navy vis-à-vis the Interior Department (after 1951):

> The Navy . . . did . . . the environmental health—mosquito control, flies, plants, and things like that. It's more or less on a forced type of thing. The Department of Interior, when they took over, we changed that system into attacking—in other words, teach the people—make the people understand why we do these things. . . . Preventive medicine, or health education.

Another change in approach to medical programs by the Interior was in training *abroad* for "islander medical personnel." The Naval Administration concentrated on the training of "health aides, dental aides, and nurses aides for service in the public health program, [which] was conducted at the various civil administration dispensaries and was one of the most important functions of the senior medical officers," the last-named being U.S. Naval physicians.[2] The Interior Department went a step further and sent selected Micronesians to the Fiji School of Medicine at Suva, in the early 1950s. Kansou was one of those to be sent to Fiji. After a five-year course of study at the School of Medicine there, Kansou and his fellow students were graduated as "medical officers," the difference in that title and "medical doctor" being that the Fiji School was not considered as advanced as those medical schools in the United States.

Notwithstanding the continuing emphasis on health programs under both the Navy and Interior, in turn, the World Health Organization (WHO), in 1965, after touring Micronesia, reported that the Americans, as Kansou recalls, "weren't doing enough in health services, [in] taking care of the Micronesians." Efforts since the mid-1960s to improve such conditions have included the use of "paramedical people" to augment the limited medical personnel available in the islands. Some Micronesians have attended medical school in the United States; however, the "brain drain" syndrome has been operative. Two islanders who completed their residency training in recent years opted to practice in Hawaii and Seattle, respectively. A School of Nursing has been available on Saipan for several years, graduating practical nurses.

Medical facilities have improved recently. William D. Jackson, Program Development Officer in the Community Development Division, Trust Territory Government, says that the new hospital in Ponape, with 115 beds, is a major "referral hospital" for the Trust Territory, thus relieving Guam of that added responsibility. High Commissioner Winkel, in his report to the U.N. Trusteeship Council in June, 1977, said that completion of that hospital in Ponape early in 1977 thus assures not only the Ponape District of needed services, but would be both a "referral and training center for the rest of the [Trust] Territory. When fully staffed with appropriate specialists, it will become the nucleus of inservice medical training within [Micronesia]." Winkel also spoke of a new 50-bed hospital in Yap District (expected to be completed by January, 1978); a hospital in Kosrae almost ready; a new addition to the Palau Hospital (to be ready by August, 1977); and renovations to the sub-hospital on Ebeye, in the Marshalls. Winkel concluded that "adequate medical care to the outer-island communities" remained as "one of the major problems" facing the Trust Territory Government's Health Services Division, but expressed appreciation for the availability of "federal grant programs," which, he said, "have assisted materially in the improvement of health services."[3]

WAR CLAIMS SETTLEMENT: NO . . . AND YES

The Naval Administration from the outset in 1944, as islands were captured first in the Marshalls, and then westward, attempted to return the Micronesians to their home islands. "There was probably no action taken by the Navy in the immediate postwar period which impressed the Micronesians more" than such a policy, as Richard recorded in her third volume of "Naval Administration." She mentioned the words of King Tomeing, on Wotje, in the Marshalls, when he gave a speech at the raising of the American flag during November, 1945:

> It was on February 2, '44 that we [the islanders] ran away from our oppressors. We have been under their rule for many very trying years and had to suffer and put up with many insults. Because of these things we decided to sail out in our canoes to try and contact the Americans [i.e., the military forces] whom we have always liked and loved since childhood. On June 9th [1944] we were all together under the American flag on Erikub Island [in the Marshalls] and now today for the first time the flag flies from this island [of Wotje].[4]

Unfortunately, the "goodwill" expressed by Chief Tomeing, as well as Micronesians throughout the areas when, one by one, the U.S. Naval Administration assumed control over the formerly Japanese Mandated Islands, was to evaporate in a very important—to the Micronesians—sector: the matter of *claims* arising over damage incurred both during the War and in the period of occupancy by U.S. forces immediately thereafter. Maynard Neas, whose initial assignment to the western Pacific was to serve as a member for four years (1947-51) on the Philippine War Damage Commission, believes that the long history of "war claims" problems which was to plague the American Administration in Micronesia down to the late 1970s could have been resolved *early* had the U.S. Navy taken a different course of action. What was Navy's emphasis immediately after World War II? Actually, the Naval commanders declined to apply the Foreign Claims Act in 1944 and 1945, presumably on the assumption that the payment of claims to islanders should be placed upon the defeated Japan. However, the State Department had other plans: namely, that Japan should be left out of "reparations" payments in order to be built up, in Neas' analysis, as a "bulwark against Russia."

The Navy did not ignore Micronesian material needs after the War entirely. Thus, while avoiding the problem of "war claims," the Naval Administration did permit its officials to "turn over war materials" to the Micronesians. Neas gives an example of such "giveaways":

> When the Americans came up from Peleliu and Angaur, and established military government at Koror [in Palau], there were 1,000 or 2,000 Quonsets in crates on Peleliu and Angaur. And they [the Navy] made those available at somewhere around $20 [each] . . . [or] some minor nominal sum that they could call it a shipping cost, to ship it up there. And they turned over Japanese materials to Micronesians in food and housing that was left. . . . [on Saipan,] they divided up San Antonio Village, that [had been] . . . a big housing area for [Japanese] troops and supplies, . . . and gave them [the islanders] village lot homesteads and the Quonset that was on there. By doing all of that, a lot of the Americans figured that they had liquidated all losses that the Micronesians had sustained.

When queried whether such above transactions were recorded, Neas says that there was "nothing in writing. . . . [The United States] did not get any kind of quid pro quo out of it." Richard wrote that "no claims for noncombat damage were filed during the period of the war. The Micronesians philosophically accepted their losses as part of their experience of living." She also noted that "no settlements for use of properties were made with any local inhabitants during the war period either through a lease or as a result of a claim. A major problem in assessing ownership was the almost complete lack of property records."[5]

Did Interior become involved early (after 1951) in the settlement of damage claims by the Micronesians? Neas recalls that the islanders submitted numerous petitions to the U.N. Trusteeship Council for during the War and afterward. Interior sent out a survey team in the 1961-62 period, headed by George R. Milner (now Deputy Director of the Office of Territorial Affairs in the Carter Administration). That team estimated that the "war damage claims" were between $5 million and $10 million, based on the value at the time of loss. In 1967, a War Claims Office was established within the Office of the Attorney General in the Trust Territory Government. Neas was asked by the then Attorney General, Robert Shoecraft, to "collect claims on post-secure damage," meaning those claims arising from damage *after* the island areas were declared "secure" by the occupying military. Thus, Neas spent two years "going through all the districts and collecting claims. . . . I reached the conclusion that there was somewhere in the neighborhood of, I estimated that I had a total of pretty close to $20 million" in claims, and he accordingly reported that amount and helped prepare the draft for what became the "Title II Claims" (differing from those under Title I, which involved the "combat losses" suffered by the islanders).

How were the above "damage claims" eventually resolved by the Trust Territory Government? Terry L. Garrett, Director of Finance at headquarters, gives the following breakdown of claims settlements effected by the fall of 1976 (when the Foreign Claims Commission Branch "certified" the claims and then disbanded its operation), with an indication of how the Japanese Government participated in the "Title I" payments:

> Title I turned out to be $11.6 million, approximately; Title II was $20 million. . . . [The Japanese Government] in 1968 [signed] an agreement . . . wherein they contributed $1.8 billion yen which, in 1968, was valued at $5 million. The agreement between the U.S. and the Japanese Government says that each of us [the Japanese and Americans] would contribute a "corresponding amount." The Japanese contribution [was] to be in the form of goods and services to be distributed as an ex-gratia payment to the citizens of Micronesia, for the benefit of Micronesian development in the Post-War period. . . . Because of the interest, . . . the Japanese contribution turned out to be $6.6 million rather than the original $5 million. We [the U.S.] contributed dollars. . . . In other words, Micronesia got both the goods [from Japan] and the dollars [from the U.S.].

Yoshiaki Kotaki, in the First North American Division of the Japanese Ministry of Foreign Affairs in Tokyo, feels that the above payment for Title I by the Japanese, through "goods and services," had a "terrific result"; and after reflecting on the three decades' delay before such claims were resolved, adds: "and overly regrettable."

The last has apparently not been heard with regard to "Micronesian damage claims" under Titles I and II, above. High Commissioner Winkel informed the U.N. in mid-1977 that, while "all funds authorized by the 1971 [War Claims] Act have been expended and final payments of the awards have been made," a case was still pending in a U.S. District Court involving "a Micronesian War Damage claim," and a bill was in the U.S. Congress to amend the above 1971 Act so that islanders would receive larger settlement amounts from the United States than awarded previously.[6] Thus, the matter remains unresolved at this point.

"WHY HAVE A MICRONESIAN FLAG?"

An entry in Richard's final volume on the "Naval Administration" (for 1947-51) indicates that the Navy was pushing for adoption of a "Micronesian" flag, but failed: "The choice of a design for the [islander] flag resulted in a tie vote. The difficulty had not been resolved before naval administration ended so that enforced use of the flag did not become the Navy's problem."[7] It was not until the era of the Council of Micronesia that a successful "flag contest" was conducted. The 1961 session of that forerunner to the Congress of Micronesia (see chapter 1) passed a resolution promoting such a contest, and, in 1962, the High Commissioner (M. Wilfred Goding) approved the winning design and an official flag of the Trust Territory was adopted. Professor Meller further noted that, before leaving office, Goding amended, by an executive order (No. 100) the *Code of the Trust Territory* so that "all locally registered vessels" would be required "to fly the Trust Territory flag."[8]

Untold in the above accounts is the view expressed more recently by Dwight Heine, a Marshallese and the Chairman of the Council of Micronesia at the time the above flag was adopted. Heine remembers that several of the Micronesians attending the Pacific Islands Central School (PICS) in Truk (which high school brought islanders together from throughout the Trust Territory), had opposed the original Naval Administration recommendation for a Micronesian flag during 1948-49. Why? They (the students) did not want a flag until they could *feel* a "territory-wide" nature developing among the islands. "We knew that it takes a long time to build" that sense into a reality, Heine recounts. "That school give us ideas. We begin to think in along those lines. We begin to speculate. And, of course, we have American friends who would held the same idea as we did, and they also threw in the seeds here and there that propagated and give us ideas." Navy, Heine says, "told us we were not ready" to become involved in Territory-wide matters. Instead, Heine recalls, the Naval Administration decided to begin chartering the municipalities (discussed in chapter 1).

Heine gives the rationale for the earlier Micronesian opposition to a flag (during the Navy Period) as follows:

> When they [the Navy] asked us if we have a flag for our Trust Territory, we do not want to make a flag. . . . We didn't want to have one because, we said, "Gee whiz, we fly the U.N. flag. Why don't they give us that? A flag stand for something. And what does this [proposed] flag stand for?" (Laugh.) We don't know. Why will flag that means something? And this flag will be so meaningless, because nobody wants it. So we were against it.

He also recalls Interior's support of a Micronesian flag in 1961, when there was another contest. The reason for Interior's concern for a Territory-wide flag was apparently for a "commercial" reason:

> Many years later [in 1961], when I become the Chairman of the Council of Micronesia, there was a contest. . . . And a little later we find out why. When the Interior took over [in 1951], they send out copra to San Fran-

cisco by ship. When they [the ships] arrived, the union got on board and immediately asked those fellows [the islander crewmen] how much they are paid? What do they eat? What kind of treatment do they receive? So they [the union officials] said they [Interior] cannot do that [the kind of conditions of the Micronesians on ship] under the American flag. . . . When they go to California, they [the islanders] should be subjected to those union rules, and so on. So when the Marshallese fellows and Carolinians when they come back, thought they were rich, because of all the back pay they [Interior] had to pay them. (Laugh.) Well, at least we know it was not an honorable thing [i.e., Interior's backing of a Micronesian flag], and it was not all some noble thought that a flag we should have. It was a businessman who brought out copra and who operated on a ship.

Heine also recalls his response when the editor of the *Micronesian Independent*, Joe Murphy (not to be confused with the Editor of the Guam *Daily News* by the same name), inquired of Heine *why* the islanders had rejected the earlier Naval bid for a Micronesian flag (in the late 1940s). Heine's reply to Murphy: "Well, we were younger and not as wise as we are now." Heine reflects more recently and says of his reply to Murphy's question, above: "More foolish thing. But that was a reason. We suspected something, and we couldn't put our finger on it, why they [the Navy] wouldn't grant us what we asked for [i.e., Micronesian involvement in Trust Territory-wide affairs]."

The official flag of the Trust Territory is appealing in its simplicity: six white stars forming a circle on a blue field. One is reminded of the stars and field portion of the flag design approved for the original 13 states in America, except for the number of stars involved and the shade of blue—the Micronesians' field being darker. Ironically, with the forming of the interim Government of the Northern Marianas in April, 1976, and that pending commonwealth's own flag being adopted shortly thereafter, such would seem to warrant a *change* in the design of the Trust Territory flag; however, with Kusaie becoming the District of Kosrae on January 1, 1977, the sixth star remained intact and no "interim" Micronesian flag was involved during that nine-month period.

THE CONTINUING IMPACT OF CHRISTIAN MISSIONARIES

The impact of Christianity on Micronesia dates back to the Spanish Period and continued, with modifications, throughout the succeeding German and Japanese eras, as noted in the introductory chapter. The Naval Administration did not let foreign missionaries return to Micronesia until the post-War period began.[9] Reverend Vincent I. Kennally, S.J., was the first such American missionary to return after the War, and was named Interim Apostolic Administrator of the Carolines and Marshalls Vicariate, with headquarters on Moen. (Bishop Kennally still served as Vicar Apostolic in that area in mid-1977.) Richard wrote that "the natives never ceased to request" the return of foreign missionaries to Micronesia; however, the Navy remained adamant on that ban until "some months after the end of hostilities."[10]

Once returned, the foreign missionaries were treated with respect by the Naval Administration officials but, at the same time, the clergy was *not* under the sponsorship of the Government: "The Navy continued to assist religious activities and missionaries with the means at its disposal but desired that the native people understand that the missionaries were not sponsored by military government." Further, when the American Board of Commissioners for Foreign Missions (which the Navy asked to "supervise" the work of returning German Protestant missionaries) approached the Secretary of the Navy for permission to resume the work of the ministry in the islands, and indicated interest in developing a program of "educational and welfare work," in addition to the religious activities, that board was *denied* the opportunity to duplicate Naval Administration programs in Micronesia. Thus, the Commander-in-Chief of the Naval Command in the Pacific (CinCPOA) responded to the American Board with regard to relations between the Navy and the missionaries in which he indicated that "the mutual responsibilities and areas of action of each group [the Navy and the clergy] is basic. This will obviate overlapping action and the undesirable consequences which follow such overlapping. . . . Such programs [in education and welfare] are already established under [the Naval Administration]," and the CinCPOA concluded: "It is recommended that no commitments be made relative to missionary participation now or in the future" in educational and welfare matters.[11]

Another policy statement by the Navy on the privileges of missionaries is instructive on the extent to which those clergymen traveled and their desire to procure military aircraft for their labors: "Further privileges as requested [beyond "traveling in the interests of the government"], . . . such as excessive baggage allowances, free air transportation in the area whenever desired, free transportation to the United States and beyond for foreign missionaries, and sale or donation of naval craft for interisland traffic," were all denied.[12] Possibly, one clergyman interested in the "sale or donation" of Naval aircraft "for interisland traffic" was Reverend Edmund Kalau, now assigned on Guam and previously a longtime pastor of the Lutheran mission in Yap. Reverend Kalau, a German Liebenzell, had been a pilot in the Luftwaffe during World War II and, during his years in Micronesia, came to be known as a "flying parson," as he would pilot his small aircraft (most recently, a twin-engine, nine-passenger STOL aircraft), named the *Evangel,* used for medical evacuations, air and sea search, and "mission work in the islands of Yap, Truk, and Ponape."[13]

Over the three decades since the U.S. Navy first administered in Micronesia, a number of Christian missionaries, mostly from the United States, have served in the Trust Territory. As of mid-1977, the earlier American Board of Commissioners for Foreign Missions had been replaced by the United Church Board of World Ministries for the predominant Protestant churches, which are the United Church of Christ (or Congregationalists, who first came to Kusaie in the mid-nineteenth century), the Liebenzells (or German Lutherans, in Yap and Palau), and the General Baptists (only on Saipan). Other groups in Micronesia include Independent Baptists, the Seventh Day Adventists, the Jehovah's Witnesses, the Assembly of God, and, beginning in 1975, the Church of Jesus Christ of Latter-day Saints (Mormons). The Catholic missionaries are represented by the Society of Jesus, under the direction of Bishop Kennally (mentioned earlier), and the Capuchin Franciscans (only in the northern Marianas, with their ecclesiastical headquarters on Guam). Approximately 50 percent of the Micronesians are Catholic (predominantly in the western areas of the Marianas, Yap, and Palau), and an equal percentage are Protestants (mainly in the Marshalls, Kosrae, and Ponape), with Truk more or less equally divided as well.

Three of the main Protestant churches—the Congregationalists, the General Baptists, and the Liebenzells—have formed as the Conference of Micronesian Churches and have met in recent years to discuss matters of concern to all of the islanders. At the 1975 session of that conference, Reverend Mack Williams, Pastor of the Community Church on Saipan (until his rotation back to the U.S. in the summer of 1977), recalls that all of the pastors with the exception of two—Reverend Kalau (mentioned earlier) and himself—were Micronesian. When the Congress of Micronesia called a Constitutional Convention to convene on Saipan that year to consider a constitution (see chapter 1), Reverend Williams was elected by his conference to be the "liaison officer for the Protestant churches" to that convention. Specifically, he was then designated by the Congress of Micronesia to be the Protestant chaplain for the convention.

Reverend Williams recalls four main "positions" the Conference of Micronesian Churches requested that he take with regard to provisions in the proposed Constitution for the Federated States of Micronesia. On the "separation of church and state" issue, he says that he, and Reverend Kalau, the German, *differed* with the islander clergymen on the latter group's stand: "Being of the American Baptist background, I feel very strongly in the separation of church and state to the extent that Government should not subsidize schools, etc. But the Micronesian Protestant leadership does not feel that strongly. . . . They [the indigenous ministers] feel that the Government should encourage the Christian faith." Reverend Williams attributes the Micronesian clergymen's attitude on the "separation of church and state" matter to the schooling those islanders received under church sponsorship:

> Most of them have been educated in church schools. . . . The early Protestant missionaries in the Marshalls and Ponape Districts . . . were the ones that started the schools, and almost all of our [islander] leadership in Micronesia today are products of Christian schools: Protestant schools in the eastern half of Micronesia and Catholic schools in the western half. . . . And since they are products of Christian schools, they believe that you need Christian schools to hold the morality and the Christian influence; and, therefore, they believe it is proper for the Government to also help [the church schools].

Even before the above constitution was drafted in 1975, the Trust Territory Government was already granting "aid-to-parochial schools" (to be discussed in chapter 4).

On the issue of "capital punishment," the Conference of Micronesian Churches instructed Reverend Williams to state that the Protestant leadership was opposed to the taking of life. "This is foreign to our custom." Parenthetically, Reverend Williams indicates that "capital punishment" may *not* be so "foreign" to the Micronesians' customs: "I have had a number of incidents referred to me, and I have full reason to believe that 'capital punishment' has been practiced in one of the districts since I have been here in three years [since 1973], for an offense. . . . It was handled 'native custom, native way'—bang, over with, it's hush, hush, nobody talks about it." The difference in the "native custom" approach to "capital punishment," Reverend Williams adds, is that it is "carried through the traditional leaderships," meaning the tribal or clan chiefs. An American official observes that "tribal executions" occurring in recent years would not surprise him, but adds that such "would have to be [on] an outer island, and even that is a fairly risky business, because even the remotest islands have magistrates and school teachers who are required to keep records on the population. And in the event that somebody disappears, they'd have to have some excuse for it, . . . [and be in] a very strong traditional community in which the Chief told everybody to keep quiet, and everyone does."

For two other issues at the Constitutional Convention on Saipan in 1975—one, economic, the other, political—the Protestant leadership had Reverend Williams state a firm position with regard to the "law of the sea" and the "future political status" questions. On the former, the Conference of Micronesian Churches followed the Congress of Micronesia's position in wanting to see a 200-mile economic zone based on the archipelago approach (see chapter 1); on the latter, Reverend Williams says the clergymen saw the advantage of Micronesia "sticking together in unity, . . . with some kind of relationship with the U.S., but they did not desire the close union that the northern Marianas would have [i.e., a commonwealth], . . . [or] an 'independent' idea of wanting to separate from the U.S."

Reverend Henry Dykema, Pastor of the Faith Presbyterian Reformed Church on Guam, has worked with hundreds of Micronesian students attending the University of Guam since his arrival in that area in 1965. Additionally, he has traveled throughout the Trust Territory periodically. How do Micronesian youths react when away at school, so far as maintaining the standards of their homes?

> I think that most of the Micronesians, when they leave their districts and come to Guam, they enjoy the freedom that Guam provides to them: freedom away from the control of the home, and freedom from the control of the church, and freedom from some of the standards and mores of the community. So the students, the young people that come to Guam, sometimes don't really know how to use this new-found freedom that they are suddenly experiencing, and it gets some of them into trouble, and trouble basically in terms of alcohol. Alcoholism has become a problem with many. . . . Also, many students may stop going to church while in Guam, . . . whereas, back home, they may have gone very regularly or very faithfully—not necessarily always by choice, but simply out of custom to the requirements of the family in the community.

(Reference to alcoholism by Reverend Dykema, above, reminds one of the annual purchase of alcoholic beverages in the Trust Territory, which totals $1 million, as mentioned in chapter 2.)

Perhaps the leading scholar among the Catholic missionaries in Micronesia over the past decade has been Reverend Francis X. Hezel, S.J., on Moen. Father Hezel, in an article entitled "Micronesia's Hanging Spree," which he authored in 1976, details the "epidemic proportions" which suicides have reached. Using statistics based on lists compiled by students and faculty at the Xavier High School in Truk of "all individuals known to them as having taken their own lives during the previous year [1975-76]," and verified with "other informants outside the school," Father Hezel placed suicide, as a form of death, number one among young islanders: "Today, it is the number one cause of death among Micronesians between the ages of 15 and 30, surpassing auto accidents, gastro-intestinal diseases, and heart disease as a killer." Father Hezel's research found 23 such deaths in that year, but he indicated that "there may well have been more, perhaps as many as 30." To what does Father Hezel attribute this relatively high suicide rate among young Micronesians? He blames, mainly, the "plight of the family" in being unable to exercise *more* "control" over the youths, and in saying this, proceeds to place that on the roles now being performed by other decision-making bodies in the island communities, including the Trust Territory Government:

Over the past years the Micronesian family has gradually relinquished to other agencies many of the roles that it once exercised on behalf of its members. The school has assumed the responsibility for educating and even feeding its children. The police station and the court have increasingly taken on the responsibility of restraining them and correcting them when they misbehave. The hospital or dispensary cares for them when they are indisposed. Government recreation boards are assigned the task of occupying them during their leisure, and the government administration is expected to employ them during their working hours. No wonder parents feel their direct control over their young slipping away!

Another Catholic missionary to express himself on the weaknesses found in the Micronesian society is Reverend William McGarry, S.J., in Ponape, who, in a personal letter to this writer in early 1977, indicated his own view on seven points which, fulfilled, would, in Father McGarry's view, lead to "a happy, developed society" in Micronesia:

FIRST, *sufficiency of material prosperity.* In general, Micronesians are quite well off when compared to most of the world. . . . They would be just as well off without all the pumping in of American money. Life would have less tinsel, but sufficiency and equitable distribution might be fine. The one contribution has been US medical services. The economy at present, of course, is very largely dependent on *give-away* programs. There is little real economic progress.

SECOND, *adequate self-respect or esteem.* In this I find the most distressing situation. The dependency syndrome has had its effect. The education system leaves large numbers of *second class* citizens behind. We have been working on this self-esteem matter here in Ponape. I am not sure there has been much progress.

THIRD, *participation in decisions about one's life and future.* The rank and file Micronesian has little understanding about what is happening. Most leave it to those who have been to school. These latter are a new class of *magicians.* I would like to see an anthropological study on past and present levels of participation. It is my suspicion that past seemingly autocratic traditional chiefs were *more* sensitive to and open to the wishes of the "commoners" than the legislators at any level "democratically" elected in the present system. Congressmen and legislators [of the District Legislature] are *rarely* seen among their constituents.

FOURTH, *human love and friendship.* The family is breaking down. Communication between the generations is not good. Suicides and youth crime is high.

FIFTH, *a certain security from fear.* Although any place in Micronesia is a lot safer than an American city, fears seem to be creeping in. Crime, alcoholic violence, etc., are on the increase.

SIXTH, *a reasonable fulfillment of hopes.* Young people are urged to study to get to high school where there is no room for them. Then they expect jobs which don't exist. Manual labor and hard work on the land are losing their dignity.

SEVENTH, *an openness to the transcendent.* Here you have a Missionary's view. . . . People locked in to the limits of the empirical and the limits of a short span of life will likely not remain happy. Materialism is taking over in Micronesia. (Italics mine.)

Father McGarry, who had previously (in 1971) corresponded with this writer on the subject of "unity" in Micronesia, concluded the above 1977 letter by observing: "The unity question is a mess. My own view is that all negotiations should cease completely. A plebiscite should be held after one year of thorough grass-roots discussion on unity. . . . Perhaps each district should first draw up its own constitution and then put them together in some form of federation, if unity is decided upon."

This writer commented to a secretary in the Trust Territory Government, on Capitol Hill, Saipan, in the fall of 1976 that he felt strange riding a bicycle around that island. She responded: "Well, you shouldn't feel so strange. The Mormon missionaries, with their white shirts and ties, have been riding all over the island for the past two years!" The northern Marianas saw the arrival of the first Mormon missionaries to the Trust Territory in early 1975. For those readers familiar with the proselyting program of the Church of Jesus Christ of Latter-day Saints, or Mormons, as the members are commonly called, this extension of missionaries to that area of the central and western Pacific might not be surprising, as the Mormon Church has some 25,000 young men and women in over 100 areas of the world doing missionary labors. However, until 1975, none of these had been sent to the Trust Territory. (Guam has experienced such missionaries for a number of years, as have such other Pacific areas as Polynesia, New Zealand, Australia, Indonesia, the Philippines, Singapore, Hong Kong, Taiwan, Japan, and Korea.)

William W. Cannon, President of the Hawaii Honolulu Mission, headquartered in Honolulu, when queried as to the recent presence of his young missionaries (the men called "elders," a title for the priesthood they hold) on Saipan and in the Ponape District, explains why Micronesia is now being proselyted by those missionaries, each of whom serves for two years at his own expense: "Our [church's] responsibility is to reconcile the children of our Heavenly Father with His family. This is an on-going duty, and we feel that we have an obligation to share this message with all people everywhere." Hence, the Mormon presence in Micronesia.

JFK'S CHARISMA IN MICRONESIA

Within a relatively short period following the assassination of President John F. Kennedy in November, 1963, a monument was erected to him on the grounds of the Mt. Carmel Church, on Saipan. To some members of the present generation of Americans, President Kennedy may be only vaguely remembered, for the distance from late 1963 to mid-1977 covers almost 14 years. A number of islanders were asked why such a monument to a slain American Chief Executive who served as

President less than three years and never visited Micronesia elicited an apparent charismatic reaction when his death was known some 8,000 miles away from Washington, D.C. The responses vary. For example, Dwight Heine, a Marshallese who has lived on Saipan, the capital of Micronesia, for most of the time from the early 1960s, gives a more general impression: "He [Kennedy] is the only person, non-Micronesian, when we heard that he was dead, assassinated, all the islands, on their own, they ring the church bells—the Micronesian people. The Government would send the word later—much hours later—but the Micronesian flag was at already half-mast. The American flag followed it. I've never seen—talk about charisma—I've seen all these definitions, they're inadequate." JoeTen, the leading Saipanese entrepreneur, points to Kennedy's Catholicism and the heavy Catholic concentration in the northern Marianas (close to 99 percent) as the principal catalyst for the monument action: "Mainly because he's a Catholic, and he's the first Catholic to become a U.S. President, . . . and I think it's nothing more than that, because nobody knows about Kennedy other than he's a Catholic. And this is the reason why . . . the people here put up the monument right in front of the [Mt. Carmel] Church, which . . . you can never find this elsewhere." JoeTen also discounts the doubling of the annual appropriation (from $7 million to $15 million) during the Kennedy Administration as a principal reason for the ground swell of adulation among the Saipanese after the assassination, recalling the northern Marianas had just recently (in 1962) reverted from the Naval Administration back to the Interior Department: "Maybe [the Saipanese] were different than the other people feel, the other districts, because over here [in the northern Marianas] is almost 100 percent Catholic. Of course, we just got in—at the time he was the President—we just got into the new Government [i.e., under Interior], so you cannot notice the difference other than he's just a Catholic."

The person most closely involved in the *permission* to erect a bust of the slain President on the grounds of the Mt. Carmel Church on Saipan was Father Arnold Bendowske, who, as a Capuchin Franciscan, was the Pastor of the church and responsible for the Catholic activities on Saipan from 1952-68. Father Arnold, in mid-1977 the Associate Pastor of Mt. Carmel, remembers the emotionalism expressed by the Saipanese schoolchildren, as well, when news of President Kennedy's assassination was received, and their desire for an appropriate remembrance:

> The municipality put that [monument] up. The people asked to put that up. When Kennedy, the news [of his death] came in, . . . it was a Saturday morning, about 7 o'clock [on Saipan]. . . . A number of the [students], at that time they had no high school except our [Mt. Carmel] high school here, and those kids heard about it. By 10 o'clock in the

morning, they had already taken up a collection, they come in here, and have a mass for President Kennedy. For some reason, he [Kennedy] . . . captured their imagination more than any other President. As part of it, the fact that he was Catholic. But I think it was something else. There was something [in] . . . the way he spoke and acted, and his experience, also, during the War,[14] that he had the facility of making the people feel that he was one of them. So then they [the Saipanese] took up this collection and decided to put up the monument. They were having all kinds of debates as to where they should put it. Then they finally came and asked me if they could put it up on church property, in front of the church. And they put it up there. . . . But the municipality took care of everything.

A subject lesson in the *closeness* of the "separation of church and state" in the northern Marianas, including Guam, is also gleaned from Father Arnold's reply over whether it was *unusual* to place monuments to political leaders on Catholic Church property:

No, we have monuments in Guam to war dead on church grounds. It's unusual in the sense that the [Saipan Municipal] Government would ask the church, because the Government built it. But we have to understand one thing here: the church—we have separation of church and state, eh? But we do not have separation of the people; and the people do not feel that they, as Catholics, belong to the church, and as citizens, they belong to the Government. They feel that they are one. They feel that the church is very much a part of their normal life. So, to them, that would not be at all strange.

THE PEACE CORPS ARRIVES IN MICRONESIA "WITH A BANG"

On August 12, 1966, Micronesian Senator José R. Cruz, of the Marianas, read on the floor of the Senate a copy of a letter written to Jack Vaughn, then Director of the Peace Corps, from President Johnson on May 5 of that year. The President began his letter: "Dear Jack: I am writing to call your attention to a new development in the Trust Territory of the Pacific [Islands] and to urge the greatest possible involvement on the part of the Peace Corps." Johnson's letter continued by indicating what that "new development" was: "On May 3 [1966], there was relayed to me by Secretary [of Interior] Udall a request from members of the Congress of Micronesia for Peace Corps Volunteers to serve in the fields of education, health, public works, and community development."[15]

The question arises, was the "request from members of the Congress of Micronesia for Peace Corps Volunteers to come," as quoted in the above from President Johnson's letter, an *official* action in behalf of the Micronesian Congress? Or was President Johnson's Administration perhaps acting *unilaterally* in the matter? Senator Borja has a photo in his

"To Promote the Social Advancement of the Inhabitants ..."   179

Saipan office, in the rear of his supermarket, showing him and a group of other Micronesians gathered with President Johnson in Washington, D.C. Borja reflects on what prompted that photo session: "I was instrumental in bringing the Peace Corps here [to Micronesia] back in 1965, ... when I went over to the State Department, and we [the islanders and Washington officials] talked about it, and they were asking if there is a plan for [the Peace Corps] coming into the Trust Territory." Senator Borja recounts returning to Saipan after the above 1965 visit to Washington, D.C., and he "prepared and adopted the resources of the Congress of Micronesia that we welcome it [the Peace Corps program]. The Director [Dr. Ross Pritchard] came and give us a speech in the joint session [of the Congress of Micronesia], and so forth, so [we were] very, very happy with things because we need more qualified teachers, more lawyers, and all these things."

Ruth G. Van Cleve, appointed Director of Territorial Affairs (DOTA) in May, 1977, and the then Director of Territories (1964-69) when the Peace Corps was sent to the Trust Territory, wrote in 1974 that, "in '66, the Peace Corps came [to Micronesia] with a bang." She said that the Peace Corps' assignment to the Trust Territory was "inspired by State Department representatives," and was "what the Peace Corps called the saturation technique, designed to use hundreds of volunteers at once to improve conditions in the TT as close to overnight as possible." She concluded with what one may read into the matter a certain amount of pique over Interior's role—or lack of such—in the above decision-making process:

> If Interior had wanted to object, which it did not, it would not possibly have succeeded, for once the Peace Corps juggernaut was in motion, nothing could stop it. Any questions raised were instantly brushed aside, to be answered tomorrow, if ever; legal impediments were dissolved forthwith; any problem that required money to solve could be quickly disposed of, for fiscal constraints seemed nonexistent. Nothing could be permitted to arise that would thwart the forward motion. The Peace Corps was then small, as federal agencies go, but when fired up to get something done, its power was peerless. The only thing to do was relax and enjoy it.[16]

The DOTA's observation, above, points to some concerns that were expressed immediately before the deployment of the Peace Corps to Micronesia and through the years following the "saturation technique" of sending hundreds of volunteers at once to those islands. Michael F. Caldwell, at the University of Guam, was a legislative aide to Congressman John Conyers, Jr. (Democrat, Michigan), in 1966, and recalls that the Peace Corps' project at that time was to bring some 1,600 volunteers to Micronesia: "Some of us raised a little hell over that, in those days. We thought the numbers [1,600] were a little too big, and I think they were. You're talking, really, one volunteer for about every 60 people! That's a horrendous amount of social change." Roger Gale, now in the Tokyo area for the Quaker International Affairs Program, reflects on the "American influence" penetrating deeply into Micronesia, and indicates how impractical it would have been to have, *proportionately*, the same number of Peace Corps volunteers assigned to the Trust Territory in, say, some heavily populated underdeveloped country: "When there were a thousand Peace Corps volunteers in Micronesia, there was one volunteer for every hundred people, and if you try to do the same thing in India, you'd have to have 5 million people [as volunteers]. You can't do that. There's just no way Micronesia is going to escape completely, because it is so small."

After the Peace Corps arrived in Micronesia, the then Senator McCarthy (Democrat, Minnesota), raised the question of whether the Trust Territory is "foreign" or "domestic," realizing that such volunteers were to be deployed to *foreign* areas. McCarthy indicated that "the Peace Corps finally decided it could operate in Micronesia because the [Trust] territory is not a U.S. possession."[17]

The actual number of Peace Corps volunteers sent on two-year tours to Micronesia has ranged from a low of about 200 (in the 1976-77 period) to a high of about 800 (in 1968). Initially, the volunteers, principally young liberal arts graduates, were drawn to Micronesia through the rather "colorful" approach used by Peace Corps recruiters on college campuses. Professor Robbins, the first Legislative Counsel to the Congress of Micronesia, referred to that appeal:

> During the past year [1966-67] an extensive Peace Corps program has been undertaken in the Trust Territory. The presumptuous Peace Corps advertisements in college newspapers more than a year ago, with the announcement that "There Is Trouble in Paradise"[18] and the implication that one should join up for two years of joyful experience and service to help clear up the trouble, produced applicants in such large numbers that an excellent army of volunteers could be selected by a careful screening process.[19]

Professor Robbins later (in 1971) told the Micronesian House of Representatives that the 1966 publicity on Micronesia, by Peace Corps recruiters, was *misleading* in two basic aspects: "[First,] that Micronesia is Paradise, when indeed it is a bewildering 'Wonderland'; [and second,] the implication that the Peace Corps could clear up troubles in a jiffy."[20]

Pritchard's speech before a joint session of the Congress on Saipan in the summer of 1966, to which Borja alluded earlier, was useful in letting those legislators know what the Peace Corps volunteers could expect to be accomplishing among the islanders. Using "five years of statistics" worldwide (as experienced in 50 "host countries during 1961-66") as a

"To Promote the Social Advancement of the Inhabitants..." 181

basis for Micronesia, that Peace Corps official said: "One could say that 50% of all these Volunteers will be classroom teachers, 25% will be working in rural community development, 10% will be in health programs and 10% will be in agriculture programs. ... The average Volunteer lives and works and enjoys life on less than $100 per month."[21]

The last point raised by Peace Corps Director Pritchard, in the above speech, with regard to the average volunteer receiving "less than $100 per month," was probably more applicable to the *outer* islands than the district centers. The average volunteer living in Chalan Kanoa Village, on Saipan—probably the *most* expensive area in the Trust Territory —was receiving (in 1970) $140 per month as a "living allowance" from the Peace Corps, in addition to a "readjustment allowance" of $75 for each month of service, the latter sum paid at once ($1,800 for 24 months) when the volunteer would return home.[22] By mid-1977, Betty Sackbauer, a Peace Corps volunteer also living in the Chalan Kanoa Village, says that the "living allowance" had increased to $180 a month and the "readjustment allowance" (a forced savings account in Washington, D.C.) from $75 to $125 a month. After taxes, that "readjustment" is a net of about $2,300 for the two-year tour. Surprisingly, the $180 "living allowance" is taxed by the Micronesian Congress. (By way of contract, members of the U.S. military either assigned in overseas locations or in stateside posts receive "quarters" and "subsistence" allowances—averaging considerably more than the above Peace Corps "living allowance"—which are nontaxable. American Foreign Service employees also receive attractive nontaxable allowances.)

To have *some* say in the deployment of volunteers throughout the islands of Micronesia, the Congress of Micronesia passed a joint resolution (S.J. Res. 1) in 1966 to establish a "Peace Corps Advisory Council." The late Senator Francis Nuuan, of Yap, in introducing that resolution, warned the Senate that, "if the Congress did not establish it [the council], the Administration would—and then they [the legislators] would have no say in the matter." The resolution passed after two days of debate (with no committee referrals involved) and the House of Representatives accordingly convened as a committee of the whole to consider the Senate resolution. None of the legislators in either house was opposed to this resolution, and the Congress of Micronesia thus established its advisory body.[23]

The Peace Corps volunteers began ariving in Micronesia during October, 1966, the first group totaling some 445 young people. John Pincetich, the first Director of Peace Corps/Micronesia, addressed a joint session of the Congress of Micronesia nine months later (in mid-1967) and expressed his view that the "early doubts" over whether the Peace Corps program would work in Micronesia had "diminished, if not faded"; and he proceeded in that address to indicate that those volunteers were *welcomed* into the islanders' homes, that each corpsman was able to live on the spartan allowance made available (i.e., $80 per month average, with an additional $10 if rent was required), that volunteers were being assigned that first year to many *remote* islands (with some of them serving "on more than 80 of the 97 inhabited islands of Micronesia"), and that *every* volunteer had "some language proficiency, ranging from a working knowledge to fluency," with regard to the "nine different languages" (and numerous dialects thereof) spoken in the islands. As anticipated, the majority (280) of the first 445 volunteers to arrive were assigned to the Trust Territory educational system. Pincetich concluded his remarks to the Congress by stressing that those young volunteers were *not* all "paragons" either of accomplishment, dress, or conduct (the last two characteristics being deficiencies which the Soviet member on the U.N. Trusteeship Council was to criticize a few years later[24]); rather, that they were "individuals who have stepped out of their individual career patterns to be of service to others. They share a strong sense of nonconformity; but they also share a strong conformity of concern for their fellow men; they are action oriented; and . . . dedicated."[25]

HOW OTHERS VIEW THE PEACE CORPS

At the outset, this writer can state that the *consensus* of opinion among American and Micronesian officials, teachers, businessmen, and the youths is that the *impact* of Peace Corps volunteers in the Trust Territory during the first 11 years (1966-77) has been more positive than negative. One reservation articulated by many observers is with regard to the "political" involvement of *some* of those young volunteers, especially in the first few years (which coincided with the Vietnam War). Representative of that latter view is Dennis L. Duncan, who, as mentioned earlier, travels extensively throughout the Pacific:

> The Peace Corps' a tough one to evaluate. I think that it has probably done more good than what you read about in the press. The people tend to be very dedicated. The problem that I see with our Peace Corps volunteers in Micronesia has been that they come down there to do a basic mission and they get caught up in the political side of trying to assist the politicians in expressing their views. And, of course, our young educated university graduates who join the Peace Corps tend to be very vocal in their thought process, and I don't think that that's healthy. But I do think the education, the nursing care, their assistance in agriculture, in sum, their general clerical help to some of the companies: they give courses in accounting to businessmen—things like this, I think, are very beneficial. But on the other side—the involvement in politics—I think, is very dangerous, because it's done by young people who have all the right thought

processes going for them, but they don't really fully understand the Micronesians. And the Micronesian culture is totally different. Any island culture is going to be totally different than the United States of America. It must be.

Andon Amaraich, of Truk, feels that the *influence* in great numbers of Peace Corps volunteers "overwhelmed the Micronesians." He says that the volunteers were "poorly trained," the Administration was not ready to receive them (lacking programs for them to implement); "thus," Amaraich believes, "the volunteers were frustrated" for the most part. Referring to the political involvement, the former Trukese senator recalls that "many of the Peace Corps criticisms were legitimate, which the Administration did not like." Overall, he feels that the volunteers "did good work in Health and Education" areas. Lazarus Salii, from Palau, adds that "the greatest impact that the Peace Corps had on Micronesians was to say, 'You deserve more. Ask for more. Make these people [islanders] critical.'" Salii believes that, in general, such was "an irresponsible impact. The volunteers couldn't influence basic American policy for the Trust Territory. I think they turned off most of the responsible officers. A lot of them [the volunteers] were liberal, radical-type of people; young people who really had no sense of responsibility in terms of what the United States was involved with in Micronesia." Salii, the former chief negotiator for future political status (from 1967-76), acknowledges that such thinking as the politically motivated portion of the volunteers exhibited was "something that was coming" among the islanders, themselves; however, Salii believes that Peace Corps involvement in the political realm "actually accelerated the dissatisfaction between Micronesians with the United States." Again, Salii agrees with the consensus: "In terms of their impact on education I think they may have done a lot of things to fill the gap in the Trust Territory." He questions, however, whether the educational involvement of many volunteers "is really a lasting effect on Micronesia."

N. Neiman Craley, Jr., former U.S. Congressman (1965-67) and Director of Public Affairs in the Trust Territory (1967-72), then a Special Assistant to the High Commissioner (1972-76) before serving in the interim Government of the Northern Marianas (from April, 1976), believes that the Peace Corps volunteers were "a real thorn during the years '66, '67, '68, '69, largely because . . . there were far too many of them, but, primarily, it was the Trust Territory wasn't prepared for them. And we had such a large number here, and there was no coordination. The people [volunteers] were wandering around and didn't know what to do." Craley feels that, when the volunteers were in that kind of a situation (during 1966-69), they became "disenchanted, dissatisfied, unhappy, and the people that they were working with in Government were obviosuly unhappy. But I think, on the whole, they've been a definite asset." Craley, from his vantage point for so many years in the Trust Territory headquarters on Capitol Hill, Saipan, recalls that "the biggest problem," originally, was "an incompatibility between the Administration and the Peace Corps . . . to blend and work out people. There was a competition going on. Peace Corps wanted to get as many volunteers as it could, . . . [and] the Trust Territory [Government] many times was trying to prove that they didn't need them, didn't want them."

Two Trust Territory Government officials who previously were former Peace Corps volunteers to South America and Africa, respectively, and who later served as professional staff members for the Peace Corps, are Samuel McPhetres and William D. Jackson. McPhetres, who was a volunteer in Ecuador (1962-64) before being a professional in the Ivory Coast and Somalia (1966-70), first arrived in the Trust Territory to be the Peace Corps Director for the Truk District (1970-72). McPhetres, a researcher in the Political Affairs Division's Education for Self-Government (ESG) Program, believes that "there was a definite switch in Peace Corps philosophy about 1970" in Micronesia, by which time the numbers of volunteers were receding. He agrees with those quoted earlier that, when the total was running around 700 during 1967-69, "the place was over-saturated with volunteers." McPhetres also notes an "anti-Vietnam War" syndrome experienced by some of the Peace Corps workers in the islands:

> There was a lot of the anti-Vietnam, anti-Administration types who got very much involved in what they saw here as perhaps not in conformity with the best ideals of American Government, who saw U.S. Administration as being primarily for the U.S. goals and conflicted with the Peace Corps philosophy rather strongly. I think you can mark the turndown of the Vietnam War with an increase in more passive volunteers. You just don't have the activists here. I saw the last of them, I think, when I was in Truk. Most of them [the volunteers] now are carefully selected as to type. There are very few—very few—"letters-to-the-editor" writers, outspoken people, as had existed previously. . . . When I came out here [in 1970], you were constantly running across a volunteer who was speaking out on one or another issue. . . . The switch-over from Peace Corps to ACTION [in July, 1971] had a big effect on how things were developed out here. Then, with the reduction in numbers, volunteers generally tended to have more to do.

Jackson, in the first group of Peace Corps (and third to be sent overseas, to Nigeria), elaborates on the "effects of the Vietnam War" on some of the volunteers he saw come through the Peace Corps training program, when he was a staff instructor during 1965-66:

> [We] began to get a type, with the Vietnam War being so tremendously unpopular, you really had people trying to join Peace Corps as a haven, to avoid being drafted. This is a reality. And these people weren't neces-

sarily as idealistic, or as committed, as we felt, say, we were in 1961, because they would just tell you, "Hey, man, I'm trying to avoid the 'Nam!" And that's why they were there in training. . . . I would say this [draft dodging] was around a good 30-40 percent.

Jackson also considers the "single-most impressive thing about the Peace Corps volunteers in Micronesia" has been their ability to "learn the languages." He observes that Europeans, and some Americans, hold to the "myth" that "Americans are incapable of learning foreign languages," and he gives examples of volunteers he trained, or saw in training, who were able, through the "oral method" (i.e., you hear, you speak; you hear, you speak; you hear, you speak—instead of the traditional writing-and-reading approach), to become conversant in so-called "exotic" languages: "[Volunteers learned] such tongues as Hausa and Ebo and tongues here in Micronesia—Mokileze, Pingelapese, Trukese, and Palauan—you name it, they learn it; and they do a remarkably good job. . . . I've seen Peace Corps volunteers from countries all around the world . . . learning and using these so-called 'impossible languages.' "

Jackson believes that the "hardest part" of being a Peace Corps volunteer in Micronesia, especially in the outer islands, is the *isolation,* which he feels is worse than that he experienced in Africa as a volunteer teacher:

> I lived in the bush 500 miles up-country and 180 miles from the nearest electricity. But it was quite possible to get into a Jeep, or to a mammy wagon, or an African bus. And rough trip though it was, you could get to so-called "civilization" in several hours. In Micronesia, remember, when you're assigned—particularly in an outer island—you are totally cut off. You don't even get daily mail; in fact, you're lucky if you get mail every three months. . . . If there's been Peace Corps problems, it's related to the isolated, outer-island assigned volunteer.

Maynard Neas, while being "pretty much turned off" by the "initial impact group" of Peace Corps volunteers for the first four years (1966-70), in hindsight, expressed admiration for what some of the outer-island volunteers have accomplished: "Looking back, I'd say that the elementary schoolteachers that went out into Yap—I mean, out to Ulithi and Bulubul [both in Yap] and into Kili [in the Marshalls], and places like that—they have my admiration and respect. I couldn't have done what they did, . . . [which was] an immense amount of good."

THE SUCCESS OF PEACE CORPS LAWYERS

Senator Borja lauds those young American attorneys who volunteered to be Peace Corps lawyers for the same "living allowance/readjustment savings" arangement for all other volunteers. Borja says that "a good example" of such lawyers "is Michael White, who is recently the Counsel for the Congress of Micronesia. Now he has become the private [practitioner on Saipan, in a law firm]. He's helping as a consultant to a lot of people here." The untiring work of three volunteer lawyers in Peace Corps Legal Services—Thomas L. Whittington, Sharon N. Ruzumna, and Donald T. Bliss—resulted, during their two-year tours in the late 1960s, in what should prove to be of *lasting* importance to a developing Micronesia. These young people edited the "opinions of the High Court of the Trust Territory" (both the Appellate and Trial Division levels) for the period of 1951-68, their completed efforts eventually published in four volumes by the Equity Publishing Corporation, in Orford, New Hampshire (beginning in 1969). Professor Robbins commented on the "unusual satisfaction and long-range importance to the Trust Territory and to those interested in it, as well as anyone interested in political and judicial modernization in the publication of the *Trust Territory Reports* under the editorship of Whittington, et al."[26] Edward P. Furber, retired Chief Justice of the High Court of the Trust Territory (from 1948-68), expressed particular joy in seeing the Peace Corps volunteer lawyers' dedication to that compilation of court cases in Micronesia.[27]

Craley recalls several volunteer lawyers who left their Peace Corps assignment—one or two of them during their tours, the rest, afterward—to join the Congress of Micronesia's legal staff, in addition to White (mentioned by Borja, above) in private practice on Saipan. Craley also says that possibly "150 volunteers . . . [have] ended up working for the Trust Territory, either for the Government or the private sector, over the 10 years that they've been here." Craley says the jobs available to former Peace Corps volunteers include the legal positions (mentioned previously), teachers, administrators, and "any number of different jobs."

Scott H. Stege, a lawyer in the Attorney General's Office in the Trust Territory Government, spent his two years (1973-75) in the Peace Corps first with the Marshall Islands District Legislature (for 20 months) and then the final four months with the Marianas District Legislature. As his desire was to remain in the islands, especially after he married a Marshallese before finishing his Peace Corps tour, he looked around for job possibilities. There was a need for American lawyers as advisers to the delegates to the 1975 Constitutional Convention on Saipan, so Stege applied for one of those positions and was accepted. In 1976, he signed a two-year contract to work in the legal office of the Trust Territory headquarters.

Stege's reflections on being a Peace Corps volunteer lawyer in recent years give an indication of the difficulties still being faced in Micronesia. He received practically no "Peace Corps training" before reporting to Majuro, in the Marshalls, for his first assignment. The "training program at that time [1973] was composed of three elements: cross-cultural, a skills acquisition, and a language ... [lasting] six weeks." However, Stege was unable to participate as the District Legislature began at the same time and those legislators had been without an attorney for two years. Thus, he was "very warmly received" by them. (Neas says Stege performed "almost superhuman professional work" for the Marshalls District Legislature during that time.) Half of the Marshallese legislators spoke no English, and the daily journals (the proceedings of the legislature) were in Marshallese. Only the bills and resolutions were in both languages. The Chamorro language was used on the floor of the legislature in the Marianas except when the Legislative Counsel, Bill Nabors (an American attorney practicing on Saipan) participated; then, "they would, of course, phrase it [the question for Nabors] in English, and he would respond in English." Another variation in the Marianas Legislature (which was replaced in 1976 by the interim legislature for the Government of the Northern Marianas) was that the journals were printed in both English and Chamorro.

THE PEACE CORPS DEPARTS THE MARIANAS

A member of the last group of Peace Corps volunteers to serve in the northern Marianas is Betty Sackbauer, who completed her two-year tour in July, 1977. Thus, after almost 11 years of the Peace Corps program in the Marianas, future volunteers will concentrate their efforts in the districts of the Trust Territory. While the apparent assumption might be that the Marianas ended their association with the Peace Corps due to the pending commonwealth status, the termination for the volunteers probably would have occurred irrespective of that political development. Why? Jean Olopai, presently the Registrar and a teacher at the Marianas High School on Saipan, and married to a Saipanese Carolinian, was a Peace Corps volunteer in the northern Marianas during 1969-71. She believes that *rapport* between the volunteers and the inhabitants of the Marianas is about the same in mid-1977 as it was in her earlier volunteer days—*poor:*

> We [the Peace Corps] don't belong here. We didn't then, and we still don't.... The problems we had then [1969-71] are the same problems that volunteers have now. We're supposed to live on the same level as the people, we're supposed to be the same as them—not better, not worse—but we always came out a little lower. At the time I came, we were always horribly criticized for the way we dressed. Before we come into Peace Corps, we're told you can only bring so many pounds of clothing, and they send us a list of what to bring: girls bring loose-fitting dresses and wear zories; boys, shorts and T-shirts. That's all the people wear. You come to Saipan and you're a bum! You dress like that, [but] ... the people here don't.

They [the islanders] dress like that when they're working around the house, or they're out in the garden; but to go to school, to go to work, you don't dress like that. We got criticized for that.

Some problems faced in the northern Marianas by the Peace Corps volunteers were unique vis-à-vis those in other districts, if at all present. For instance, the Peace Corps Director for the Marianas District during 1969-71 would not permit the volunteers to own vehicles. That *sounds* reasonable; however, on Saipan, the most developed of all district centers in Micronesia at the time, Olopai recalls that "only old people and little children walked. You could tell it was a volunteer because they were walking or riding a bicycle." Olopai indicates that condition changed in more recent years so that a bicycle is considered respectable. A more serious matter for the Peace Corps volunteers in the Marianas was the dichotomy existing between what those young workers expected (the ideal) and what they found (reality):

> One of the problems we had was being on Saipan. For instance, for myself, when I thought of going to the Peace Corps, when I read about Micronesia and all, I was ready to give up everything and try to start . . . all over. Other people, and help them. . . . I had the ideal, etc. But, I came to Saipan and everything was here! I mean, we didn't have to learn the language, because every place we went, we could use English. We had water, we had electricity in every house we looked at, and, by the end of my first year [in 1970], we had television here. Telephones. . . . So, when I went to Truk for . . . a conference workshop, . . . I did meet a lot of the volunteers [from other districts] and spent a lot of time with them down there. And when I came back [to Saipan], our Director said, "Well, are you ready to transfer?" And I said, "That's what I *thought* Peace Corps would be; but, I can't go now, because I'm *not* ready now to give up everything I was ready to give up before when I started!" (Italics mine.)

Betty Sackbauer relates the *high* attrition rate of her 1975-77 group—11 of the original 17 volunteers terminated *early*—to the *reasons* given for quitting: " 'Personal problems,' such as pregnancy, death in the family, or family needs you back home, this type of thing. [Also,] the people who 'didn't like it': a lot of their concept of where they were going was not what they found in Saipan. Maybe if they'd been on an outer island, that's more of what they were looking for."

(The Peace Corps volunteers' *main* involvement in Micronesia—in *educational* programs—is discussed in chapter 4, following.)

CAT EFFORTS: "COSMETIC" OR USEFUL?

In 1969, a 13-member Naval construction battalion (or "Seabees") arrived in the Trust Territory. This was the first of seven "civic action teams" (or "CATs") to be assigned to Micronesia within the next year. Five of those CATs were Navy Seabees; one was an Air Force military team, and the last was composed of Army military personnel. The initial CAT mission has remained consistent down to mid-1977: to labor to improve the living conditions of the Micronesians as well as instruct and then employ indigenous laborers to *assist* in building needed community projects.[28]

Naval Commander David Burt, Special Assistant to the Admiral as CinCPAC (Commander-in-Chief, Pacific) Representative for the Trust Territory, stationed on Guam, indicates that the Seabee teams (mostly composed of 13 individuals) are deployed on *vertical* construction projects: building classrooms or dispensaries; the Air Force and earlier Army teams are/were comprised of nine members each, and assigned to *horizontal* tasks (mainly, road construction).

How did the CATs happen to come to Micronesia? Were they invited by the Congress of Micronesia or the Administering Authority? Or was this a *subtle* gesture to "slip the military into the Trust Territory" in preparation for "massive troop buildups" in later years? Two islanders, both of whom were in the Senate during the 1969-70 commitment of the first seven CATs, separately agree that the effort was "cosmetic" (or transparent). For instance, Lazarus Salii, of Palau, feels that the CATs have accomplished something, "in terms of building bridges and small roads, things like that," then adds the transparent nature of the CAT program and how it was brought to Micronesia:

> This [the CAT mission] was cosmetics that they [the teams] were involved in, but, while it's here, . . . get something done. But, it's just too transparent. The U.S. military . . . was not always able to mix with the community, would get into fights with the natives. It was insulting to me, personally, I think, to try to do it this way. I would have expected an official of the military . . . [would come and say they are] going to assist the Trust Territory, assist the Congress of Micronesia, by doing this, with the Seabees, or ICC [OICC, Officer-in-Charge of Construction], or whatever it is—the best they have—the [Army] Corps of Engineers, and come in and not try to disguise this. . . . But, you couldn't refuse an official. But, I think it was a hasty, ill-conceived program.

Former Senator Andon Amaraich, from Truk, believes the "initial problem" of the CATs was one of *funding*. "Some of the work is important, but the CATs have lost their main purpose: to train Micronesians in the use of heavy equipment." Again, Amaraich concurs with Salii, in the above, that the CAT efforts were "cosmetic—that was obvious."

Craley recalls that there was "a considered effort to show the military and the Defense Department in the best possible light" back in the late 1960s, when "there was some discussion—and a great deal of speculation—

that the military had designs for the Trust Territory." He indicates that, in the thinking of some people, "the military had . . . somewhat of a bad image" in Micronesia. Thus, Craley believes that the U.S. military wanted to "neutralize" that negative image:

> I think there was some desire to kind of "neutralize" that image by putting teams out that would . . . live in the local communities and work with the local people, and accomplish some projects that weren't being done by the Trust Territory Government and, at the same time, provide some training and everything else. And I think, in the long run, it was also an asset. But I don't think we got back the dollars, or we got back the result that we spent the dollars for. A lot of those teams—and, if I recall correctly, I believe they came in for a period of eight months, one team—I think there was a fair amount accomplished by their coming in, particularly where districts were set up to deal with them. Again, it was like the Peace Corps: sometimes these teams came in and . . . nobody at the district level was prepared for them. And they [the team] sat around for a month or two, and all they did was work around their own complex, and the officer-in-charge was off trying to get the local committee to decide what priorities or what projects they [the community] wanted; [or] he was off trying to get . . . materials.

Craley verifies that "the military buildup" concern of some observers after the initial arrival of the CATs in 1969 was present: "I know that a lot of people said, 'You know, this is the first wave. And you get seven teams out here now, and the next group that comes, they're going to have 12,000 troops, and they're going to build airfields, and the Marines are coming, and the Army's coming, and everything else.' And, of course, it hasn't worked, that [buildup] plan."

Thomas E. Tavares, Chief of Roads, Harbors, and Structures Branch in the Trust Territory Government, feels that the CATs, while doing "a lot of road work," have not been as successful or effective as they might have been. The reason? Tavares sees a distinct *weakness* in the lack of "follow-through" on road projects, in particular: "They've [the CATs have] done a lot of road work, . . . [but] today, what they've done three or four years ago no longer exists. There has been no follow-through in what they had done." As an example of the road problems, Tavares cites the type of material used—*coral*, instead of asphalt: "After the first big rain, then the road all washes away, because most of the roads they [the CATs] put in are not paved. Just coral laid on the ground with a few culverts and a lot of them [the roads] don't have enough culverts to take up the water that flows in a heavy rain. So, a lot of your road system washes away."

Whose fault is the *lack* of a "follow-through" on projects such as roads when a CAT is involved? Josef Rotholz, Technical Adviser in the Community Development Division of the Trust Territory Government, and a structural engineer, became the "coordinator" at the headquarters level for the CATs almost by default. Dwight Heine originally was the "official coordinator," but, as Rotholz recalls, "he [Heine] did not go out in the field, and he was not very much involved in practical coordination; he was involved mainly in administrative coordination." It was Rotholz's involvement in housing for Community Development in the outer islands, and in the designing of small bridges and water systems which brought him into contact with the CATs in 1970: "While I was doing this, I was faced with the civil action teams because they were [also] doing these jobs. And in one of their conferences between the High Commissioner and the admiral, in Hawaii, they requested a coordinator, and they suggested me as the coordinator." Thus, Rotholz's duties since 1970 with the CATs, which consume about 10 percent of his time, are at the practical level.

Rotholz says that the lack of "follow-up" on CAT projects is *not* the fault of those teams, and indicates why:

> It's definitely not the civic action team's fault . . . there's no follow-up, because this is not their responsibility. The responsibility is up to the community. There is a problem—and this is . . . an engineering problem: when you build a road in this area and you don't cover it with asphalt, it deteriorates. But, the same thing is being done by other agencies, not only the civic action teams. The [CATs] . . . have got no control over the materials that they are using. They would definitely be in a position to apply asphalt on a coral road. They are building now a 17-mile coral road in one of the islands in Truk, in Fefan, and they are doing a very nice job. They are contacted, they give self-help [training], . . . but we know that eventually, if it's [the road's] not covered with asphalt, it will deteriorate. Another item is the growth here of all these wild, vegetation is very fast, and if you don't crop it away it will take over the road. But I disagree with the statement that . . . it's a matter of "cosmetics" [by the CATs].

Neas has seen CATs at work in three of the districts (Ponape, Palau, and the Marianas). His impression is that they work hard and have good rapport with the islanders: "They had, I thought, a very representative group of young Americans in their social habits and also in their work habits. They would work them [the Micronesians]! I'm telling you, they *worked!* Those guys, I've never seen people that tackled their job any more professionally than those teams that I actually saw in the field."

Commander Burt, stressing the "training" aspect of the CAT mission, also points to a different type of "follow-through" problem: "Micronesians have been trained [in the use of heavy equipment] . . . Unfortunately, many of the districts find themselves with many, many bulldozer operators—and no bulldozers—after the team leaves." Rotholz observes that the CATs' "job is not the main purpose. The job is only a means, of course, to provide a facility. But they [the teams] would like to train. And if they did not train people, maybe the people were not available. But most of the time they did train people. There is, sometimes, we have problems in funding . . . for the trainees."

Inflation has hit the CAT program. Initially, a team in the early days (1969-70) cost $100,000 for the six-to-eight month deployment. By 1976-77, the cost rose to $250,000 per team. The Fiscal Year (FY) 1977 budget was over $500,000 for two teams; the request in FY 1978 was $800,00 for three CATs. All costs *except* the pay and equipment come from the district budgets, which, in turn, rely on the Administering Authority's annual appropriation from the U.S. Congress. Rotholz gives a breakdown on the Trust Territory Government's part in the financial support of a team: "We pay their [the CATs'] per diem, . . . the amortization of the equipment, . . . their travel to the mainland and back, and for resupply shipment—not the resupply, itself, but the shipment of the resupply. . . . Their resupply and their equipment, their salaries, . . . are paid by the Department of Defense." The materials are also furnished by the host district.

Tavares, who earlier mentioned the "follow-through" problem, recommends that the CAT be permitted to *complete* such projects as roads *100* percent: "It doesn't have to be a big road, or a wide road. A one-lane highway would be fine, and, where it's not too expensive, put sufficient drainage in it where it would last 10, 20 years." That *lasting* condition depends on asphalt, not crushed coral.

(The reader would, at this point, be referred to the *Annual Report* for a detailed listing of the CATs' achievements since 1969; however, no entries to date have been made in the yearly reports to the United Nations. Those reports, while interesting reading, are often erroneous and incomplete.)

As a concluding comment on the visibility of the CATs in Micronesia, one of the officials with whom this writer conversed, after noting that, "generally, I think the CAT program has been very successful," and that "you're always going to have criticism of this or that," observed, in the fall of 1976: "I don't think the military should be embarrassed or ashamed that it is interested in the Trust Territory. After all, why shouldn't we be? Fifty percent of our concern in the United States comes from abroad as far as things that we need and what we do."

THE NEED FOR A "WORKABLE" CIP

The above section on the civil action teams is interesting from the standpoint of "small, community projects," for an expenditure of even $800,000 by the Trust Territory Government as a share in the expense of maintaining three CATs during FY 1978 is *minuscule* in comparison with the basic infrastructure needs at present in the six districts of the Trust Territory (including the newest district, Kosrae). High Commissioner Winkel, in his 1977 appearance before the U.N. Trusteeship Council, listed a "capital improvements infrastructure" (involving "roads, bridges, ports and harbors, airfields, plus sewer, water and power systems in every district") as *one* of the "four fronts" which the Trust Territory Government "will be moving forward on . . . simultaneously," with the goal being to have such an infrastructure "in place, at the earliest practicable date."[29]

Koichi Wong, Director of the Department of Public Works for the Trust Territory Government, reflects on the paucity of "public works projects" accomplished during the "Rust Territory" period of the 1950s, which he blames on the small budgets available (averaging around $6 million yearly for the *entire* operation of Micronesia, as discussed in earlier chapters). Wong indicates that a $145 million appropriation from the U.S. Congress was earmarked "for construction of most basic infrastructures. That's roads, docks and harbors, airfields, water, sewer, and power. Within the next five years [1976-81] we will spend $145 [million]." That amount, which Wong admits as probably down to about $138 million by late 1976, is part of the annual budget item known as "capital improvement program" (CIP). To assure that such a large funding is *properly* managed, Wong says that the U.S. Navy was given responsibility for the CIP:

> Recognizing the fact that the Navy is much more qualified to do this [CIP] program—and maybe not necessarily qualified, but maybe more efficient and [has] people for support from Guam, Hawaii, and Washington [D.C.]—maybe they [the Navy] can do this job better. Not only that, but the concern of the [then] Jackson Committee [Interior and Insular Affairs], that accountability of Micronesia was, this [Trust Territory] Administration was not very famous for having good accountability. So, concern over that [accountability problem] and recognizing that we have to maintain what we've got, . . . a division of responsibility was made so that the Navy would take care of the new construction. And we [in Public Works] are still participating in the new construction—some smaller projects and also coordination. But we [Public Works] will concentrate on the operation and maintenance which is very much neglected throughout the years because of this curtain [i.e., between Headquarters and the districts].

Van Cleve agrees with Wong's appraisal of the lack of "infrastructure" in earlier years, and noted that, even with the *doubling* of the annual budget in 1963 (to $15 million), the "capital improvement" area suffered, and, within two years, was *unfunded:* "In '63, . . . $7 million out of $15 million appropriated was available for capital improvements. The next year, $6 million out of $17.5 million was so available. The year after that all of the authorized $17.5 million was required for the costs of administration—for teachers' salaries, medical supplies, economic development, and the like. Nothing was left for further capital improvements."[30]

Lieutenant Commander James Wood, Resident Officer-in-Charge of Construction (ROICC) for the Trust Territory, and the Program Coordinator for the CIP in Micronesia, elaborates on how the Navy came to be responsible for this infrastructure program:

> In February of 1976, a memorandum of agreement was signed between the Naval Facilities Engineering Command, which is [OICC's higher headquarters] . . . in Washington [D.C.], and the High Commissioner, . . . at the urging of the Office of Territorial Affairs [Zeder then the Director], that the OICC take over all the Capital Improvement Programming. . . . The Navy would administer all of it—both the design and the construction.

Wood also repeats what Wong says about the problems of "accountability" found in Micronesia, and the then Jackson Committee's concern. (Senator Jackson relinquished chairmanship of the now defunct Committee on Interior and Insular Affairs in early 1977, and he became chairman of the newly created Committee on Energy and Natural Resources.)

Wood comments on the difficulty in *defining* what a "basic infrastructure" is in Micronesia. When the Congress of Micronesia hesitated to define that term, Commander Wood says that he defined it for that legislative body: "Something that will get products and people in [to a district center], and products and people out, provide enough utilities to run these things that we're doing, and then suppose that we decide that we have to move around with these population centers and down to whatever it is you're going to call industry, and whatever it is that agriculture's going to be."

A major problem facing the CIP has been "land ownership," especially when it comes time to construct a project. Wood gives an airfield development as an example:

> Say I'm going to build an airfield. There may be 200 owners around here. So, the first thing you do is you go out and you say, "All right. Where's your land going?" And he says, "It goes over to that rock." And so you've got to turn to his neighbor and say, "Is that right? Do you agree with that?" "Yes. That's his side, and this is my side." So then you've got to go down to that one and that one and you say, "Is that where your land is?" [Referring to other neighbors in the area.] "Yes." So everything's fine, and you get started. But you forget Joe Neighbor, who is a cousin that lives over in Ponape. He comes home and he says, "What are you guys doing? That's my land!" And they say, "Oh, yes. We forgot!" So you've got to go back, and you go through this all the time.

Another example of the difficulties involved in "land issues," especially in Micronesia, where land is a *sacred* commodity and very traditional, occurred on an outer island in the Yap District: "We were running a power line which was going to bring electricity out to this little remote village which wanted it," Wood recalls. "But, it passed through another guy's domain. And he says, 'You're not putting that—line through here!' So, all the poles were laying there, waiting to be put up. They hadn't been bought. They [the islanders] burned them!"

To avoid the above examples from being repeated as the five-year CIP effort accelerates, the OICC writes letters to the District Administrators and advises them that *they* "must give us [the OICC] 'land clearance'" before the project will begin. Thus, the pressure is placed on the laps of the district leaders to resolve any "land disputes" which might otherwise hinder CIP projects under way.

Ambassador Winkel reports in mid-1977 that a number of CIP projects are in the planning stage or under construction, including seven new inter-island ships under construction (for field trip services to the outer islands); approval of a $10 million appropriation to build a new airport for Truk; plans for an airport at Kosrae being processed, the hoped-for construction date being in October, 1978; construction of a Palau Airport, which is hoped to begin in December, 1979; and improved communications as "a priority" for the Kosrae District which, when completed, would "permit full inter-connection with the Trust Territory inter-district and Headquarters voice and data network, including the capability for overseas telephone calls." The Koror-Babelthaup Bridge, replacing the old ferryboat service, opened to traffic in the spring of 1977.[31]

Senator Jackson, in a personal letter to this writer in May, 1977, said that he believes "the United States has admirably fulfilled its commitments under the Trusteeship Agreement of 1947 in terms of . . . providing a capital infrastructure capable of supporting whatever economic development the peoples [islanders] themselves wish to pursue." In light of the foregoing problems facing the CIP during 1976-77, it will be interesting to see how correct, or presumptuous, the senior senator from the state of Washington is when 1981 arrives.

A "SKILLED FILIPINO" INVASION?

What do Guam, the northern Marianas (principally, Saipan), and the present six districts of the Trust Territory all have in common? The answer to this question is in two parts: first, the *absence* of a "skilled indigenous labor force"; and second, the *infusion* of large numbers of "alien contract laborers," the vast majority of whom are Filipinos.

The extent of alien hiring in Micronesia becomes more evident when one considers that the relatively small island of Saipan, within its population of some 10,000 includes about *1,000* Filipinos. Caldwell confirms that there is a "Filipino Club of Micronesia" organized throughout the area, with small groups of Filipinos belonging to that club in almost every district. Joe Murphy, Editor of the Guam *Pacific News,* notes that Guam, with a "background . . . much richer in the sense of being more of a melting pot of . . . aliens, coming from other areas," is at present "sort of being flooded by a lot of particularly Filipino immigrants, and, in a way, this has caused some problems on the island." Murphy estimates that there are perhaps 20,000 Filipinos on Guam, that island having an overall population of some 110,000 (about one-third being U.S. military personnel and their families). The predominately Chamorro inhabitants on Guam, Murphy feels, fear that they (the Chamorros) may become like the Hawaiians: unable to elect their own political leaders, "at least not of native blood. And this is disturbing to them."

There is *no* fear at present that the Filipinos might take over "political control" on Saipan or in the districts of the Trust Territory. What kinds of work are they contracted to perform in Micronesia? Skilled construction work is the predominant employment, although there are some *100* CPAs on Saipan alone. Laoncio Suarez, the CPA at the Hafadai Beach Hotel on that island, says that the accounting staff of the Royal Taga Hotel (owned by the Jones brothers, from Guam) is headed by a Filipino. When asked if he makes more money on Saipan than he would in the Philippines, Suarez is affirmative, and notes that he is "Number 14,116" as a registered CPA in the Philippines. (He completed his college work at the University of East, in Manila, in 1972, so his "registration number" is probably much lower than that of, say, a 1977 graduate of that university or other schools in the Philippines.) Thus, the combination of overpopulation and unemployment at home vis-à-vis a two-year contract (with renewal possibilities) to work in Micronesia at higher wages is the dilemma facing the professional and skilled Filipinos. For those who opt to come to Micronesia under contract, there is usually the separation of their families for at least two years or longer, if the workers decide to "extend" and their employers can justify such retentions.

Some Filipinos have become businessmen on Saipan. The most successful at present is Jesus B. Yumul, General Manager of the YCO (Yumul Company) Hardware and Builders. Rated as a civil engineer in Manila during 1968, Yumul remembers that, during that time, "construction companies in big Manila are hiring workers for Saipan to work for this sewer line projects here [on Saipan]. So, I was one of the lucky engineers to be sent here for that project." Eventually, Yumul married a Chamorro. The YCO business is a corporation involving three persons: Yumul's wife, his mother-in-law, and a third Saipanese. The YCO employs 11 aliens (all Filipinos) and three local laborers. Asked if the Saipanese are able to do the skilled construction work involved—the largest project to date for the YCO being the Headquarters Personnel Building, a $150,000 contract—Yumul replies: "Since 1970, we've been trying to hire local guys. And if Saipanese have experience and education, then we can rely on them. But most of the others, like those without any background experience or education, they usually don't care about work." (One of those three "local hires," in the fall of 1976, had been with YCO for a year.)

Another Filipino has a seamstress and tailoring shop on Saipan. Generally, the Filipinos on that island are either involved as skilled construction workers, clerical help in one of the levels of government (Trust Territory headquarters, district [now, the Government of the Northern Marianas], or municipal), or as a CPA. During 1976-77, four Filipinos were teachers at the Marianas High School (one each in business, English, social studies, and vocational education). The Saipanese Principal, Victorio S. Cepeda, says those four are *good* teachers.

The Sablan Construction Company, also on Saipan, employs about 300 laborers, most of whom are Filipinos. In a "joint venture" with a large Japanese concern, the Shimizu Construction Company (to be discussed in chapter 5), since 1975, there are 80 Filipinos employed out of a work force of 90. The *difference* in pay between employment for Filipinos in construction on Saipan vis-à-vis what they would receive at home, in the Philippines, is striking. Brad Nago, General Manager of Sablan Construction, and a Hawaiian himself, says: "No matter how skillful you are in the Philippines, you might make *two* pesos an hour as a highly skilled construction worker. Here, in Saipan, the *minimum* wage that we pay at Sablan Construction is $1.25, which is equivalent to about *12* pesos an hour in the Philippines." (Italics mine.) Thus, a 6-to-1 ratio in wages.

Socially, are the Filipino workers and, in the rarer cases where their families accompany them (or join them at a later time), their families accepted into the island community? First, most Filipino construction workers live in the company's compound, so that controls most frictions between the local people and the Filipinos. Yumul believes that the "work ethic" of those aliens does not allow for civil disobedience: "The main reason they [the Filipinos] are here is to work, so I don't think they'll go out looking for trouble." The Northern Marianas Immigration Officer, a Mr. Castro, when asked if the approximately 1,000 Filipinos on Saipan get into trouble, replies: "No, very little. The people who bring them—like Sablan and Block [another company]—they watch these [aliens] very carefully." Castro also observes that drunkenness is not a problem among the Filipinos on that island.

Francisco C. Ada, former District Administrator in the Marianas, articulates a view expressed by several politicians when he says that "third-nation immigration," with specific reference to the Filipino laborers, ought to be "tightened up" through legislation: "For example, if a company here [on Saipan] does not have the local resource to hire, he would be permitted to import, let's say, an accountant, with a legal provision that that accountant, who is brought in, has a timetable to train a local individual to take over." (This is also the policy for "Micronization" instituted in the Trust Territory Government, as discussed earlier.)

Commander Wood, the ROICC for the CIP in Micronesia, indicates that Filipinos are contracted in that program throughout the Trust Territory, as well as Koreans, another highly skilled labor market in the Pacific.

MICRONESIANS, ATTITUDES, AND WORK

The Social Security Office of the Trust Territory Government has records on 17,000 islanders who participate in the Social Security Program. This is out of a work force of some 50,000. Additionally, about 500 Micronesians are receiving benefit payments. Most of those involved in the work force are employed by one of the levels of government in the islands.

To state that the above workers are all diligent, conscientious, and hardworking would be to impose a standard usually reserved for the British Civil Service. Still, there are certain "character traits" among the islanders which *impede* their development in all four areas considered in this book: the political, economic, social, and educational. For instance, there is the "Micronesian time" syndrome, by which practically everything seems to start *late*. Even a movie showing this writer and his wife attended on Saipan in 1970 started 20 minutes late. (Of course, very few patrons were in the theater at the scheduled hour!) Perhaps a few other examples will reinforce some of these negative traits which, if overcome, would aid in the advancement of the islanders.

One longtime U.S. employee tells of having worked in Supply at the Ponape District Center, on Kolonia. When it came time for the Micronesian employees to inventory USDA food, they would make "estimates" of what they *thought* they had on hand and what they *thought* had been distributed. This necessitated that American make the *physical* inventory. Thus, when the use of computers is discussed as an answer for information-gathering by Health Services, Personnel, and other departments in the Trust Territory Government, one should remember that the information fed into computers is only as reliable as the efforts made by the employees gathering the material.

An entry in the *EDLF Report* of 1976 (see chapter 2) records an example of the problems experienced in administering loans in the districts. It seems one district economic development officer had only an eighth-grade education, and one of his responsibilities in that now defunct program was "to register EDLF loan security agreements with a clerk of a District Court. It took him 10 months to get the job done. The Court is less than 100 yards from his office."

Alex P. Luzama, the senior Micronesian official with Air Mike (see chapter 2), says that the drivers for the hotels in the various district centers may or may not pick up the tourists arriving at the airport terminals and expecting to be driven to the hotels: "Many times the driver will ... just come up and, if he doesn't see anyone that he might know, why then he turns around and goes back to the hotel, and the poor tourists are left there at the airport. So, that's a problem."

The problem of punctuality, as well as discipline by supervisors, is a difficult matter for the islanders to resolve. Duncan, with the Bank of America's Asia Division, feels that some of the senior Micronesian employees with that bank in the islands should be branch managers by this stage; however, he says that "the educational problems are immense for us down there because most of the Micronesians will go through the equivalent of a high school, but their high school education doesn't quite equate to what a U.S. high school would be." Then Duncan touches a sensitive point which continues to be a stumbling block for the Micronesians: "When it comes to supervision of people, the Micronesians and their culture, they have a difficult time in supervising their own people. It's not their way. It's more of a family-type of environment. The guy [islander] who has to be the boss and say you must be at work at 8:30 in the morning is the bad guy."

The following chapter focuses on the fourth, and final, goal in Article 6 of the Trusteeship Agreement of 1947: to promote the educational advancement of the indigenes.

Notes for Chapter 3

1. See Dorothy E. Richard, Cdr., USNR, *United States Naval Administration of the Trust Territory of the Pacific Islands,* III (Washington, D.C.: Government Printing Office, 1957), p. 845.
2. *Ibid.,* p. 920.
3. See *Statement by Adrian P. Winkel, Special Representative to the Trusteeship Council on the Trust Territory of the Pacific Islands,*

June 6, 1977, United States Mission to the United Nations, Press Release USUN-34 (77), June 7, 1977, pp. 14 and 15.
4. Richard, *op. cit.,* pp. 53-54.
5. *Ibid.,* pp. 239 and 235.
6. See *Statement by . . . Winkel,* p. 22; also see "War Claims Drew Support," *Highlights,* May 15, 1977, p. 3.
7. Richard, *op. cit.,* p. 382.
8. See Norman Meller, *The Congress of Micronesia* (Honolulu: University of Hawaii Press, 1969), pp. 371-72. The incoming Congress of Micronesia, in 1965, made adoption of this flag one of its first legislative acts.
9. See Dorothy E. Richard, Cdr., USNR, *United States Naval Administration of the Trust Territory of the Pacific Islands,* I (Washington, D.C.: Government Printing Office, 1957), p. 497. Meanwhile, missionaries were permitted to reenter Guam, which was "reoccupied American territory."
10. See Dorothy E. Richard, Cdr., USNR, *United States Naval Administration of the Trust Territory of the Pacific Islands,* II (Washington, D.C.: Government Printing Office, 1957), 393 and 390.
11. *Ibid.,* pp. 398-99.
12. *Ibid.,* p. 400.
13. See "Plane Starts Service to Outer Islands," *Highlights,* February 15, 1977, p. 8. Reverend Kalau also has an older plane (a six-passenger Cessna), which, in 1976, was repaired through a $100,000 appropriation from the Congress of Micronesia. There is another pilot who assists him, Maurice Pickard.
14. President Kennedy may have been influenced favorably toward Micronesia in part by his World War II Naval service in the south Pacific, where his famous "PT Boat 109" episode occurred. The President probably also reviewed some of the U.N. Visiting Mission Reports on the Trust Territory, which pointed to the need for improvements in those islands. Finally, Kennedy undoubtedly received a useful "briefing" both by Navy and the Interior prior to his signing of Executive Order 11021, which transferred jurisdiction in the northern Marianas from military to civilian rule in 1962.
15. See Trust Territory of the Pacific Islands, Congress, *Senate Journal (Third Day),* 1st Cong., 2d spec. sess., 1966, pp. 266-67. The "new development" quotation was repeated in *Report to the Congress of Micronesia by John Pincetich, Director, Peace Corps/Micronesia,* Saipan: July 19, 1967, p. 1, which was delivered in person by Pincetich.
16. See Ruth G. Van Cleve, *The Office of Territorial Affairs* (New York: Praeger Publishers, 1974), p. 181.

17. See Senator Eugene J. McCarthy, *The Limits of Power* (New York: Dell Publishing Company, 1968), p. 141. The release of this book coincided with Senator McCarthy's Presidential campaign that year.
18. Jerry D. Sherrell, a former volunteer, told this writer in 1972 that he "remembered seeing similar publicity in 1968 about 'the problems in paradise,'" although he was then applying to go to Nigeria for the Peace Corps (which assignment was changed to Micronesia due to the Biafra problem of 1968).
19. See Robert R. Robbins, "Trust Territory of the Pacific Islands: The Development of a Polity," a paper presented at the panel, "Liquidation of the American Dependent Empire," New England Political Science Association annual meeting, Amherst, April 29, 1967, pp. 11-12. (Mimeographed.)
20. See *Remarks of Professor Robert R. Robbins of Tufts University, First Legislative Counsel of the Congress of Micronesia, before the House of Representatives,* Capitol Hill, Saipan, January 18, 1971, p. 4. (Mimeographed.)
21. See Trust Territory of the Pacific Islands, Congress, *Senate Journal (Nineteenth Day),* 1st Cong., 2d reg. sess., 1966, p. 68.
22. See Gwyneth Donchin, "From Maine to Micronesia," *Micronesian Reporter,* XIX (1st quarter, 1971), p. 36. Miss Donchin was a Peace Corps volunteer on Saipan at the time she wrote this article.
23. For an indication of how the respective debates developed over this "advisory council" recommendation, see Trust Territory of the Pacific Islands, Congress, *Senate Journal (Third and Fourth Days),* 1st Cong., 2d spec. sess., 1966, pp. 268 and 274-76; also see *House Journal (Fourth Day),* p. 193.
24. In 1971, Mr. Shakhov, the Soviet Representative, referred to the *number* of Peace Corps volunteers serving as teachers throughout Micronesia (down to a total of 249 as of June, 1971) and, citing the *Pacific Islands Monthly* (Vol. 41, No. 11, 1970), said: "The parents of Micronesian students are worried . . . [that] the view of life and even the external appearance of certain volunteer American teachers 'of a hippie type' . . . is being adopted and imitated by the Micronesian youth." See United Nations, Trusteeship Council, 38th Session, June 1, 1971, *Provisional Verbatim Record of the Thirteen Hundred and Eightieth Meeting,* T/PV.1375, pp. 24-25.
25. See *Report to the Congress of Micronesia by John Pincetich, Director, Peace Corps/Micronesia,* Saipan: July 19, 1967, p. 6.
26. See Robert R. Robbins, "United States Territories in Mid-Century" (paper prepared for the Conference on the History of the Territories, National Archives and Research Service, Washington, D.C., November 3-4, 1969), p. 65.

27. See *Remarks of Professor Robert R. Robbins . . . before the House of Representatives,* Capitol Hill, Saipan, January 18, 1971, p. 4. Judge Furber, during the mid-1960s, also served as chairman of the Committee on the Code, which was instrumental in drafting the *Trust Territory Code,* which, when completed, comprised two volumes of the laws of the Trust Territory.
28. For the first three-year "scorecard" on the achievements of the CATs, with assistance from Micronesians, see U.S. Navy and JO1 Kirby Harrison, "Civic Action Teams," *Micronesian Reporter,* XX, 2 (2d quarter, 1972), p. 2.
29. See *Statement by . . . Winkel,* pp. 18, 2, and 3.
30. Van Cleve, *op. cit.,* p. 132.
31. See *Statement by . . . Winkel,* pp. 18-20.

Chapter 4

"To Promote the Educational Advancement..."

A more detailed reading of the fourth goal in Article 6 of the Trusteeship Agreement indicates *how* the American Administration would proceed to "promote the educational advancement" of the Micronesians: "[The U.S. will] take steps toward the establishment of a general system of elementary education; facilitate the vocational and cultural advancement of the population; and . . . encourage qualified students to pursue higher education, including training on the professional level." High Commissioner Winkel reiterated the above goal in his address to the U.N. Trusteeship Council, in June, 1977, when he said that the *third* of "four fronts" which the Trust Territory Government "will be moving forward on . . . simultaneously" is "the continuation and improvement of the programs of health [see chapter 3, preceding] and education, which make possible that mental and physical growth and health which are every person's right and which are essential to the total growth and health of every human society."[1]

This chapter will briefly consider the various educational approaches which have been made in the Trust Territory of the Pacific Islands since the island schools were reopened under the direction of the U.S. Navy at the end of World War II, and determine the effects of such programs on the generation of young Micronesians which has grown to maturity under American rule.

THE NAVAL ADMINISTRATION'S EDUCATIONAL EFFORTS

A concluding statement by Commander Richard on "the worth of the educational program" for Micronesia under the seven years of Naval Administration (1944-51) is useful in perceiving the "military thinking" behind Navy's approach during those early years: "The [Naval] administration recognized the basic problem arising from the conflict of both indigenous and foreign cultures in the area and aimed to set one pattern of education that would not superimpose still another alien culture [i.e., the American] upon the inhabitants."² Thus, from the outset, the Naval Administration encouraged the reopening of schools throughout the islands. The "greatest progress in reestablishment of the schools" was in the Marshall Islands, where the "long contact with American missionaries" was superior to that found in the other districts and the "success or failure" of such programs would depend mostly on the Naval officers' ability and interest in stimulating the reopenings. The Naval Commander in Micronesia (ComMars), in November, 1946, issued a directive that there should be an "immediate establishment of teacher training schools by the atoll or island commanders at Ponape, Truk, Yap, Saipan, Majuro, and Koror. 'Prompt action in establishing these schools is imperative,' he stated. 'Do not wait for perfect conditions. Build as you go along.'" The student-teachers to be trained were the indigenes, who were "to be subsisted, housed if necessary, given medical care and paid five dollars per month of attendance, at the expense of the military government." The superintendents of those teacher training schools were the Naval education officers assigned to the respective districts.³

David Ramarui, Director of Education in the Trust Territory Government at present, and a Palauan who began his education career under the Navy in 1946 and, during the seven-year period up to 1953, served, successively, in elementary school education first as a classroom teacher, then as principal, and finally as superintendent, recalls that the implementation of the above teacher training program on Koror was conducted with a noticeable variation: those Naval officers who spoke Japanese served as instructors in that training school: "The first thing that was done was to arbitrarily select teachers from all communities, brought them to Koror, and there was started a 'teacher training' program with military officers who could speak Japanese, so we begin to organize some training, and organize schools." Ramarui says that he was among a group of Palauans selected to study the English language for a few months on Koror, then he and other islanders from throughout Micronesia were sent to one-year programs on Guam for teachers, afterward returning to their home districts to teach other indigenes: "Every now and then we bring in one teacher from inside the villages to Koror and we train them and then send them back to the village, and then we get new people. And that's how we conducted our program."

Although no high schools were established in the islands during the Naval Period, some "adult education" was conducted. Richard wrote that "one group of Ponapean laborers went to Enewetok [in the Marshalls] to work on the airstrip only after being assured that a school would be set up there to teach them English."⁴ Richard also noted a *weakness* in the Navy's approach to using indigenous teachers and the native languages in the island schools: "The failure of the elementary schools to provide the children with a working knowledge of English retarded learning at higher levels so that capable English-speaking teachers could not be returned to the schools in adequate numbers to correct the error at its source."[5] Strik Yoma, a Ponapean who was to graduate from the University of Hawaii and later become the Trust Territory Government's Director of Public Affairs, feels that the *lack* of a fundamental knowledge of English at the lower grades during the Navy and later Interior days had a detrimental effect which even *higher* "annual budgets," of themselves, could not correct:

> In the late 40's, say, right after the War, and early 50's, very few Micronesians were able to speak English, in spite of the fact that we were trying to send Micronesians to bigger schools in Guam [for high school, specialized training centers, and, eventually, college] and off to Fiji, and trying to get Micronesian students to go to Hawaii. But we simply lacked the necessary educational preparation to go on to higher education—college-level education. And so, in the '50's, even if the United States had given all the money that we needed, we wouldn't be able to utilize it that effectively. Maybe they could be, if you increased the budget at that time—maybe more people would have gone to school, let's say; but I think there's an absolute limit there. You simply cannot just get people to go, because they're not qualified. So that the necessary training and preparation would have to start here in Micronesia, and we wouldn't be able to take advantage of all the opportunities even if they are there, because we simply were not prepared.

INTERIOR'S WATERSHED POINT: 1963

Ramarui recalls that there was a change in the financial support of education in the Trust Territory under Interior, beginning in 1951: "Things stayed more or less the same except that the budget began to change. Under the Navy, even up until 1951, the financing of schools in the communities was entirely by the community. After '51, when the Interior took over, we [the Government] began to pour in more school supplies, textbooks, until 1960." Other than that logistical support by Interior, other aspects—including the salaries of the *elementary* school teachers, all of whom were islanders until the first American contract teachers appeared in 1962—were "still paid by the community, and later on taken over by the district legislatures."

The intermediate schools (for grades 7 and 8) established during the pre-1963 era "were staffed both by Americans and Micronesian teachers, who were paid by the Trust Territory Government."[6] The first *public* high school in the Trust Territory was the Pacific Island Central School (PICS), which "became a full 3-year secondary school, the only

Government-operated school of this level in the Territory," in 1957.[7] Father Hezel, in Truk, in a personal letter to this writer in 1971, expressed surprise that the Trust Territory would later (after 1962) *abandon* the PICS approach of drawing students from *throughout* Micronesia in favor of *separate* district high schools: "I often think that the only real way to effect a breakthrough in cultural bias (whether it is in Micronesia or in America) is to permit as many individuals as possible to experience rewarding contact with persons from another culture."

The year 1963 became a "watershed" in education from a number of standpoints. For one, Ramarui recalls, the Trust Territory Government's announcement that, henceforth, "the English language [would] be the medium of instruction in school. This didn't rule out the teaching of local vernaculars, but it was specifically taken that the English language shall be the medium of instruction." He remembers that the then Director of Education in the Trust Territory Government, an American, was "very much opposed to it [the changeover to English in the public elementary schools], but he didn't challenge the new Administration and the new High Commissioner [M. Wilfred Goding], so he only inserted one phrase [in the directive] which says: '. . . if there are qualified teachers to teach in English.' "

One of the first American contract teachers to arrive in the Trust Territory that year was Roger Ludwig, presently the School Curriculum Supervisor in the Government of the Northern Marianas. Ludwig was recruited from Florida and arrived on Saipan to teach the seventh and eighth grades at the Hopwood Junior High School, and recalls his first exposure to those Chamorro students recently out of the all-Chamorro language elementary schools on that island: "The first year of teaching, 1963, was probably one of the most frustrating years I've ever experienced, because we had no orientation. There was no curriculum; there were no guidelines. We [the American teachers] did not speak Chamorro; the students did not speak English. And trying to teach in that kind of a situation was like running into a brick wall."

While the public elementary schools in Micronesia were making the changeover to English in the early 1960s as "qualified teachers" could be found to instruct in that language, the *parochial* schools did not have to face that trauma. Why? Father Arnold says that the Catholic Church's schools had been instructing in English beginning at the *first*-grade level. He was instrumental in starting the Mt. Carmel School on Saipan in the 1950s (first, at the elementary grades, in 1952, followed by the expansion of that school facility to the 12th grade by 1957). Father Arnold gives two basic reasons for the parochial approach to English in the island schools from the very beginning: first, as preparation for high school, where English is spoken. The second reason was a combination of

To Promote the Educational Advancement ..."

"logistical need" as well as "survival" in Micronesia, which has been administered for over 300 years by a succession of four foreign nations:

> Well, where else can you get something to read [in Micronesia] if it's not in a foreign language? I mean, if they [the islanders] don't know any foreign language, . . . if they [the foreign officials] told you, "Your cow gets sick," you can't do anything in Chamorro. . . . [Also,] they [the students] have to know a foreign language—I don't care what it is: Japanese, German, Spanish. But they have to know a foreign language; otherwise, they can't talk. . . . We [at Mt. Carmel] never did what the public schools in Guam did. We never forbade them to speak Chamorro on the playgrounds.

Also beginning in 1963 was an increase in the amount of federal funds available for the public schools in the Trust Territory. Van Cleve wrote of this turning point: "The central TT Government, with federal financing, assumed responsibility for public education. An accelerated program for the construction of elementary schools was begun . . . to accommodate all Micronesian children, who are required by law to attend school between the ages of six and 14."[8] That "accelerated construction" of *public* school facilities was to result by mid-1977 in the availability of 230 elementary (including intermediate level) and 16 high schools, in addition to the parochial school totals (17 elementary and 14 high schools).[9]

PEACE CORPS VOLUNTEERS AND TESL

The arrival of the first Peace Corps volunteers to Micronesia in 1966 complemented the Administering Authority's program to teach English as a second language (TESL). Former High Commissioner William R. Norwood appeared before the U.N. Trusteeship Council in mid-1968 and indicated to that body that the Peace Corps workers assigned to be schoolteachers (which, as mentioned in chapter 3, encompassed a majority of those volunteers) were not only participating in the TESL program to a high degree, but they were also helping to train Micronesians as English language instructors. The purpose to be served by preparing the indigenous teachers to instruct in English? Norwood saw that emphasis on English as "intended not only to provide the Micronesians with a widely useful second language [the *main* purpose of the TESL program], but to establish English as the common language of Micronesia and thus strengthen communication in the interest of political and administrative cohesiveness."[10]

Perhaps one of the most constructive purposes served by the infusion of literally hundreds of Peace Corps volunteers as principally elementary schoolteachers throughout the islands was to give the schoolchildren the opportunity to hear English spoken by Americans instead of by Micronesian teachers (a majority of whom were struggling, themselves, to pronounce the words). Ramarui discusses that impact as follows:

> The impact that Peace Corps had, I think, was much greater in English in all elementary schools. Before Peace Corps policies came in [in 1966], and before the contract teachers came into Micronesia to start some of those outlining schools [after 1962], English language was taught by Micronesians, and they only taught by books by way of reading, but most of the thing was carried on [in] Palauan conversation and translation [in that district]. So, the impact of Peace Corps upon Micronesian elementary kids was that they were, for the first time, able to hear a native English, . . . to give to them in English, and they were able to get, I guess, English first hand, and not raise English language standard greatly.

Agnes McPhetres, Deputy Director of Education for the Trust Territory Government, and the highest-ranking Micronesian woman employed by Headquarters, qualifies what Ramarui meant in the above, when he said that the Peace Corps volunteers did *not* "raise the English language standard greatly" in the schools: "First of all, the influence of TESL is based on oral English, and not comprehension. And you find out that a lot of the students will repeat, but will not understand what they say." That very reason is probably the main catalyst for *discontinuing* the TESL program, per se, in recent years. The more current approach to what Ramarui refers as a "bilingual or bicultural education," is one under which his Department of Education hopes "might blend the inevitable values influenced by the American style of education and American culture with the various Micronesian cultural heritages and values so that Micronesia's identity and its place in the world community will not be lost."[11]

As McPhetres sees the "bilingual or bicultural education" program, above, "our main approach towards language now—and this is our trend today—is that we would introduce bilingual education. We will teach our language—the local language—and teach also English. But first, local language." She also reflects on her own schooling in Saipan as a child, and feels that, although English was *supposed* to be a "second language" for the islanders, it was taught more as a *prime* language, with rather sad effects: "When I graduated from school, . . . [I did not know] how to really write well in my own [Chamorro] language, real well in my own language, because we have been pushing that aside, the local language." An American official in the Trust Territory Government sees the "bilingual" method as having some difficulty by mid-1977 due to the number of "approaches" found in the islands: "Now you have TESL in some schools, you have bilingual approaches in other schools—they're not using TESL but they're teaching the local languages through TESL techniques. You have the South Pacific [Commission] English Program, ... and you have locally developed programs in some areas. It's turned into a real octopus, a variety of things." That official indicates that funding for the different approaches is coming from the Office of Education (in HEW) as well as Congressional appropriations.

ALL NOT WELL FOR PEACE CORPS VOLUNTEER TEACHERS

As mentioned in the previous chapter, the last contingent of Peace Corps volunteers exited the northern Marianas in the summer of 1977. The main reason for removing the Peace Corps from the Marianas is the change in political status (i.e., the pending commonwealth). If some of the volunteers, themselves, who had served in the Marianas over the years, should be asked to indicate if they felt *needed* there in recent years, the responses would probably prove to be negative. Jean Olopai, now with the Marianas High School under contract and formerly a volunteer to the northern Marianas (during 1969-71), feels that the Peace Corps workers assigned as schoolteachers there were *misused* by the Marianas' Education Department:

> We came in, and we thought we were going to train local people in the job [as teachers] and the area that we were working in. But, what it turned out was, in the Education Department [of the Marianas], we were just used as people—free people. They didn't have to hire anyone in our place. Our first year [1969-70], we knew we would probably be in the classroom alone, but, hopefully, by our second year, we would have a Micronesian counterpart—someone to train in the area that we were studying. One—only one person in my group—had one, and that was because she said, "I will absolutely not go in that classroom unless you get me a counterpart!" And, so they finally found one. But it was such a last-minute deal just to keep her [the volunteer] in the classroom that the counterpart stayed only two months after she [the volunteer] left, and then quit, herself, because she really wasn't interested [in being a teacher].

Betty Sackbauer, a volunteer who completed her two-year Peace Corps tour in mid-1977, seconds Olopai's critique, above. Sackbauer, one of two physical education volunteer teachers at the Marianas High School during 1975-77, adds: "Granted, I'm doing a lot of good teaching these kids, but I'd be doing a lot more good if I were teaching teachers. I could reach a lot more people that way." These complaints are *not* limited to the Marianas. Roger Gale recalls that, in the fall of 1974 in Truk, "there were five or six new [Peace Corps] couples who were going to be teaching educational techniques to teachers, . . . [but,] at the last minute, they ended up in the classroom." Agnes McPhetres believes that some Micronesian teachers are "more experienced" than the volunteers, themselves, in the classroom and thus would not need such "teacher training" by volunteers whose only experience is having liberal arts degrees "fresh out of college." The response to her opposition by Peace Corps volunteers is that the latter group would not want to train *experienced* Micronesian teachers. Of course, one could conjecture as to how the "experience" was gleaned, realizing that classroom exposure of itself may not supply expertise in the use of learning objectives, visual/audio aids, and all the supplemental approaches to good teaching techniques.

Examples of Peace Corps volunteers involved in other-than-classroom instructional duties include some graduate degree holders in the Department of Finance at the Trust Territory Headquarters and in Finance's branch offices throughout the districts. Terry L. Garrett, Director of Finance, has been pleased with those volunteers in his area: "We do have in this particular program Peace Corps volunteers—graduate computer scientists, graduate accountants in each of the districts. I've got several of them here [at Headquarters]. . . . Some sharp people!" Josef Rotholz, Technical Adviser in the Community Development Division of the Trust Territory Government, has a book entitled *Construction Manual for Community Development Offices and House Authorities in Micronesia*, published in 1973, which was compiled when he was directing a seminar in Palau. The instructors of that seminar were Peace Corps volunteers. Rotholz says this book, which was completed with the help of those volunteers, is "sort of an abbreviated architectural graphics. . . . Any construction man could go through that book and build a house from it."

"ONLY FIFTY PERCENT GRADUATE FROM HIGH SCHOOL"

Someone once said, "you can prove anything with statistics!" This is especially the case in Micronesia, where the manually computed numbers for those attending school are suspect, at best. For instance, the *Annual Report* for 1975 (published in mid-1976) indicates that, "as of June 30, 1975," there are such-and-such totals of students enrolled in the elementary and high school levels. Those figures, incidentally, showed 30,444 in elementary schools (27,856 in *public* schools and 2,588 in *parochial*) and 7,970 in high schools (6,202 in *public*, 1,768 in *parochial*).[12] A longtime U.S. official in the Trust Territory believes that "inflated" totals are often the case in the classroom reports which eventually filter up to the Headquarters for compilation in such *Annual Reports:*

> Most [Micronesians] . . . are not trained in statistics. In fact, the logistics of gathering data here are almost impossible. If you want to get enrollment figures from schools, it should normally be a fairly simple

thing. You have to bear in mind [however,] that a teacher will accept in the first grade a lot of students on the first day and discover after he's filled out the attendance reports, the enrollment figures, that half of the kids in class are over-age or under-age, and then they'll be dropped from the classes. So you have inflated figures where, in fact, you have a lower number of people going to school, and they never report this attrition. And then, of course, you have the probably field trip service [statistics]. ... The fact [is] that people really don't like to write things down here.

Having said the above, the "statistic" for the number of Micronesian young people who enter the first grade and eventually graduate from the 12th is 50 percent. Ramarui remarks that "maybe it's a safe figure to say 50 percent." The consensus of opinion is that the best of the original six districts (including the northern Marianas as one, but keeping Kosrae as part of Ponape here), so far as educational programs, are the Marianas and Palau (with upwards of 99 percent of the elementary students in those districts going on to high school). The poorest districts from the standpoint of production of students are the Marshalls and Truk (the latter being the most populous of all the districts). Yap is in between, with Ponape somewhat better than Truk and the Marshalls, educationally speaking. Ramarui indicates that more eligible young people would *like* to attend high school in Truk and the Marshalls, but there simply is not enough classroom space for them: "They want to go to high school, they're qualified, but they cannot get in." Transportation problems for such scattered islands in Truk and the Marshalls also add to the classroom shortages.

EBEYE: A SUBSTANDARD ENVIRONMENT

Picture 7,000 people crowded onto a *one*-square-acre-mile area and you have described Ebeye, a speck of an island barely off the east coast of Kwajalein, in the Marshalls. Here, the "extended family" (with all the coattail relatives, it seems) has moved in on the wage earners employed by the Kwajalein Missile Test Range Center. Ebeye is characterized by many observers as "Micronesia's ghetto."[13] Agnes McPhetres, during a trip to Washington, D.C., in 1975, was asked by the Office of Territorial Affairs to stop off on her way back to Saipan and "make an assessment" of Ebeye's educational needs. Following are her conclusions: the school enrollment in the past year has dropped from 1,000 to 900, due in part to some Marshallese being encouraged to return to their respective outer island homes; only about 20 percent of the students graduating from the elementary school on Ebeye are able to go on to high school on Majuro (the district center some 270 miles southeast of Ebeye); the vocational school on Ebeye is very limited, possibly due to being ignored by the district education department; and there is a need to train the teachers. She inquired during her stay on Ebeye if it might be possible to have some American wives on Kwajalein, "either on a local hire basis or on a volunteer basis," come over to Ebeye and conduct that teacher training. The school's principal on Ebeye lacks a bachelor's degree and some of the teachers "can hardly read [English]." Pausing in her reflections on the above, McPhetres raises the question: "Looking to the future, . . . we really don't know what the future will be. But one of the goals would be to see that the teachers in all schools are accredited."

PATS, MOC, AND CCM

There are three specialized schools in Micronesia which have been established since the late 1950s and have met with successful, moderate, and questionable results, respectively: Ponape Agriculture and Trade School (PATS), a secondary vocational school with male students from throughout the Trust Territory; the Micronesian Occupational Center (MOC), a post-secondary institute on Koror, in Palau; and the Community College of Micronesia (CCM), a two-year school also located in Ponape. Father Hugh F. Costigan, of the Society of Jesus, who, in early 1977 celebrated his thirtieth year as a missionary in the islands, initially planned PATS in 1958. In response to a query on PAT's "role in vocational education," Father Costigan reflects as follows:

> I would hope that it is one of leadership, intelligently aimed at preparing the technical competence in young men which is the infrastructure of any developing society. We have preached this gospel continuously over the past few years in the various committees [of] the Congress of Micronesia and the Department of Education [of the Trust Territory Government], with the hope that the public secondary education programs would contain more vocational preparation of both boys and girls.

PATS has a campus spread over 200 acres, with the facilities including, besides the two-story administration building, the following: classrooms, dormitories, a dining hall, a machine shop, an automotive shop, a carpentry shop, a construction center, and an agriculture and nutrition center with a nursery and seedling area. An audiovisual center is also available. The student body of some 200 boys is a cross section of the six districts. Jeffrey J. White, an American contract teacher at the Marianas High School, visited the PATS campus in early 1976 and believes that PATS "is one of the schools for the future, as far as the Trust Territory is concerned. It's a school that concentrates on each of the kids. . . . It's so practically oriented." White also recalls that the seniors are permitted to have their own garden plot, the policy being for those students that

To Promote the Educational Advancement..."

"everything you make from your vegetables pays your tuition.... So, you defray the cost of tuition by growing foods. It gives you that added incentive. Same thing with raising pigs." Caldwell's opinion, considering the problems faced by so many other schools in Micronesia (including the MOC and CCM, to be discussed shortly), is: "PATS is still in business, thank Heaven!" P. Terry Edvalson, Student Assistance Officer in the Trust Territory Government, agrees that PATS has "a good program," noting that the public schools in the Trust Territory have emulated some of PAT's innovations: "[PATS is] ... different in scope, certainly, than the public schools can be, because they're [PATS is] involved with a limited number of students. A lot of their innovations and the like, I think, are being picked up by the public schools. They do work in curriculum development, [and] they work in adult programs which public schools have used as models, in some instances." Again, the consensus is that PATS is *highly* successful.

The MOC, Ambassador Winkel told the U.N. Trusteeship Council in 1977, "had its final visitation by the Western Association of Schools and Colleges for the purpose of gaining full accreditation. It is anticipated that they will take positive action on accrediting this important vocational institution."[14] Ramarui says that his department is "very proud" of the MOC, and that the Trust Territory Government has connections "with many community colleges in Hawaii that deals largely in vocational area, so we send our teachers, at the Micronesian Occupational Center, to Hawaii to be trained further, and [they] come back and improve our training in Koror [at the MOC]."

The "moderate results" evaluation for the MOC, mentioned earlier, comes from the counseling—or *lack* of adequate counseling—given to the approximately 350 students in attendance. While Agnes McPhetres says a 1975 survey by the MOC showed that "80 percent of their graduates are presently employed in all the districts," Caldwell, who was an adviser to the Director of Education in Palau for a year (1972-73), questions MOC's *heavy* emphasis on the "technical" trades:

> I have a little bit of trouble understanding whether we're going to have the needs for auto mechanics and air conditioner repairmen and all these things ... in terms of what we're paying to do the training. What frequently has happened [is that] people who become skilled in those areas discover that there are other academic [opportunities]. And you find the goal becomes, "I've got some basic skills in English language and reading in my vocational program, but now I'm going to get my B.A. in political science!" So, you've got that goal.

The CCM is an outgrowth of the Micronesian Teacher Education Center in Kolonia, Ponape. By mid-1977, the CCM was granting associate of science degrees in a number of disciplines, including the Nursing

School (on Saipan), business management, special education, elementary teacher education, and secondary vocational teacher education (the last-named "offered in conjunction with [PATS] . . .").[15] The CCM, "now run entirely by the [Trust Territory] Government, has an enrollment of approximately 200 students."[16] The "questionable results" evaluation for CCM mainly centers on an Oregon College of Education letter, written in September, 1976, as a result of a contract from the Trust Territory Government to provide some technical assistance to the CCM. After visiting the CCM campus for two or three days, the authors of the Oregon critique concluded that the CCM should either be closed or completely revamped and reprogrammed, for the college apparently was *not* meeting the needs of the students. A strong recommendation in that Oregon College of Education correspondence was that the CCM be placed under the Trust Territory Government Student Services Office. Another source indicates that there have been other rather negative evaluations with regard to the CCM's performance.

The accrediting institute, which is Western Association of Schools and Colleges, did give the CCM a "candidate for accreditation" status in 1974; however, *if* Palau should separate from the rest of the Trust Territory as a result of the Palauan request (in September, 1976) for "separate negotiations" with the United States (see chapter 1), then the CCM would be the *only* form of higher education in the Trust Territory. Should the CCM's present administration be inadequate, corrective action by the Trust Territory Government would be an imperative.

ISLANDERS' HIGHER EDUCATION "ABROAD"

Approximately 2,000 Micronesian students by mid-1977 were abroad attending various colleges and universities. The "abroad" for the islanders, of course, is anywhere outside of the Trust Territory. The most popular schools are the University of Guam (where an average of 300-400 Trust Territory young people have been found in a student body of 3,300-3,400 in recent years), the University of Hawaii, and a relatively large number of "stateside" schools. Until 1974, Trust Territory Government scholarships were made available; however, that program was discontinued and, as Edvalson observes, "our [Trust Territory Government] program has been reoriented to reflect the real world of student financial aid. This year [1976-77] I estimate that we'll need over $9 million to support some 2,000 students that are abroad." Edvalson adds that money from federal programs include the "basic grant, supplemental grant, [and] college work study, . . . through the institutions."

Prior to the cancellation, or discontinuance, of Trust Territory Government scholarships, the student applying for such financial aid was placed in a position where he would "commit" himself to a number of "priorities" which, listed in order, were obviously incompatible for his proposed major. Edvalson comments on that untenable situation:

> A student would make application for a [Trust Territory Government] scholarship based on an advertised list of manpower needs within the Trust Territory—which was developed by the Manpower Advisory Council. So, consequently, a student would see a list and it would say "Priority One is medicine; Priority Two is auto mechanics; Priority Three is, whatever." And a student would, consequently, when he filled out his application, would apply for Priority One, apply for Priority Two. You would [thus] have a guy applying to be a brain surgeon or a diesel mechanic.

Some colleges and universities have attempted to be as accommodating to the Micronesians as possible. The East West Center, in Honolulu, is a good example. Also, five small schools stateside have formed what is called the "Micronesian Mainland Education Project," comprised of Suomi College, in Hancock, Michigan; Lake Superior State College, in Sault Ste. Marie, Michigan; Northern Michigan University, in Marquette, Michigan; Wagner College, on Staten Island, New York, and Texas Lutheran College, in Sequin, Texas. Caldwell, while Dean of Students at Suomi College, formed the "Pacific Micronesian Cultural Aid, Inc.," at that school in 1969, which encouraged Micronesian students to attend Suomi, where the male islanders lived in the "Pacific House" next to the campus. Caldwell's involvement there ended in 1975; the "Pacific House" was phased out in 1972-73 as the islanders were encouraged to integrate with American students in housing.

Mention was made in chapter 1 of several of the prominent Micronesian leaders in mid-1977 who received their bachelor's degrees in political science. That has changed over the years, with a number of graduate degrees being achieved by islanders in such fields as medicine and law.

In summary, the three decades under American rule have seen considerable advancement in the educational areas for the Micronesians, beginning with the U.S. Navy at a time when schools had ceased to function as a result of the Second World War. A strain was introduced when the "language" direction saw indigenous teachers at the elementary grades replaced in the 1960s by American contract personnel and, in many instances, by Peace Corps volunteers. School buildings were constructed but were still insufficient in numbers to meet the needs in two of the districts, the Marshalls and Truk. Micronesians in large numbers have attended college abroad, with limited opportunities for training within the Trust Territory itself; namely, the secondary vocational school (PATS), the post-secondary center (MOC), and the associate degree two-year college (CCM).

The final chapter will focus on Japan's present interests and possible future involvements in Micronesia.

NOTES FOR CHAPTER 4

1. See *Statement by Adrian P. Winkel, Special Representative to the Trusteeship Council on the Trust Territory of the Pacific Islands, June 6, 1977,* United States Mission to the United Nations, Press Release USUN-34 (77), June 7, 1977, pp. 2 and 3.
2. See Dorothy E. Richard, Cdr., USNR, *United States Naval Administration in the Trust Territory of the Pacific Islands,* III (Washington, D.C.: Government Printing Office, 1957), p. 1031.
3. See Dorothy E. Richard, Cdr., USNR, *United States Naval Administration in the Trust Territory of the Pacific Islands,* II (Washington, D.C.: Government Printing Office, 1957), p. 372.
4. *Ibid.,* pp. 381-82.
5. Richard, *op. cit.,* III, p. 1032.
6. See David Ramarui, "Education in Micronesia: Its Past, Present, and Future," *Micronesian Reporter,* XXIV (1st Quarter, 1976), p. 11.
7. See U.S., Department of Interior, *Annual Report of the Secretary of the Interior, for the Fiscal Year ended June 30, 1957* (Washington, D.C.: Government Printing Office, 1957), p. 363.
8. See Ruth G. Van Cleve, *The Office of Territorial Affairs* (New York: Praeger Publishers, 1974), p. 135.
9. See U.S., Department of State, *28th Annual Report to the United Nations on the Administration of the Trust Territory of the Pacific Islands, for the Fiscal Year ended June 30, 1975* (Washington, D.C.: Government Printing Office, 1976), p. 211.
10. See Office of the High Commissioner, *Opening Statement by High Commissioner W. R. Norwood to the 35th Session of the Trusteeship Council, May 28, 1968,* released by the Department of Public Affairs, Saipan: [1968,] p. 7. (Mimeographed.)
11. See "Education in Micronesia, Its Past, Present, and Future," p. 13.
12. See U.S., Department of State, *28th Annual Report to the United Nations . . . [for] 1975,* pp. 211-12.
13. An American official who also visited on Ebeye in 1975 gives the following impression of what he found there: "As I recall the figures at the time, there were approximately 7,000 people crowded into this little island, not unusual for anywhere from 10 to 20 people to be living in a one-room house. They sleep in shifts, and it was really a ghetto. [The wage earners on Ebeye work for the U.S. Government

headquartered on Kwajalein. The arrival of outer-island relatives occurred in 1968-69.] In Marshallese culture, the end result was that they came—the Marshallese came—from all of the other outside islands—to move in with their relatives, who were making the $1.50 an hour. And the end result is that you had one wage earner who was then, in effect, supporting anywhere from 10 to 15 people. They [the relatives] came to the island voluntarily. . . . This is now really a problem. You could have an epidemic and it would be really catastrophic—the number of people that could die because of the insufficient health services that are being offered. My understanding is that they [the District Administrator, Oscar DeBrum] are attempting, voluntarily, to get people to move back to the islands from which they came. . . . These people cannot continue to stay there. We [the Trust Territory Government], in 1973, decided that there must be more to life in Ebeye than playing roulette and bingo—which is what they seem to do all day long—and maybe some of the older people would be interested in making handicraft in Ebeye. The Marshallese are very well known for their handicraft. We attempted to get a handicraft organization going there, and the result was complete inertia: why should they bother to work because it wasn't necessary. . . . The lure of—I think it was quoted in the paper [the Guam *Pacific News*]—the lure of the bright lights (they even have television now) and beer, and many of the other consumer commodities, is the incentive. But, I personally can't visualize why anyone would want to leave an [outer] island to live in the ghetto of Ebeye.

14. See *Statement by . . . Winkel*, p. 14.
15. See U.S., Department of State, *28th Annual Report to the United Nations . . . [for] 1975*, p. 104.
16. See "Education in Micronesia, Its Past, Present, and Future," p. 18.

Chapter 5

Japanese Interests in Micronesia at Present and in the Future?

The reader will note that the above title ends with a question mark. It is somewhat difficult to determine what the Japanese interests are at present; it is almost impossible to "guesstimate" what the future may hold at the mid-1977 point. Nevertheless, the writer's month in the Tokyo area (September, 1976), followed by research on Guam and on Saipan, enabled him to interview several Japanese Government officials and businessmen as well as others associated with the Japanese in advisory capacities or as scholars also studying Japan's development in the Pacific Basin. These views were then juxtaposed with what American and Micronesian officials and others in the islands perceived the Japanese endeavors to mean. The following brief comments are simply expressed as an avenue of allowing the reader to share in the general views formed at present.

THE JAPANESE GOVERNMENT POLICY ON MICRONESIA

This was the *easiest* "position" to establish, and it may be expected to remain so long as the Trusteeship Agreement of 1947 is in force. As Yoshiaki Kotaki, an official in the First North American Division, American Affairs Bureau of the Ministry of Foreign Affairs in Tokyo, observes:

> We [the Japanese Government] consider the Micronesia affairs as one of the American domestic affairs, and the diplomatic part is determined by the United States Government, and we always negotiate anything about Micronesia through the U.S. Government. . . . The so-called Micronesian Agreement [regarding the $10 million "war claims" settlement] was reached between the U.S. Government and the Japanese Government. In

that sense. So, I think that it is the U.S. Government desire that we, the Japanese Government, doesn't contact directly with the Micronesia Government.

Kotaki, in answer to a question on how his Government feels about "business contacts" Japanese companies may have with the Micronesians, replies: "Well, we [the Government] do not have any reason to object to dealings, business dealings, of Japanese firms with Micronesians. But, we do not encourage or discourage such."

Examples of those occasions when the Japanese Government has, or would, "negotiate through the U.S. Government" with regard to matters concerning the Trust Territory include the approval for Continental/Air Micronesia to land in Japan as a result of the Civil Aeronautics Board (CAB) and President Ford approving the direct flights between Saipan and Tokyo (see chapter 2). Although Kotaki says Senator Tosiwo Nakayama, President of the Micronesian Senate, visited the Ministry of Foreign Affairs Building to discuss that matter, such a conversation is *not* considered a point of "negotiations" between Japan and Micronesia. Craig G. Dunkerley, Second Secretary of the United States Embassy in Japan, who accompanied this writer on the above interview with Kotaki, places the "Saipan-to-Tokyo route case" as part of a "larger problem" for the United States and Japan to consider:

> The Saipan route is considered a part of the larger U.S. civil aviation question, and there are a number of problems right now, regarding continental U.S.-Tokyo flights. . . . We are about to start negotiations on the overall agreement, so the Saipan route question is really part of this larger issue which involves . . . problems that we share also with the British in terms of frequency of flights, questions of that. It's not solely a Micronesian question. . . . [For example,] continental U.S.-London flights, . . . not just a question of flights from Saipan to Tokyo, but also, frequency and landing rights, say, for JAL, Pan Am, Northwest to Tokyo [and] Okinawa. It's part of much larger ball of wax which is quite sticky at the moment.[1]

Another instance in which the Trust Territory would be a subject of discussion between the American and Japanese Governments is with respect to the 200-mile offshore limit on fishing restriction which the United States imposed on other nations effective March 1, 1977. Again, Dunkerley indicates the 200-mile fishing limit in a wider perspective than the waters of Micronesia (which, incidentally, were exempted from the above restriction in early 1977) : "I would suspect that most of the attention, in terms of U.S.-Japanese fishing problems, is more related to the northern Pacific, off the Alaskan coast, northwest America. . . . I haven't seen as much reference how this would affect Japanese fishing efforts in the Micronesian area."

THE JAPAN MICRONESIA ASSOCIATION: A "GO-BETWEEN"

Through whom do "unofficial" visitors from the Trust Territory, such as Senator Nakayama, in the above example of the "Saipan route case," make contacts when visiting in Japan and desiring to see various Governmental or business sources? In Nakayama's situation, he arranged his contact with the Foreign Ministry though Izumi Kobayashi, Secretary General of the Japan Micronesia Association (JMA), in Tokyo. The JMA, a part of the Asia Center of Japan, was founded in 1973. It has a Board of Directors consisting of members in 30 businesses. One of those directors is an official in Japan Air Line (JAL).

Kobayashi, only one of three paid officials in the JMA, operates at present on a $30,000 annual budget. Each of the above 30 directors of Japan's largest businesses must pay a yearly $300 membership fee. Suekazu Hamanaka, Consul General of Japan in Agana, Guam, was the individual who obtained the permission from the Ministry of Foreign Affairs to establish the JMA, although the latter organization is nongovernmental. Kobayashi hopes that the JMA may, in the near future, receive financial support from the Government just as other groups within the Asia Center of Japan do: "We have many kinds of associations [in the Asia Center], like associations in South East Asia, for example—the Japan Singapore Association, the Japan Vietnam Association, the Japan Cambodian Association, for five years. These kind of associations already gets funds from the [Japanese] Government."

In addition to serving as a "third-party go-between" for foreign visitors (which is the *preferred* way to approach individuals in Japan), the JMA in the summer of 1976 sponsored a "children's exchange tour" between Palau and Japan, in which 100 children from Palau were flown to Japan for a week while, at the same time, a comparable group of young people from Japan were escorted to Palau. Kobayashi recalls that initial exchange program as "a very big success." (That Palau should be selected as the district involved in the above "exchange" program is not surprising. The "central terminal storage facility"—to be discussed in the concluding pages of this chapter—involves Palau.)

JAPANESE "JOINT VENTURES" WITH MICRONESIANS

Lazarus Salii, of Palau, who, in his capacity as a senator in the Congress of Micronesia (1966-77), visited in the Tokyo area on several occasions, believes that the two main interests at present for the Japanese businessmen in Micronesia are fishing and tourism. Optimistic that the "Saipan route" case will eventually be resolved, Salii observes that the Japanese "like to do things in a big way," but that Micronesia is *not* that way for them. Father Robert J. Ballon, S.J., Chairman of the Sophia University Socio-Economic Institute in Tokyo, and a Belgian who has resided in Japan for 28 years and traveled extensively throughout the Pacific as part of his Socio-Economic Institute responsibilities, has studied the activities of Japan's general trading companies. Ten of those organizations account for 40 percent of Japan's overseas investments. Father Ballon indicates that the usual approach such trading companies will make in developing areas is to form a "joint venture" with an indigenous company in the host country: "Usually, the Japanese partner will be one of those 10 large companies. The local [indigenous] partner usually is a nobody in economic terms. . . . That is the way of the Japanese in a number of developing countries."

Senator Borja made reference to one of the "joint ventures" in which he and his wife, Carmen, after beginning with a "mom and pop" store on Saipan following World War II and expanding that to a larger enterprise, called the Carmen Safeway Enterprises, decided, in early 1976, to become a partner with a Japanese department store chain in Japan, the result being one of the three supermarkets on Saipan at the present time. Stating that the Micronesian businessmen "are trying to encourage outside investors to really help us beyond our capability," Borja reflects on his and his wife's "merger" with the Meitetsu Store, as follows:

> I did ask for Meitetsu Store, in Nagoya, who is always a prime developer, [and] one of the top five [such enterprises] also in Japan. They have railroad company, they have real estate, they have marketing, retails, and so forth, they have transportation, air service. . . . So I am, right now, establish a foreign cooperations with them, with the management with me [i.e., Borja's the manager]. And also several years after, 51 percent. Right now, we're 50-50%, but complete management is with the understanding that I will be taking Micronesian [majority ownership] . . . with the approval of the Government [of the Northern Marianas]. . . . I believe in local people have the . . . most shares—in other words, the majority for any participation—but, when I found out that we need to develop department stores for complete dry goods [in the Borja's present store], . . . and develop second story or go out more, it's pretty hard for one man to own it, to really go to the bank and get it, especially when the banking here [on Saipan] are very much limited to land matters. They [the banks] cannot mortgage because of legalities. . . . So, the only way to do that is to really get together [with outside investors].

Elizabeth Udui, Chief of the Foreign Investment Branch in the Department of Resources and Development of the Trust Territory Government, says that, as of late 1976, while there had been "several investments in Micronesia" by foreign sources, "they've all been in the Mariana Islands. We have not seen any business permit applications for the other districts with the exception of one in Truk [relating to a fishing enterprise]. . . . But there are Japanese businessmen coming through here all the time and meeting with Micronesian businessmen."

The *most* successful "joint venture" as of mid-1977 between Japanese interests and Micronesian firms has been the forming of the "S.C. Corporation of Micronesia Ltd.," which involves the Shimizu Construction Company of Japan and the Sablan Construction Company on Saipan. (Thus, one may read into the "joint venture" title *either* "Shimizu Construction" or "Sablan Construction"—both being "S.C.") Shimizu, unlike the Meitetsu Store in the above example, owns 70 percent of the joint venture; Sablan has the remaining 30 percent. Shimizu's position is that it employs some 9,000 and grosses about $2 billion a year in construction projects. Takahisa Oguma, General Manager of Shimizu, says of his company's standing in Japan: "We have five big companies in Japan. Maybe five big companies in Japan may be biggest companies in the world [in] construction." Sablan, meanwhile, employs 300 workers (mostly Filipinos), and operates on a diversified base: a service station, repair shop, a hardware store, and a quarry (from which rock quarry products, including ready-made concrete, are extracted), all on Saipan.

Brad Nago, General Manager of Sablan Construction Company, recalls that the first "joint-venture" project for the "S.C. Construction Company, Ltd.," was to build the Peace Monument on the top of Suicide Cliff in the northern end of Saipan. That was a $50,000 job in early 1976. At present, the S.C. Construction Company is engaged in two multi-million dollar projects on Saipan: the Grand Hotel (a $4.7 million, five-story structure with 120 rooms for which S.C. is the general contractor), and the Nauru Building (a $6 million, eight-story structure with a revolving restaurant on top, with S.C. being the major subcontractor, doing about 96 percent of that project), both of which are on Saipan. Owners of the Grand Hotel will be Japanese. The Nauru Building is owned by the Nauru Railroad Company, a private operation on Nauru. (Nauru has also purchased a controlling interest in the Eastern Gateway Hotel, on Majuro, the Micronesian partner in that hotel being the senior senator in the Congress of Micronesia from the Marshalls, Amata Kabua.) Being so small in comparison to Shimizu's organization (which is *181* years old), Sablan's agreement in the joint venture is to supply the labor, materials, and equipment, as such is available to Sablan.

That the Shimizu Construction Company, with $2 billion in gross profits annually, would be willing to come to Micronesia is a welcome, albeit rather surprising, development. Consul General Hamanaka, mentioned earlier, feels "Japanese investment in the Trust Territory" is "very difficult" to achieve, due to the lack of an adequate infrastructure in the various districts:

So many Japanese businessmen wanted to invest money in Micronesia, but, unfortunately, all the districts in Micronesia have no infrastructure. . . . Whenever they [the Japanese] want to invest money in some, such as Palau, Ponape, Truk, you see, they are always failing, because no suitable [Micronesian] counter-partner, and no skilled labor, and so forth. . . . So, for the time being, I think, there will be no big money invested in Micronesia by Japanese.

Oguma, Shimizu's General Manager, concurs with the Consul General in the above appraisal, and notes that the "logistics" of doing business in Micronesia is also difficult:

I think this island [of Saipan], in districts [of the Trust Territory], there is no product—industrial product—and if we want some material, industrial material, we have to order overseas: Japan, America, and other— the Philippines, Taiwan—overseas order we have to make. After we order, we have to wait. The shortest time is two months. In case of Japan [when his firm in Japan needs materials], . . . the next day we can get some materials, very many materials.

The Sablan Construction Company, in its responsibility of providing the labor for the Grand Hotel project, recruits *heavily* in the Philippines. Of the 90 employees on that contract, only six—all administrative types —are Japanese (which includes Nago, a Hawaiian), four are local hires (Saipanese), and the remaining 80 (with the building supervisor, or foreman, Domingo Sarabalia), Filipinos.

Two other hotel projects, with different parties involved both in Japan and on Saipan, met with varying degrees of failure during the period of 1974-77. Manuel S. (M. S.) Villagomez, President of the M. S. Villagomez Enterprises on Saipan, decided to have a three-story (124-room) hotel built within a five-minute driving distance of the new $10 million Saipan Airport. To secure a Japanese partner for his proposed "Villa Hotel," Villagomez says that he made *four* trips to Tokyo in 1974, but failed in his attempts; thus, the $3 million Villa Hotel remains one-third completed. Another source tells this writer that part of Villagomez's problems in completing the hotel on his own stems from his habit of "changing his mind" on the design and construction phases. The other hotel on Saipan to face difficulty is the White Sands, which was the site for the Constitutional Convention in 1975. The problem here is alleged "stock manipulation" on the part of a Micronesian employee. This charge was to result in litigation, the ownership of the White Sands not being decided in court until the spring of 1977. Meanwhile, the White Sands stood vacant (except for the 1975 convention proceedings) for two years.

Japanese businessmen also have minority shares in the Inter-Continental Hotel (a Pan American subsidiary) on Saipan and the South Park Hotel in Kolonia, Ponape.

FIVE MILLION JAPANESE TOURISTS SOON?

The total number of Japanese "overseas visitors" during 1976 exceeded three million. A spokesman for the Japan Association of Travel Agents in early 1977 predicted that the annual number "will soon reach the 5,000,000 mark."[2] May one assume that the *majority* of the Japanese overseas visitors are tourists? Robert S. Webb, Executive Vice President of Hitachi Zosen CBI Ltd. (a joint venture between Chicago Bridge and Iron from the United States and the Hitachi Engineering Company, the tenth largest corporation in Japan), has been in Japan since 1974. Webb believes that the above figure for "overseas visitors" (i.e., the three million) refers *more* to businessmen than tourists:

> Most of them are Japanese businessmen who travel overseas, and most—at least it's my understanding—that most large companies in Japan, by the time a man reaches managerial level, he is allowed two overseas trips a year. . . . He goes alone, mostly. Occasionally, some of them want to take their wives, but that's the younger, more modern-looking guys. Most, not all, Japanese travel alone as businessmen at company expense.

Father Ballon points to the *pressures* of a homogeneous life for young Japanese in a nation of some 115 million crammed into space less than half the size of California: "[Tourism overseas] is a tremendous break, in particular for the young [Japanese] people to get away for a time from the social controls that a homogeneous society exercises on its members, whether you agree to it or not. So, for them, it is temporary escape. . . . Now, they can travel abroad." Consul General Hamanaka indicates why Guam, a favorite vacation spot of the Japanese in the earlier years of the 1970s, has more recently fallen on harder times: "[The] eight Japanese hotel managers always are telling me that if someone die—hotels [close]—they would like to go back to Japan, because number of Japanese tourists decreasing year after year." Hamanaka indicates that the Japanese tourists' total for 1975 was 160,000 down 50,000 from 1974. He projects that the announced figure for 1976 would show a further downswing. Reasons for the lagging tourist trade to Guam? Hamanaka says that "many Japanese tourists always complain that Guam has no tourist attraction. That's the main reason." (As mentioned in chapter 2, the *high* air fares also affect the number of Japanese tourists to Guam, and especially to Saipan and other parts of the Trust Territory until JAL's direct flights to Saipan are finally approved.)

JAPAN'S FUTURE INTERESTS IN MICRONESIA?

Joint ventures, fishing, tourism—these are "present interests" which, to a considerable degree, await final determination of the future political and economic status of the Trust Territory before the Japanese businessmen are expected to "commit" themselves in the future. However, one must remember that Micronesia, as an overseas *market* for Japan is not really in the mainstream. Father Ballon gives the following advice when one considers those areas which would hope to be overseas suppliers for Japan's domestic markets:

> When you export to Japan, just try to imagine that your market is 110 million people. And you say, "Now, just a minute. I have 110,000 people [as in Micronesia]!" Well, what you don't have is Japan. In the Western economy, you can more or less figure that out, since we are individualists, and you have 110,000 individualists, and you have a market of 110,000. But here, you have 110 million members of Japan. Forget about your small market here. That is a major problem. . . . I would say that, currently, there is not yet an answer to that problem here, and that can certainly be a major problem for Micronesia.

Gregory Clark, an Australian economist, and Visiting Lecturer at Sophia University's International College in Tokyo, has a particular interest in Japanese investment overseas. He feels that Japan's interest in Micronesia at present and in the future is "in tourism and fishing," and he gives a frank appraisal of *where* Japan's main thrusts are in the Pacific:

> It seems to me that I ought to be perfectly frank that the Japanese have been ignoring . . . Micronesia and have given much more interest to the south Pacific, considering Micronesia central Pacific. In particular, Papua New Guinea. I assume that they're keeping out of Micronesia because they feel they can't compete with the Americans. But they are showing real interest in Papua New Guinea since it became independent, and the south Pacific—such places as Fiji and [Western] Samoa.

PALAU: A CENTRAL TERMINAL STORAGE (CTS) FACILITY FOR JAPAN?

Perhaps the most discussed topic in Japan in recent years (aside from the events involved in former Premier Tanaka's forced resignation and later trial) is the *fuel* crisis, and especially, the problem of obtaining a central terminal storage (CTS) facility. It was as a result of the "fuel crisis" of 1973-74 that the Japanese Diet (the national legislature) declared that Japan would increase its oil reserve storage from 60 days to a 90 days' capacity. A study was made by the Ministry of International

Trade and Industry (MITI), which made recommendations as to how much additional storage capacity each of the oil companies should accordingly provide. The international oil companies showed reluctance to install additional storage; hence, the search for a suitable location for a CTS. The possible sites considered involved a number of points in Japan or one or more strategic reserve terminals outside Japan. Two main arguments against domestic CTS locations for Japan center on the environmentalists' argument (i.e., oil spills would pollute the fishing beds) and the necessity for deepwater ports (the Japanese supertankers being planned for up to one million tons each).

Attention was turned to the deepwater ports in the Palau District, which, if utilized, would enable the supertankers to dock there with their oil being stored between 20-30 days, after which smaller Japanese freighters would then transship the supplies to Japan. Former Senator Lazarus Salii, of Palau, is in favor of Palau becoming involved as a CTS facility. Salii, while a senator in recent years, has visited the Middle East and Japan to confer with business officials on the Palau possibility. His preference for *how* an arrangement in Palau should be made is as follows:

> I would like Palau to own one-fourth of all of it [the CTS facility], in addition to controlling the port itself, the reef area out in the water, without contributing any money to it. They [the Palauans] recognize this. Japan would like to have as much control [as possible]. . . . Japan is the most nervous of the four [concerned parties]—between Iran, the United States, Japan [and Palau]. . . . I'd like to see, more or less, the United States and Palau be the partners in some future pattern [of the CTS], under [the Palauans'] control.

Fred M. Zeder II, while Director of Territorial Affairs (DOTA) during 1975-77, spoke in favor of the multimillion dollar possibilities of a CTS in the Palau District. In September, 1976, the Palauans overwhelmingly voted in a plebiscite to request "separate negotiations" with the United States (see chapter 1), which brings those islanders one step closer to the supertanker storage facility. Still to be conducted with regard to a CTS in Palau is a $5 million "feasibility study," the costs therein shared among the Iranians, Japanese, and Americans. As of mid-1977, the CTS possibility for Palau remains just that—a "possibility." Meanwhile, the Japanese businessmen involved in the oil business may have to turn to other possible locations—including "floating oil platforms." In Palau, there has been some opposition from environmental groups; however, the economic impact would seem to outweigh such opposing views. In the likelihood of a CTS in the Palau District, a time lag of probably four years (until 1981) would be required before that structure would be ready.

Meanwhile, the foregoing interests of the Japanese—in joint ventures, fishing, and tourism—will probably continue to be nourished even as the termination of the Trusteeship Agreement approaches in the early 1980s, if not in the targeted 1981 cessation point.

Notes for Chapter 5

1. Still, the Congress of Micronesia continues to contact the Japanese Government, even directly, with respect to the pending question of "landing rights" for Continental/Air Micronesia in the Tokyo area. In March, 1977, President Nakayama and his counterpart in the House of Representatives, Speaker Bethwel Henry, of Ponape, "sent a cable to the [U.S.] State Department's Office of Aviation, requesting that a message be conveyed to both the U.S. and Japan negotiators [in Washington, D.C.]. They also sent an identical message to the Micronesian Washington Office, asking Liaison Officer Leo A. Falcam to pass it on to the Japanese representatives." This "message" expressed the Congress of Micronesia's concern over the "uniqueness and special situation" of the Saipan-Tokyo air route. See "COM to be Heard on Air Route," *Highlights*, April 1, 1977, p. 6.
2. See "Japan Plans First Travel Congress," *Pacific Travel News*, February, 1977, p. 3.

Conclusions

How *well* has the United States fulfilled the four main goals of Article 6 in the Trusteeship Agreement of 1947? The answer to that question is especially apropos as American and Micronesian negotiators in mid-1977 resumed their "rounds of negotiations" in the hope of resolving any outstanding disagreements which might impede the expected termination of this strategic trusteeship—the only such arrangement in the history of the United Nations—by the end of 1981. However, in so stating the imperative of having "the answer," one must realize that *no* single treatise has received a consensus of opinion by the many observers who have watched developments in the far-flung islands of Micronesia that such *is* the proper course of action. Having said the above, this writer is structuring the following pages as though he, a professor by trade, were actually evaluating the American efforts in Micronesia over the past three decades (1947-77) for the purpose of issuing a "report card." Thus, the four areas to be judged within the context of their strengths and weaknesses are those listed in the titles for the first four chapters: the political, economic, social, and educational goals. A concluding paragraph will also be added for the present and future interests of the Japanese businessmen as the latter appear to perceive the economic future of Micronesia.

First, the "course" in *political development* ("[To] foster the development of such political institutions as are suited to the Trust Territory and . . . promote the development of the inhabitants . . . toward self-government or independence as may be appropriate to the particular circumstances . . . and the freely expressed wishes of the peoples concerned"). Beginning with the U.S. Naval Administration (1944-51 and, in the northern Marianas only, the additional years of 1953-62), and continuing with the Department of the Interior (from 1951-present, except in the northern Marianas, as noted above), the Administering Authority approached its tasks as though it were dealing with a people almost totally lacking in political sophistication. That assumption was correct. The preceding Spanish, German, and Japanese Administrations (beginning in the mid-seventh century and ending, for the Japanese Mandate, with the close of World War II in 1945) failed to develop those disparate islanders—spread over an expanse of some three million square miles in the central and western Pacific—to a point at which they (the Micronesians) assumed major leadership roles. That earlier pattern was altered by the American Administration in the late 1940s as district legislatures and municipalities were chartered. The real catalyst for bringing the islanders into a territory-wide "decision-making" posture occurred in 1965, with the election of a bicameral legislative body, the Congress of Micronesia. That was followed in 1967 with the first of eight "rounds of negotiations" over the future political status for the Micronesians; then, the process of appointing the indigenes to all district administrator positions and all but a few key departmental directorships within the Executive Branch of the Trust Territory Government. On a few occasions, Micronesians have served as Acting High Commissioner.

Whereas the above political achievements are lauded, there have been shortcomings. For instance, the Congress of Micronesia has yet to exercise an "override of a veto," due to the qualified restrictions placed on that body. That the Micronesian legislators, as well as the district authorities and those indigenes in positions of authority within the Executive Branch, have *not* always acted with discretion, may be expected in a polity where the inhabitants are still learning their responsibilities. Frequent changes in the U.S. Presidency (from the Democratic Party to the Republicans, then back again) have kept an even keel from proceeding. Thus, as regularly as new Presidents took office, a new High Commissioner would be appointed. Only one—Edward E. Johnston (a Nixon appointee in 1969)—was to serve over four years. With such changeovers in officials would come different approaches to policies and programs. This resulted in *frustration* for those American officials in the Trust Territory who attempted to keep the area running smoothly. When conflicts appeared between Interior in Washington, D.C., and the Administering Authority on the scene in the islands, the Micronesian leaders—especially in the Congress of Micronesia—were quick to *exploit* such differences. A prime example is the unconscionably slow negotiations over the future political status, which have dragged on for 11 years (as of mid-1977).

That the United States would permit the northern Marianas to enter "separate negotiations" in the early 1970s, culminating in the "commonwealth" option now pending, tends to be a tactical error. By mid-1977, both Palau and the Marshalls Districts have voted to request similar "separate negotiations"; thus, further *fracturing* of the Trust Territory looms as attempts are made to form a "unified" Micronesia. As a "letter grade" for this *political* "course:" *C+*.

Second, the "course" in *economic advancement* ("[To] promote the economic advancement and self-sufficiency of the inhabitants, and to this end . . . regulate the use of natural resources; encourage the development of fisheries, agriculture, and industries; . . . and improve the means of transportation and communication"). This endeavor has been the *weakest* of American achievements in Micronesia. Under the earlier Jap-

Conclusions

anese Mandate Period (officially, from 1920-45, although the Japanese military occupied Micronesia from 1914 when the Germans were driven from the Pacific with the outset of World War I), the economy in Micronesia *boomed*. By 1940, however, there were more Japanese, Okinawans, and Koreans in Micronesia than there were indigenes, and there was no question that such was a *Japanese* economy, geared for exporting to Japan. The U.S. Navy's Administration in Micronesia was characterized by *largess*. "Giveaways" were more obvious than efforts to make the islanders "self-sufficient." This was to continue somewhat into Interior's Administration, although this civilian administration was unable to duplicate Navy's logistical support, and Interior received a "Rust Territory" characterization for the decade of the 1950s which was descriptive, if somewhat unfair, given the lack of funds with which to work. Indigenous businessmen were small in volume and proceeds, with rare exceptions.

The "big employer" became the Trust Territory Government, where salaries for the islanders so employed would range three or four times *larger* than that found in the private sector. The advent of tourism and Air Micronesia gave a slight spark of self-sufficiency in the late 1960s; however, the annual budgets (more than $100 million by the time various federal grants were added) in the mid-to-late 1970s developed a philosophy in the islands that "Uncle Sugar Daddy" could solve all problems. A ray of hope came with a new Director of Territorial Affairs (DOTA), Fred M. Zeder II, in 1975. The fruits of his efforts at bringing in industrial development to the islands will have to await further evaluation (for the period of 1976-81). Foreign investment was still sparse by mid-1977. A "letter grade" for this *economic* "course" is a rather dismal $D+$.

Third, the "course" in *social advancement* ("[To] promote the social advancement of the inhabitants and to this end . . . protect the rights and fundamental freedoms of the population, . . . [and] protect the health of the inhabitants . . . and protect the inhabitants against social abuses"). The health and welfare of the Micronesians received a *high* priority under both the Naval and Interior Administrations, with particular emphasis on the establishment of dispensaries and strategically located hospitals. However, the *lack* of an infrastructure throughout the islands made transportation dependent on the Trust Territory Government's "try-weekly" airplane schedule and periodic field trip vessels for most of this period. The advent of Air Micronesia helped considerably in the late 1960s.

Two great contributors to the social development of the islanders have been the Christian missionaries—dating back to the mid-seventeenth century in the western areas, when the Catholic fathers began arriving, and the mid-nineteenth century for the Protestant missionaries in the eastern areas—as well as the later (beginning in 1966) saturation effort to bring in Peace Corps volunteers. The *lack* of a "work ethic" among the majority of the islanders is a failing which ties in with the economic problems of assisting the islanders to become "self-sufficient." A "letter grade" for the *social* "course:" *B* —.

Fourth, the "course" in *educational advancement* ("[To] promote the educational advancement of the inhabitants, and to this end . . . take steps toward the establishment of a general system of elementary education, facilitate the vocational and cultural advancement, . . . and encourage qualified students to pursue higher education, including training on the professional level"). Education has always been an important part of American life, and was a great achievement of the Second Continental Congress when it passed the "Northwest Ordinance" in 1787, with regard to setting aside land in the new territories to be devoted to "public education." The U.S. Navy reopened schools as World War II ended, and American missionaries were encouraged to return and reinstate the parochial schools. The construction of school buildings was always a high priority.

Unfortunately, the Administering Authority did not see the importance of teaching English in the elementary school grades until into the 1960s; then, the "teaching of English as a second language" (TESL) was somewhat confusing in its implementation. Nevertheless, some 1,500 Micronesians have graduated from two or four-year colleges, trade schools, and other specialized institutions "abroad" as well as through the limited facilities in the Trust Territory. The Congress of Micronesia, in 1965, was probably the *highest*-educated legislative body to come forth in a less-developed area during this century. By mid-1977, some 2,000 islanders were "abroad" attending to their higher education needs. Also by mid-1977, TESL had given way to a "bilingual, bicultural" approach to education. A "letter grade" for the *education* "course:" *B*+.

Thus, the "report card" for American rule in Micronesia during 1947-77 would appear, in this writer's evaluation, as follows:

Political development	C+
Economic advancement	D+
Social advancement	B—
Educational advancement	B+
LETTER GRADE AVE. (1947-77)	C+

The above "grades" would be sufficient for graduation from a four-year college, but insufficient for admission to most graduate schools. Perhaps the *interim* five-year period (1976-81) before the Trusteeship Agreement is expected to be terminated will see that *"C+"* improve to a more respectable *"B"* average. Time will tell.

Conclusions

Another development to watch in future years is the attitude of Japanese businessmen toward Micronesia. Although the "favored-nation" treatment for the Trust Territory was dropped by the U.S. Government in early 1974, the amount of foreign investment (including that from Japan) by mid-1977 was not so large as might have been expected. There have been joint ventures in the construction of hotels. Approval of a Saipan-Tokyo air route will improve tourism from Japan, and a possible "central storage terminal" (CTS) facility in Palau for the benefit of the Japanese may prove to be an economic lift if built by the early 1980s.

Index

Acapulco, 4
Ada, Francisco C. (Frank), 50, 70, 72-73, 92, 123-24, 198
Administering Authority. *See* High Commissioner, Office of
Adolph Capelle Company, 6
Advertiser, Honolulu, 44
Agriculture, training under Spanish, 4; under Japanese, 12-13, 15; under Americans, 116-17
Air Micronesia, Inc. (Air Mike), and transportation, 129-42, 149, 162nn.42-44, 198, 227, 231
Akina, Arthur, 77
Alcoholism, 84, 174
Aliens, 8, 14-15, 159n.10
Aloha Airlines, 133
Amaraich, Andon, 48, 64, 69, 74, 145, 156, 183, 189
American Board of Commissioners for Foreign Missions, 16, 171-72. *See also* United Church Board of World Ministries.
American flag, 166
American (Eastern) Samoa, 37, 43, 45-46, 49, 63, 70, 83, 104n.5, 105n.23, 154
America's Paradise Lost, 32n.10. *See also* Price, Willard
"Annexation theory," 60-61
Armed forces, U.S. occupational, xi, 38-40
Army and Navy view (1945), 27
Asao, F. Kazuo, 155
Ashman, Mike, 141
Asia Center of Japan, 220
Asia Foundation, 85
Aspinall, Wayne N., 108-9n.62
Assembly of God, 172
Atherton, Alexine L., 34-35n.52. *See also* Jacob, Philip E.; Wallenstein, Arthur M.
Atlantic Charter, 27
Atomic Energy Commission, 51

Austin, Warren R., 28, 46-47
Australia, 142, 155

Ballon, Robert J., 221, 224-25
Balos, Ataji L., 137
Bank of America, Asia Division, 73; Saipan Branch, 145
Bank of Hawaii, Saipan Branch, 123; Ponape Branch, 144
Bank of Tokyo, 14. *See also* California First Bank
Bauxite, 12
Beck, Donald L., 138
Bennett, Paul J., 96, 100
Beverages, alcoholic, 12, 14
Bicycles, 20, 176
Bikini Island, 47
Bingham, Jonathan B., 65
Bliss, Donald T., 186
Block Construction Company, 197
Bonnet, Richard, 150
Borja, Olympio T., 15, 21, 23, 88-89, 91, 101, 115, 118, 153, 179, 185-86; with wife, 155, 221
Boston Harbor, 5; Mission School, on Kusaie, 16
Boughton, George J., 94
Bowden, Elbert V., 161n.24. *See also* Nathan Report
Bower, James M., 123
Bowman, Isaiah, 34n.51
Boyer, David S., 5, 31n.9. *See also National Geographic*
Buddhism, 16. *See also* Religion in Japan
Budgets, including annual, 50-51, 53, 75-76, 93-94, 114-16, 122, 124-29, 141-43, 152, 177, 193-95, 205, 231
Burns, George, 145
Burt, David, 189
Burton, Philip, 85
Businessmen, Micronesian, 13-15, 155. *See also* Entrepreneurs

235

Cabranes, José A., 112n.95
Cabrera, Gregorio C., 156
Cairo Conference (1943), 26-27, 34n.49
Caldwell, Michael F., xii, 17-18, 22, 41, 94, 130, 179-80, 196, 213, 215; Sue, xii
California, coast of, 4
California First Bank, 14. See also Bank of Tokyo
Campbell, John C., 34n.49
Canham, Erwin D., 92-94, 102-3
Cannon, William W., 176
Capital Improvement Program (CIP), 142, 160n.14, 192-95
Capital punishment, under Germans, 7-8; under Americans, 173
Capuchin Franciscans, 4, 17, 172
Capuchins, Spanish, 6. See also Missionaries
Carnegie Endowment for International Peace, 59
Carolines, acquisition by Germans, 6; Carolinians, 5, 93
Carpentry, training under Spanish, 5
Carter, Jimmy, and administration, 84-85, 96
Cash crops, 120, 156
Catholic Spain in Micronesia, 6
Catholics in Japan, 16
Census (1793), 30n.1, 129
Central America, 4
Central Intelligence Agency (CIA), 49-50, 123-24; spying charges against, 102-3, 113n.101
Chamberlain, Charles, 107-8n.50
Chamorros, 4-5, 10, 14-15, 22-23, 196-97; culture of, 4
Chatroop, Henry, 118
Chiang Kai-shek, 26-27; China, 27; Chinese workers, 12-13; Chinese population in Micronesia, 14
Children's exchange tour, 220
Chinese Nationalists, training of, 49-50, 106n.33
Christianization, under Spanish, 4, 6; under Germans, 9
Church, under Germans, 7, 9. See also Religion
Church and state, separation of, 172-73, 178
Church of Jesus Christ of Latter-day Saints, 172, 176. See also Mormon missionaries

Civic Action Teams (CATs), 188-92, 202n.28
Civil administration units, 47
Civil Aeronautics Board (CAB), 130, 136-38, 140, 162-63nn.43, 46
Civil government, under Spanish, 5-6
Civil Service, U.S., 76, 79
Clark, Gregory, 225
Clergy, Protestant, 5-6. See also Missionaries
Cleveland, Harlan, 58, 61
Cocchilla, Mike, 150-51
"Cold War" between Protestants and Catholics, 5-6
Cole, W. Sterling, 43-44
Coleman, Peter T., 54, 78, 147-48
Collier, John, 44. See also Institute of Ethnic Affairs
Collier's Magazine, 105n.18
Colonialism, 27
Commission on Future Political Status and Transition, 48
Commission on the Future Political Status of the Trust Territory of the Pacific Islands (Micronesia), 108n.61
Commonwealth status. See Northern Marianas
Community College of Micronesia (CCM), 212-16
Compact of Free Association, 96-99
Condon, John F. X., 114
Conference of Micronesian Churches, 172-74
Confucianism, 16. See also Religion in Japan
Congregationalists, 5-6, 172. See also United Church of Christ
Congress of Micronesia, 61-78; unicameral vs. bicameral, 62-63; titles of houses, 63-64; 73-74; 81-82; 85-86; 90-92; 95-97; 99; 101; 103; 107n.49; 108n.59; 110n.80; 111n.91; 113nn.101, 103; 124; 131-32; 137; 144-47; 149; 151-52; 155-57; 159; 162n.38; 163n.53; 178-82; 186; 189; 194; 200nn.8, 15; 201nn.21, 23, 25; 220-22; 227n.1; 230; 232
Congress of Micronesia, xi, xiii. See also Meller, Norman
Congressional Enabling Act (1954), 52
Constabulary, under Japanese, 11, 18-19; under Americans, 40. See also Policemen

Index

Constitution of Federated States of Micronesia, 96-99; Constitutional Convention (1975), 172-74, 186
Continental Airlines, 129, 132-41, 149, 162nn.42-44, 163n.46, 227n.1. *See also* Air Micronesia, Inc.
Continental Congress, Second, 232
Contract employees, U.S., 76, 205-6, 215
Conyers, John, Jr., 179-80
Cooper, Richard, 107-8n.50
Copper, 12
Copra, development of trade, 5, 7, 117
Corporal punishment, under Japanese, 19
Corrugated sheet metal, 160n.15
Costigan, Hugh F., 145, 154, 156, 212
Council of Micronesia, 57, 61-63, 65, 107n.44, 169-70. *See also* Inter-District Advisory Committee
Craley, N. Neiman, Jr., 73-74, 76, 81-82, 92, 101, 183-84, 186, 189-90
Credit unions, 155-56, 163n.60
Cruz, C. S., 20, 40, 50
Cruz, José R., 178
"Current Topics," Station WGGL-FM, Houghton, Mich., 162n.35

Dale, Paul, 107-8n.50
Davis, James P., 49
De Broff, Gary, 155
De Brum, José, 6
De Brum, Oscar, 6, 56, 107n.49, 216-17n.13
Decentralization, 75, 78-81, 83, 140-41
Defense, Department of, and interests, 58, 99-101
Demobilization, 120
Deutsche Südsee-Phosphat-Aktien-Gesellschaft, 7
De Villalobos, Ruy Lopez, 4
Dinell, Tom, 42, 63
Discrimination, under Japanese, 17-21; in reintegration with Guam, 89
District governments, chartering of, 102, 113n.100
Donchin, Gwyneth, 201n.22
Driver, Marjorie G., 88-89
Dublon, island of, 33n.34, 38, 104n.9
Duggan, Barrie G., 138
Dumas, Jean-Pierre, 156-57
Duncan, Dennis L., 73, 135-36, 182, 198
Dunkerley, Craig G., 218
Dykema, Henry, 131, 174

East West Center, 215
Ebeye, conditions in, 211-12, 216-17n.13
Economic development, under Spanish, 4-6; under Germans, 6-9; under Japanese, 11-15, 17-22, 25-26, 117, 119-20; under Americans, 114-63
Economic Development Loan Fund (EDLF), 146-50, 156, 199
Economic Development Plan for the Trust Territory of the Pacific Islands, 124-26, 132, 145-46, 161nn.24, 26. *See also* "Nathan Report"
Economic (or Marine) Resources Zone, 99, 219
Education, under Spanish, 4-6; under Japanese, 19, 21, 23-26; under Americans, 34n.48, 38, 203-17
Education for Self-Government (ESG), program of, xiii, 95-99, 111n.85, 184
Edvalson, P. Terry, 213-15
Eisenhower, Dwight D., and administration, 49, 52, 56
Elliott, Thomas A., 162n.36. *See also* Robbins, David S.
Energy and Natural Resources, Committee on, U.S. Senate, 100, 194
Enewetok Proving Ground, 47, 51
Engle, Clair, 44-45, 105n.20
Entrepreneurs, 13-15, 155. *See also* Businessmen, Micronesian
Everyman's United Nations, 34-35n.52
Explorers, Spanish, 4

Faith Presbyterian Reformed Church, Guam, 174
Falcam, Leo A., 56, 83, 107n.49, 110n.80, 227n.1
"Fallback position," for military, 100-101
Father Arnold Bendowske, 4-5, 7, 17, 22, 48, 87-89, 144, 153, 177-78, 206-7
Federal Aviation Administration (FAA), 142, 161n.31
Fiji Islands, 7, 70, 225; School of Medicine in, 165, 205
Filipino Club of Micronesia, 196
Filipinos, skilled, 4, 143, 195-98, 223
Firzzell, Kent, 92
Fisheries and fishing, under Japanese, 14, 15; under Americans, 116-17, 128; Japanese interests in, 219. *See also* Skipjack
Five-Year Indicative Development Plan, 30n.1, **157**

Florida, 4
Fong, Hiram L., 67
Forbis, William H., 33n.36. See also *Japan Today*
Ford, Gerald R., and administration, 84, 92, 112n.95, 138
Foreign Claims Acts (1944, 1945), 167
Foreign investment, 157-59, 163n.63, 231, 233
Foreign Investment Act (1970), 158-59
Foreign Relations of the United States, 1947, Vol. I, 35n.57
Foreigners, under Germans, 7
Formosans, population in Micronesia, 14; as workers, 119-20
Forrestal, James V., 34n.51, 43
Forrestal Diaries, 104n.14
France, 27
"Friends of Micronesia," 58-59
Fukuda, Takeo, 138-39
Functions and Policies of American Government, 35n.54
Furber, Edward P., 42, 186, 202n.27
Future political status, issue of, 173-74
Future Political Status Commission, and Report of, 66-68, 109-10nn.71-72, 111n.86

Gale, Roger, 142-43, 180, 209
Gallemore, Roy T., 42
Galleons, Spanish, 4
Garrett, Terry L., 53, 79-80, 168, 210
General Baptists, 172
Gereben, Janos, 108n.51
Germans, 4; language, 9; clergy, 16, 171-72. See also Liebenzeller Mission
Germany, political struggle with Spain, 5-6; research in, 31n.4
Gilbert and Ellice Colony Medical Service, 15
Gill, Thomas P., 42, 63
Goding, M. Wilfred, 56-57, 60, 63, 81, 169
Gold, search for, 4
Government of the Northern Marianas, 22, 30n.1, 46, 72-74, 92-95, 156, 170, 197
Grants-in-aid, federal, 142-43, 231
Great Britain, 27; and Japan, 11
Gruening, Ernest, 67
Guam, location of, xi, 105n.23; discovery of, 4; Chamorros in, 4, 22, 25; ceded to U.S., 6; fall of, 11, 17; Wartime conditions in, 22-23; U.S. Navy's return to, 36; status of, 30n.1, 37, 43, 45-57, 49, 52-53, 83, 87-89, 91, 99, 104n.5, 111n.87, 114, 121, 123, 130-32, 135, 140-42, 149, 154, 156, 160n.14, 171-72, 174, 176, 178-79, 195-96, 200n.9, 204-5, 224; University of, xii, 17, 22, 31n.4, 94, 174, 179, 214

Hamanaka, Suekazu, xii, 21-22, 34n.41, 220, 222-24
Handicraft industry, 118-19
Haneda Airport, Tokyo, 138
Harrison, Kirby, 202n.28
Hassing, Gene D., 133, 135, 138-40, 149
Hawaii, University of, 56-59, 205, 214-15
Health care, under Americans, 164-66, 231-32
Heim, Hans J., xii
Heine, Carl, 71-72, 89, 111n.89. See also *Micronesia at the Crossroads*
Heine, Dwight, 13-16, 20, 23, 39-40, 49, 54, 56-57, 62, 64, 68, 76, 81, 87, 107n.49, 114-15, 122, 127, 169-70, 177
Henry, Bethwel, 56, 103, 107n.49, 227n.1
Hezel, Francis X., 5-6, 9, 23, 31n.8, 32n.12, 127-28, 161n.29, 174-75, 206
Hickel, Walter J., 76, 110nn.74-75
Hicking, Arobate, 15, 33n.35
High, Daniel J., 75, 78, 148
High Commissioner, Office of, 65-66, 74, 76-78, 81-85, 110n.83, 111-12n.91, 159, 230
Hill, A. Spencer, xii
Hispanicization, influence of, 6
Hitachi Zosen CBI Ltd., 138
Hospitals and sub-hospitals, 166
Hughes, Daniel T., ed., *Political Development in Micronesia,* 30n.2, 47-48, 142. See also Lingenfelter, Sherwood G.

Ickes, Harold L., 43-44, 105n.16
Iehsi, Ambilos, 103
Ihlen, Joseph, 141-42
Ilo, Jesus, 20, 24
Independent Baptists, 172
India, 180
Infrastructure, basic, under Japanese, 38; under Americans, 122, 160n.16, 194-95, 231
Institute of Ethnic Affairs, 43-44

Index

Institute of Pacific Relations, 43
Inter-District Advisory Committee, 57, 61-63, 65, 107n.44, 169-70. *See also* Council of Micronesia
Interior, Department of the, 42; civilian rule of, 48-103, 128, 165, 177, 205-7, 229-33
Interior and Insular Affairs, Committee on, U.S. Senate (also called "Jackson Committee"), 100, 194
International College, Sophia University, 225
Italy, research in, 31n.4

Jackson, Henry M., 100-101, 194-95
Jackson, William D., 79, 133, 165, 184-85
Jacob, Philip E., 34n.52. *See also* Atherton, Alexine L.; Wallenstein, Arthur M.
Jaluit-Gesellschaft, 7
Japan, and Great Britain, 11; U.S. bases in, 101; Micronesian war claims, 166-68; oil storage needs of, 220, 225-26, 233; Saipan air route, 137-39, 163n.46, 219-20, 233
Japan, Consul General on Guam, xii. *See also* Hamanaka, Suekazu
Japan Airline (JAL), 140-41, 220, 224, 227n.1, 233
Japan Association of Travel Agents, 224
Japan Cambodian Association, 220
Japan Micronesia Association (JMA), and Secretary General, xii, 220
Japan Singapore Association, 220
Japan Today, 33n.36. *See also* Forbis, William H.
Japan Vietnam Association, 220
Japanese, population in Micronesia, 13-14; Diet, 138, 225-26; Ministry of Foreign Affairs, 168; Ministry of International Trade and Industry (MITI), 225-26; as tourists, 141-42, 150; as actors, 150; present and future interests of, 218-27
Japanese Mandated Islands, 10-15, 26-28, 44; Mandate Period, 10, 14-15, 18-20, 26-26, 90, 119, 154, 230-31; violations during Period, 11-12; local government under, 11; civil government of, 13
Jehovah's Witnesses, 172
Jennings, William F., 119

Jesuits, Spanish, 16, 172. *See also* Society of Jesus
Johnson, Lyndon B., and administration, 65, 67, 105n.16, 108-9n.62, 178-79
Johnston, Edward E., 76, 81-83, 91, 95, 97, 110n.76, 230
Johnston, Emilie G., 22, 25, 88
Joint Committee on Future Status, 85, 97, 110n.73
Joint ventures, 158, 220-24
Journal of Pacific History, 30n.5. *See also* Purcell, David C.

Kabua, Amata, 222
Kalau, Edmund, 171-72, 200n.13
Kansou, Ngas, 11, 15, 18-19, 24-25, 33n.34, 41, 48, 69-70, 164-65
Kennally, Vincent I., 170-72
Kennedy, David M., 91, 112nn.92-93
Kennedy, John F., and administration, 50-51, 56-58, 60-61, 105n.16, 123-25, 127; charisma of, 176-78, 200n.14
King Tomeing, 166
Kluver, Wally, 144
Kobayashi, Izumi, xii, 21, 220
Koreans, population in Micronesia, 14, 231; discrimination involving, 18, 21; as workers, 119-20, 198
Koror, Palau, 13-14
Kosrae, District of, 5, 78, 140, 149, 157, 170, 192-93. *See also* Kusaie
Kotaki, Yoshiaki, 168, 219
Krock, Arthur, 35n.54
Kuchō, 11
Kuribayashi, Tokuichi, 12, 33n.24, 154
Kusaie, 5; German control in, 5; during World War II, 15, 32n.35. *See also* Kosrae, District of
Kuwano, Masao, 14, 21
Kwajalein, island of, 6; Missile Range, 100; Kwajalein Importing and Trading Company (KITCO), 117

Labor, under Japanese, 13
Lake Superior State College, 215
Land matters, under Germans, 8; under Americans, 194-95
Lane, Franklin Knight, 105n.16
Law of the Sea, 173
League of Nations, Mandate of (1920), 10-11; withdrawal from, 12

Legislatures, district, 48, 53, 106n.29, 124, 186-87, 205
Lessa, William A., 4, 30-31n.3, 32n.10. See also *Ulithi: A Micronesian Design for Living*
Liebenzeller Mission, and Liebenzells, 16, 171-72. See also German Clergy
Limits of Power, 201n.17. See also McCarthy, Eugene J.
Lindholm, Donald, 107-8n.50
Lingenfelter, Sherwood G., ed., *Political Development in Micronesia*, 30n.2, 47-48, 142. See also Hughes, Daniel T.
Local government, 53
Loesch, Harrison, 111n.87
Los Angeles Times, 113n.101
Ludwig, Kurt, 61-62, 108n.55
Ludwig, Roger, 206
Luzama, Alex P., 133-35, 199

Mackenzie, J. Boyd, 51-52, 55, 70, 95, 122, 130, 161n.33, 206n.33
MacQuarrie, Alan, 41-42
Magellan, Ferdinand, 4
Mailo, Petrus, 117-18, 159n.5
Malone, Mike, 112n.94
Management and Budget, Office of (OMB), 94
Manchuria, invasion of (1931), 11
Mangone, Gerald, 58
Manila, 4
Mansfield, Mike, 44, 105n.19
Marianas, islands of, 3, 5; Legislature, 15, 89-91; Northern, 4, 7, 49-50, 72-73, 85-95, 102-3, 111n.85, 112n.95, 123-24, 140-41, 172-74, 195-96, 200n.14, 209-210, 221-23, 229
Marianas Political Status Commission, 85-87
Marshall Islands, invasion of, xi; political struggle in, 5-6; German occupancy of, 6-7
Maxwell School, Syracuse University, 58
May, Ardith G., xiii
McCarthy, Eugene J., 180, 201n.17. See also *Limits of Power*
McConnell, J. Knox, 149-51
McGarry, William, 175-76
McGrath, William A., 33-34n.40
McHenry, Donald F., 59, 84. See also *Micronesia: Trust Betrayed*

McKinley Administration, 6
McPhetres, Agnes, 208-13
McPhetres, Samuel, xiii, 96-97, 184
Medical officers, Micronesian, 165
Medical programs, under Japanese, 15
Meller, Norman, xi, xiii, 42, 48, 63, 107n.44. See also *Congress of Micronesia*
Mexico, research in, 31n.4
Michigan Technological University, xii
Micronesia, location of, xi, 3; population of, 3, 6; gold in, 4; Spanish rule of, 3-6; German rule in, 6-10; Japanese rule in, 10-26
Micronesia Area Research Center (MARC), xii, 22, 31n.4, 88
Micronesia at the Crossroads, 71, 111n.89. See also Heine, Carl
"Micronesia Club," 55-57
"Micronesia Day," 108n.59
Micronesia Development Bank (MDB), 149-51
Micronesia: Trust Betrayed, 58. See also McHenry, Donald F.
Micronesian flag, 168-70, 200n.8. See also Trust Territory flag
Micronesian Mainland Education Project, 215
Micronesian Occupational Center (MOC), 212-13, 215-16
Micronesian Products Center, 146-47
Micronesian Seminar, 31n.8
Micronesian Teacher Education Center, 213. See also Community College of Micronesia
Micronitor (later, *Micronesian Independent*), 59, 161n.21
"Micronization," 52-53, 75-80
Midkiff, Frank H., 62, 81, 122
Militarization by Japanese, of Truk, 11-12, 19; of Micronesia, 13, 16-17, 25-26
Milner, George R., 167
Mining operations, under Japanese, 12-13, 33n.29
Mink, Patsy T., 67, 108-9n.62
Missionaries, Spanish, 4; Jesuit, 4; Jesuit Order, 4; American Protestant, 5-6, 16-17, 24; "cold war" between Protestants and Catholics, 5-6; Congregationalists, 5-6; Capuchins, 5-6; under Germans, 9; under Japanese, 15-17; under Americans, 170-76, 200n.9, 231-32

Molasses, 12
"Mom and pop stores," 118
Moos, Felix, 11, 32-33n.23
Mormon missionaries in Micronesia, 176
Morton, Roger C. B., 159, 163n.63
Moses, Artie, 118
"Mr. Tanaka," in Marshalls, 19
Mt. Carmel Church, 4, 176-78
Municipalities, chartering of, 53-54, 106-7n.43, 169
Murphy, Joe (Guam), 87-89, 91, 94-95, 112n.93, 170, 196
Murphy, Joe (Majuro), 170
Murray, James N., Jr., 35n.55
Murray, Steve, 106n.33

Nabors, Bill, 187
Nago, Brad, 197, 222-23
Nakamura, Daiziro, 97
Nakamura, Mamoru ("Mo"), 75
Nakatsukasa, Pedro T. (Pete), 22
Nakayama, Tosiwo, 56, 103, 107n.49, 136-37, 219-20, 227n.1
Nango Dendo Dan, 16-17
Nanyo Boeki Kaisha, 19, 33-34n.40
Nanyo-cho Government, 11-13, 15, 17, 26
Nanyo Kohatsu Kaisha, 11-12, 21, 33nn.24, 27. See also South Seas Bureau
Nanyo Takushoku Kaisha, 21
Narita Airport, Tokyo, 138
Nathan Report, and mission (1966), 124-26, 132, 145-46, 161nn.24, 26
National Geographic, 31n.9. See also Boyer, David S.
National University, Canberra, 7-8
National War College, 100
Nauru, investments of, 222
Navy, Japanese Imperial, ix, 15, 20, 24, 38
Neas, Maynard, Foreword by, ix, xiii, 4, 8-10, 12, 18, 27, 31n.4, 32n.18, 38, 42, 52, 59-60, 74, 104n.8, 115-16, 145-46, 166-68, 185, 191
"Negative" reinforcement, under Japanese, 17-18
Negotiations, rounds of, 68, 96, 98-99, 111n.85, 112n.98, 113nn.99, 102. See also Options, political status
Nixon, Richard M., and administration, 85, 108-9n.62, 110n.75, 136-37
Northern Michigan University, 215

Northwest Ordinance (1787), 232
Northwest Orient, 138, 163n.46
Norwood, W. R., 66-67, 81-82, 109n.67, 132-33, 162n.40, 207, 216n.10
Nucker, Delmas H., 56, 62, 81, 130
Nuclear testing, in Marshalls, 47, 55. See also Bikini Island and Enewetok Proving Ground
Nufer, Marian M., xii, 198
Nuuan, Francis, 181

Office of Education, in HEW, 209
Office of Micronesian Status Negotiations, 91
Office of Territorial Affairs, Director of (DOTA), 4
Office of Territorial Affairs, 31n.7. See also Van Cleve, Ruth G.
Oguma, Takahisa, 222-23
Oiterong, Alfonso R., 25, 34n.48, 56, 107n.49
O'Keefe, David, 8-9; daughter of, 32n.18
Okinawa, 134
Okinawans, population in Micronesia, 14, 231; joined with islanders, 15; discrimination involving, 18, 21; as workers, 119-20
Olopai, Jean, 187-88, 209
Olter, Bailey, 56, 67-68, 107n.49
On Active Service in Peace and War, 35n.53. See also Stimson, Henry L., and Bundy, McGeorge
Options, political status, 68, 87-90, 95-103. See also Negotiations, rounds of
Oregon College of Education, evaluation by, 214
Organic Act (1950), 94
Organic legislation, 45
Orientals, 14

Pacific Area Travel Association (PATA), 141
Pacific Far East Line, 129
Pacific House, 215. See also Pacific Micronesian Cultural Aid, Inc.
Pacific Islands, 4; defined in late 1940s, 105n.23
Pacific Islands Central School (PICS), 169, 205-6
Pacific Micronesian Cultural Aid, Inc., 215. See also Pacific House

Pacific Micronesian Line, 129
Palau, and U.S. bases, 101; and a central tanker storage (CTS) facility, 158, 225-26, 233
Palau Handicraft and Woodworkers Guild, 146
Palaus, under Germans, 7
Pan American Airlines (Pan Am), 133, 136, 140-41, 163n.46
Pangelinan, Edward del G., 85
Papua New Guinea, 34-35n.52, 67, 70, 225
Paradise in Trust, ix. See also Trumbull, Robert
Paramedicals, Micronesian, 165
Paris, Treaty of (1898), 6, 30n.1
Park, Robert L., 136
Peace Corps: programs, officials, and volunteers of, 79, 97, 142, 178-88, 200n.15, 201nn.18, 22-25; and TESL, 207-10, 215, 231-32
Pearl Harbor, sneak attack on, xi, 15, 36
Pearling, Arafura, 12
Pedrus, Podis, 77, 80
Peltason, Jack W., and James W., 35n.54
Pentagon Papers and the Courts, 106n.33. See also Shapiro, Martin
"Pentagon Papers" case, 50
Pepper, in Ponape, 150
Perez, Joe, 149
Peter Paul Company, 119
Philippines, 4-5; research in, 31n.4, 143, 195-98, 222-23; War Damage Commission, ix, 166
Phosphate, mining of, 7, 12, 120
Pickard, Maurice, 200n.13
Pincetich, John, 181-82, 200n.15
Plebiscites, 67, 87-89, 91, 112n.94. See also Referenda
Policemen, under Japanese, 18-19. See also Constabulary
Political offices, under Germans, 9-10
Political parties, under Americans, 101
Political Status Delegation, and Reports of, 111n.87
"Political warfare," between Navy and Interior, 42-45, 50-51, 65
Ponape, German control in, 5
Ponape Agriculture and Trade School (PATS), 145, 154, 156, 212-16
Pope Leo XIII, adjudication by, 5
"Positive" reinforcement, under Japanese, 17-18

Potsdam Conference (1945), 27
Practitioners, native, 15
Presidential vote, for Guam, 94-95
Price, Willard, 5, 32n.10. See also *America's Paradise Lost*
Pritchard, Ross, 179-81
Protestants, American, 5-6, 32n.10. See also Missionaries
Puerto Rico, 67-68, 92, 94, 112n.95
Purcell, David C., Jr., 4, 13, 30n.5, 33n.28. See also *Journal of Pacific History*

Quaker International, Affairs Program of, 180

Radford, Arthur W., 48
Rakestraw, Lawrence, xii
Ramarui, David, 9, 13-14, 18, 23-25, 31n.6, 68-69, 204-6, 208, 211, 213, 216n.6
Rechecebei, Ramon, 128
Rechucher, Eusebio, 80, 123, 157-58
Referenda, 67, 87-89, 95, 102. See also Plebiscites
Reimers, Bob, 155
Religion, under Germans, 7, 9
Religion in Japan, 16. See also Shintoism; Buddhism; Confucianism
Remengesau, Thomas O., 154
Revenue, local, 118-19; income, 151-52, 156, 163n.57. See also Taxation
Rice, 14
Richard, Dorothy E., xi, xiiin.1, 11-12, 14, 16-17, 24, 32n.17, 36-40, 103n.1, 103-4n.3, 116-17, 120-21, 164, 167, 171, 203-5. See also *United States Naval Administration of the Trust Territory of the Pacific Islands*
Rising Sun, 33n.33. See also Toland, John
Robbins, David, 130, 162n.36. See also Elliott, Thomas A.
Robbins, Robert R., xiii; 32n.21; 50-52; 55; 64-65; 70; 103n.2; 106nn.35, 39; 108 n.59; 111-12n.91; 121; 131; 160n.15; 162n.37; 180; 186; 201nn.19, 20, 26; 202n.27
Roman Catholicism, 6
Roosevelt, Franklin D., 27, 105n.16
Rota, Island of, 4; Rotanese, 4, 93
Rotholz, Josef, 190-92, 210
Russia, 27, 28, 35n.57, 167. See also Soviet Union

Index

"Rust Territory" period, 121-22, 231
Ruzumna, Sharon N., 186

Sablan, Vincente, 91
Sablan Construction Company, 197, 222-23. *See also* Shimizu Construction Company
Sackbauer, Betty, 181, 187-88, 209
Sailing ships, *Morning Star*, 5
Saipan, Island of, 4; Chamorros taken from, 4; population of (1900), 4
Saipan and Japan, air route between, 138-39, 163n.46, 219-20, 233
Saipan Community Church, 16, 128, 172
Saipan Farmer's Market Cooperative Association (FMCA), 156
Saipanese, 14. *See also* Chamorros
Salii, Lazarus, 40-41, 55-57, 60-61, 63-64, 67-68, 72, 81-82, 97, 99, 101, 107n.49, 143, 183, 220-21, 226
Samoans, 70
Sanchez, Pedro, 107-8n.50
Santos, Ben
Sarabalia, Domingo, 223
Sawaichi, Jacob, 67, 109n.70
Schnoor, Howard, 107-8n.50
Schools of Military Government, Army and Navy, 37-38, 46, 104n.8
"Security restriction," 50
Select Committee on Intelligence, U.S. Senate, 102-3
Separate negotiations, 86-87, 214, 229
Setik, Raymond, 81, 110n.78
Seventh Day Adventists, 172
Shapiro, Martin, 106n.33. *See also Pentagon Papers and the Courts*
Sherrell, Jerry D., 201n.18
Shimizu Construction Company, 197, 222-23. *See also* Sablan Construction Company
Shintoism, 16. *See also* Religion in Japan
Shoecraft, Robert, 167
Shook, Cleo, 107-8n.50
Sicard, Charles, 155-56, 163n.60
Skipjack, under Japanese, 12. *See also* Fisheries
Small Business Act, 146-47, 163n.52
Social advancement, under Americans, 164-202
Social Security Office, and programs, 198
Society of Jesus, 16, 172. *See also* Jesuits, Spanish

Socio-Economic Institute, Sophia University, 221
"Sokehs Rebellion," 7-8
Solang, Mitch, 17-18
Solomon, Anthony M., 58
Solomon Mission, and Report, 57-61, 107-8n.50, 125, 161n.21
Sonchō, 11
Sosonchō, 11
South America, 4
South Korea, War in, 47
South Pacific Commission, programs of, 209
South Seas Bureau, 11
Soviet Union, 27-28, 35n.54, 167. *See also* Russia
Spain, 3-6; political struggle with Germany, 5-6; research in, 31n.4
Spanish, 3-4; missions and missionaries, 4-5, 30-31n.3; vocational education under, 4-6; religion under, 4-5; culture under, 5; language, 5; lack of political development of islanders, 6
Spanish-American War, settlement of, 6
Spies, Marshallese, 39. *See also* Heine, Dwight
Spivey, John, 130
Stalin, Josef, 26-27
Stassen, Harold E., 34n.51
State Department view (1945), 27
Steele, Percy D. (Red), 42
Stege, Scott H., 186-87
Steincipher, John Richard, 35n.59
Stettinus, Edward R., 27-28
Stewart, William H., 31n.4, 117, 128-29, 147, 151, 161n.30
Stimson, Henry L., and Bundy, McGeorge, 34n.51, 35n.53. *See also On Active Service in Peace and War*
Stores, "mama and papa" type, 13
Students, Micronesian, xi, 5, 206
Suarez, Laoncio, 196
Subsistence economy, 120
Sugar, 12
Sugarcane, fields, 15
Suicides, 174-75
Sunday-School children, American, 5
Suomi College, 215

Taitano, Richard, 107-8n.50
Taiwan, and U.S. bases, 101; supplies from, 222

Tamag, Joseph, 155
Tangantangan, on Saipan, 123, 160n.18
Tavares, Thomas E., 74-75, 143-44, 190, 192
Taxation, local, 118-19; income, 152-53, 156, 163n.57. *See also* Revenue, local
Taxis, under Japanese, 20
Teaching English as a Second Language (TESL), 207-9
Tenorio, José C. (JoeTen), 13, 18, 23-24, 73, 115, 118, 123, 155, 177
Texas Lutheran College, 215
Thomas, Elbert D., 81
Tinian, Island of, 4; Tinianese, 93; and U.S. bases, 101
Tman, Luke, 69
Toland, John, 15, 33n.33. *See also* Rising Sun
Tordesillas, Treaty of (1494), 4
Tourism and tourists, 50, 131-32,137-42, 162n.45, 199
Trade deficits, 142
Trades, training under Spanish, 5
Trans World Airlines (TWA), 134
Transocean Air Lines, 129
Travari, David, 56
Truk, German control in, 5
Truk Lagoon, Japanese Imperial Navy in, xi
Truk Trading Company (TTC), 117-18
Truman, Harry S., and administration, 27-28, 36-37, 43-46, 104n.10, 105n.16, 129
Trumbull, Robert, ix. *See also* Paradise in Trust
Trust Territory Code, 35n.59, 169, 202n.27
Trust Territory flag, 168-70, 200n.8. *See also* Micronesian flag
Trust Territory Government. *See* High Commissioner, Office of
Trust Territory of the Pacific Islands, location of, xi, 105n.23; legislative bodies in, xi
Trust Territory Reports, compilation of, 186
Trusteeship Agreement (1947), xi, 3, 26-30, 35n.58, 36, 44-45, 65-68, 85, 91-92, 95-97, 102, 105n.20, 121, 159, 195, 203, 227, 229, 232; strategic significance of, 3, 29-30, 32n.21, 47
Tufts University, xii-xiii, 64

Udall, Stewart L., 72, 105n.16, 178
Udui, Elizabeth, 137, 158-59, 221-22
Udui, Kaleb, 82
Ulithi: A Micronesian Design for Living, 30-31n.3. *See also* Lessa, William A.
Ulochong, Raymond, 76
Uludong, Francisco, 58-59
Unions, 170
United Church Board of World Ministries, 172
United Church of Christ, 172. *See also* Congregationalists
United Micronesia Development Association (UMDA), 133, 136-37, 140
United Nations, Charter of, xi, 35n.59; Security Council, xi, 3, 26, 28, 30, 34-35n.52, 35n.58, 90; San Francisco charter-structuring, 27; trusteeship, 27; General Assembly, 34-35n.52; U.N. flag, 169; Trusteeship Council, 54-55, 62, 67, 78-79, 81, 83, 85, 89-96, 103, 104n.9, 110n.84, 111n.90, 113n.103, 124, 132-33; petitions to, 54-55, 143, 151, 156, 160n.20, 162n.40, 167, 182, 193, 200n.14, 201n.24, 203, 207, 213, 216nn.1, 10; U.N. Development Plan (UNDP), and task force, 156-57, priorities of, 157, meeting of, 124, 160n.19; Visiting Mission, 54-55, 62, 65-66, 87, 109n.63, 111n.88, 112n.95, 162n.39
United States in World Affairs, 1945-1947, 34n.49. *See also* Campbell, John C.
United States Naval Administration of the Trust Territory of the Pacific Islands, 3 vols., xiiin.1. *See also* Richard, Dorothy E.
University of the East, 196
U.S. Congress, 30, 65-67, 72, 76, 85, 92-95, 109n.69, 112n.95, 113n.101, 127, 131, 142, 146-47, 152, 168, 193
U.S. Department of Agriculture (USDA), food from, 152-54, 163n.58, 198
U.S. Court of Appeals, Ninth Circuit, 94
U.S. District Court, 168
U.S. Embassy, in Tokyo, 219
U.S. Naval Administration, xi; initial, 26, 36-45; interim, 45-49; in Alaska, 103-4n.3; 114-21, 123-24, 129, 164-65, 169-71, 203-5, 215, 229, 231-32

Index

Van Cleve, Ruth G., 4, 11, 22, 31n.7, 49, 55, 58, 62-63, 79, 84, 96, 99, 112n.98, 143, 179, 193-94, 207. See also *Office of Territorial Affairs*
Vandenberg, Arthur H., 27; Vandenberg, Arthur H., Jr., ed., *Private Papers of Senator Vandenberg*, 34n.51
Vaughn, Jack, 178
Veto, absolute nature of, 82, 110n.79
Vicariate, for Carolines and Marshalls, 170-71
Villagomez, Manuel S. (M.S.), 13, 28, 40, 155, 223
Virgin Islands, 67-68, 79, 83, 94, 111n.87

Wagner College, 215
Wallenstein, Arthur M., 34n.52. See also Atherton, Alexine L.; Jacob, Philip E.
War claims, 54-55, 166-68
Washington Post, 102-3. See also Woodward, Bob
Webb, James H., Jr., 6, 32n.14. See also *Micronesia and U.S. Pacific Strategy*
Webb, Robert S., 138, 224
Welch, John, 134
Western Association of Schools and Colleges, 31n.4, 214
Western Carolines Trading Company (WCTC), 117
Western Samoa, 225
Whalers, from New England, 5
White, Jeffrey J., 38, 212-13
White Sands Hotel, on Saipan, 223
Whittington, Thomas L., 186
Williams, Franklin Haydn, 85-86, 91, 97
Williams, Mack, 128, 172-74
Wilson, Woodrow, 105n.16
Windsor, Paul, 145
Winkel, Adrian P., 85, 95-96, 99, 110nn.83-84, 140, 143, 151, 155-57, 162n.45, 165-66, 168, 193, 199-200n.3, 203, 213, 216n.1
"Witchcraft" practices, 164
Wong, Koichi, 193-94
Wood, James, 121, 160n.14, 194-95, 198
Woodward, Bob, 102-3. See also Central Intelligence Agency, spying charges against
World Health Organization (WHO), 165
World War I, effects of, 7, 10
Wright, Carlton H., 46, 105n.24

Yale University, 112n.95
Yap, German control in, 5; stone money, 8
Yap Cooperative Association (YCA), 117, 156
Yarborough, Ralph W., 67
Yaws, 15
Yoder, Steven D., 163n.59
Yoma, Strik, xii, 43, 57, 62-63, 70-72, 76-78, 80, 205
Young Micronesian, 58-59
Yumul, Jesus B., 196-97
Yumul Company (YCO), 196-97

Zeder, Fred M., 11, 12, 33n.24, 78-80, 83-85, 96, 104n.9, 110nn.80-82, 124, 142-43, 149, 154, 160nn.19-20, 226
"Zederization process," 83-84